THE WISCONSIN PINE LANDS
OF CORNELL UNIVERSITY

 Fall Creek Books is an imprint of Cornell University Press dedicated to making available again classic books that document the history, culture, natural history, and folkways of New York State. Presented in new paperback editions that faithfully reproduce the contents of the original editions, Fall Creek Books titles will appeal to all readers interested in New York and the state's rich past. Some of the books published under this imprint reflect the sensibilities and attitudes of an earlier era; these views do not necessarily reflect those of Cornell University Press. For a complete listing of titles published under the Fall Creek Books imprint, please visit the Cornell University Press website: www.cornellpress.cornell.edu.

The
WISCONSIN PINE LANDS
of CORNELL UNIVERSITY

A Study in Land Policy
and Absentee Ownership

By
PAUL WALLACE GATES

Fall Creek Books
AN IMPRINT OF CORNELL UNIVERSITY PRESS
Ithaca and London

Originally published in 1943

Copyright © Cornell University
First Fall Creek Books edition, 2011.
All rights reserved. Except for brief quotations in a review,
the Foreword to the 2011 Fall Creek Books edition may
not be reproduced in any form without permission in
writing from the publisher. For information, address Cornell
University Press, Sage House, 512 East State Street,
Ithaca, New York 14850.

PRINTED IN THE UNITED STATES OF AMERICA

TO MY MOTHER

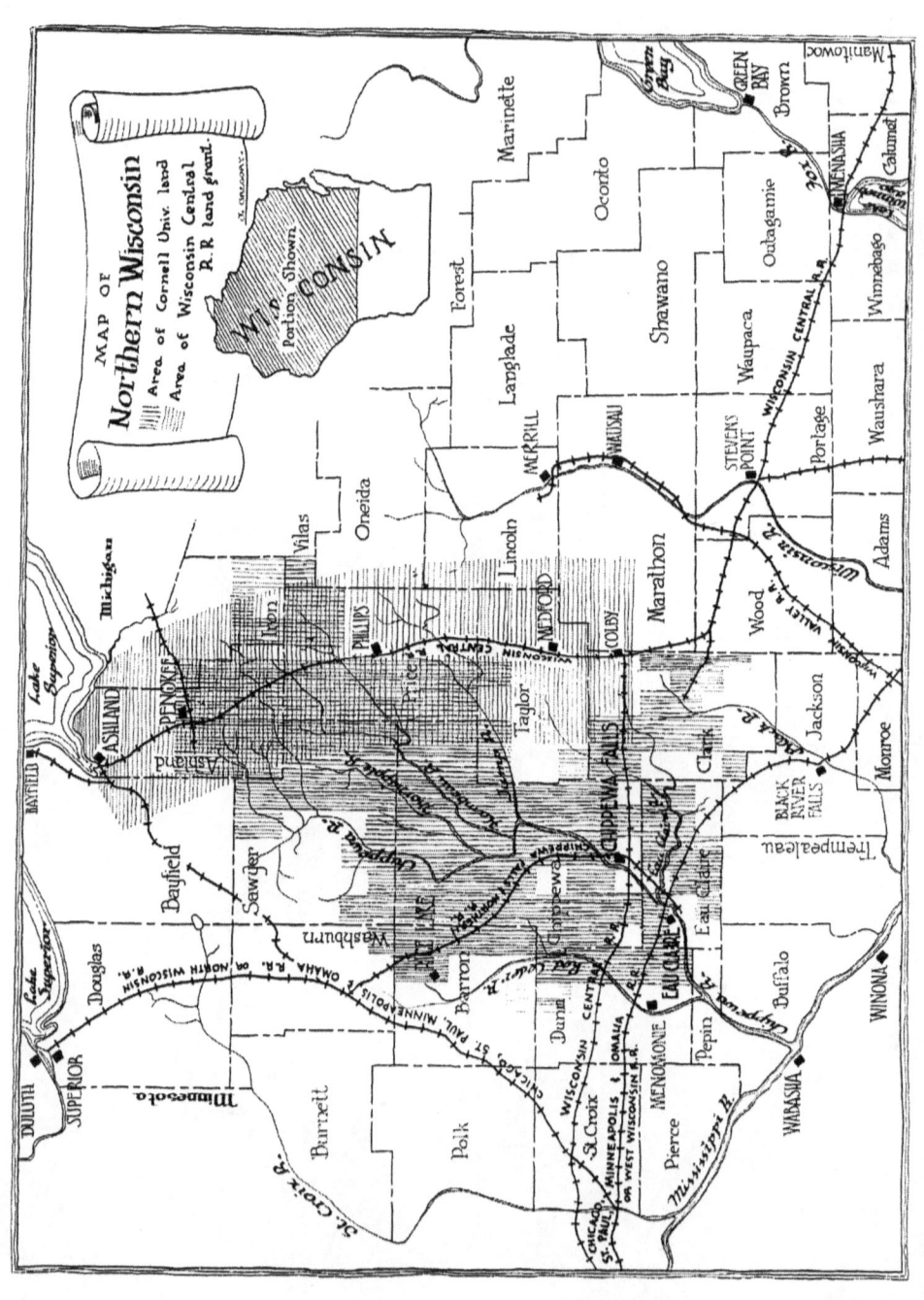

PREFACE

THIS study is an outgrowth of a larger project, a history of the disposal of the Public Domain, which was begun in 1933 with the aid of a fellowship granted by the Social Science Research Council. Some fifteen months were devoted to a systematic investigation of the land-entry books, then in the General Land Office, with the result that the astonishing extent to which speculators had intervened between the Government and actual settlers was revealed. The land companies, loan sharks, and individual speculators, who were the middlemen in government land disposal, left records of great value for reconstructing the story of the land business, the actual process of settlement, and the shaping of the patterns of land ownership and land use. Fortunately, historical societies and university libraries have gathered together an impressive quantity of these records, which were next examined. The gaps in these collections have been partly filled in by an examination of many hundreds of volumes of deed and mortgage records stored in county vaults.

It soon became apparent that before a history of the disposal of the Public Domain could be written, special and regional studies would have to be prepared to show the functioning of the land system in a number of fairly typical states and smaller subdivisions. It was also seen that more work needed to be done on Federal and state land legislation, especially with respect to its actual effects in practice. Considerable progress had been made on such an intensive study of land-disposal policies in the prairie states when the opportunity arose of using the unique collection of records concerning the half million acres of pine land entered in Wisconsin and Minnesota by Ezra Cornell for the university he founded. Use of these records, plus other collections in Wisconsin, has made possible the preparation of this study of the pine-land business.

In Wisconsin the land and lumbering business developed in much the same way as it did in Michigan and Minnesota. Consequently, what is said here of Wisconsin will, on the whole, apply to the other lake states. In them all, speculation and large-scale purchasing were widespread; "rings" were formed to control land sales; combinations were established which came to dominate the lumber industry; land values were forced upward by the publication of the Putnam report, and absentee ownership drained the pineries of their wealth.

A study of the Cornell land business or of the land speculations of any other individual, land-grant railroad, or land company inevitably leads one to consider such basic issues as taxation, extension of local government, construction and financing of roads, canals and railroads, and competition for sales among the large holders of land. All of these issues have been given attention in this study to make more understandable the problems with which Ezra Cornell and his successors had to contend in administering the university's lands. The study is offered for what it may be worth in the fields of land policy, exploitation of pine lands, absentee ownership, taxation, and local government on the frontier, and as part of the history of Cornell University.

PAUL WALLACE GATES

Ithaca, New York
February 1, 1943

PREFACE TO THE SECOND EDITION

When this study was undertaken there was little in print on the pine land business and the lumber industry in the Lake States, but since then parts of their history have been investigated and what was once a closed book has been thrown open to all who would read. I refer to the fine studies of Agnes M. Larson (*History of the White Pine Industry in Minnesota*), Robert F. Fries (*Empire in Pine: The Story of Lumbering in Wisconsin, 1830–1900*), Ralph W. Hidy, *et al.*, (*Timber and Men: The Weyerhaeuser Story*), and to other works by Richard N. Current, Arthur R. Reynolds, Larry Gara, Alice E. Smith, Kenneth W. Duckett, Merle Curti *et al.*, Vernon Carstensen, and Arlan Helgeson. All these books add to the background of my story but none require modification in it.

Readers of this monograph will perhaps recognize how much I was influenced directly or indirectly by Benjamin H. Hibbard, George S. Wehrwein, Frederick Merk, Lewis C. Gray, Frederic L. Paxson, and Joseph Schafer. I should also add to this list Lillian F. Cowdell.

PAUL WALLACE GATES

Ithaca, New York
July 27, 1964

CONTENTS

		PAGE
Preface		vii
I	Land Policy and the Agricultural-College Act	1
II	The States Dispose of Their Land Scrip	27
III	Ezra Cornell Founds a University	49
IV	Hazards of Land Speculation in Wisconsin	65
V	Cornell Acquires Wisconsin Pine Land	90
VI	The Pine-Land Ring	107
VII	The Chippewa Lumber Industry	121
VIII	Tax Warfare	137
IX	Cornell Against the Railroad Lobby	177
X	Sales of Pine Land	208
Conclusion		245
Bibliography		251
Index		259

ILLUSTRATIONS

A selection of pictures illustrating various facets of the Wisconsin lumbering industry follows page 146. With the exception of the portraits of Ezra Cornell and Henry W. Sage, all are drawn from the Iconographic Collection of the State Historical Society of Wisconsin.

CHAPTER ONE

Land Policy and the Agricultural-College Act

AMERICAN land policy has developed through a series of conflicts between opposing groups representing different philosophies, different sections, and different economic interests. The group dominant at the outset looked upon the public lands as a national treasure which should produce revenue for the government and thereby minimize the need for taxation. It favored limited sales at high prices, wanted to restrict the area open to settlement, and was not disturbed if speculators monopolized public lands that were opened to sale. The agrarians, representatives of the landless poor in the East and of the small farmers in the West and South, opposed the revenue feature of the land system, wished to open the lands freely to settlers, and resented the ease with which speculators acquired great tracts and seemed to control land policy.

As the agrarians grew in numbers and political power after 1800 they extorted from a reluctant Congress, still revenue-minded, a series of measures which gradually liberalized the national land policy. The smallest unit of sales was reduced from 640 acres to 40 acres; the minimum price was lowered from $2 to $1.25 an acre in 1820, and to 12½ cents an acre, for certain lands, in 1854; squatters were granted pre-emption rights which protected their claims against speculators; and finally, in 1862, the capstone of the agrarian demands was attained in the Homestead Act, which promised actual settlers a free grant of 160 acres.

Running counter to this agrarian trend in land policy was the practice of granting public land to aid schools, highways, canals, railroads, and other public institutions. The lusty young nation, growing in size and numbers at an amazing rate, was too impatient to wait for private initiative or local government to satisfy these demands. The inadequacy of Federal income and credit prevented money grants, but the nation possessed a gigantic quantity of land which was used instead. This grant-in-aid policy has been followed since the beginning of the national period, although haltingly at first, and more than three hundred million acres have been given to the public-land states and to private corporations for various purposes. The grantees were expected to sell their land at the government minimum price or better, and of course were interested in receiving the highest possible return from their subsidies. Such grants-in-aid weakened the land reforms which the agrarians were obtaining because they led to the creation of innumerable land agencies whose disposal policies were the antithesis of that towards which the Federal Government was working.

It was in the Lincoln administration that the free-homestead and grant-in-aid policies clashed most seriously. At the very moment that Congress adopted the Homestead Act it was considering making grants to western railroads, which were to take more than one hundred million acres out of the public domain. Furthermore, thirteen days after the Homestead bill became law, Congress passed the Agricultural-College Act, which offered to the states some nine or ten million acres for the endowment of colleges of agriculture and mechanical arts.

"Never since the formation of our government has a more important measure been submitted to Congress . . . , none that contemplated weightier interests, or . . . would be fraught with more salutary and widespread benefits." [1] Thus spoke the West of the Agricultural-College Act while it was still under consideration. Yet, when it came to the final vote, the representatives and senators of this area either opposed the measure or supported it with extreme reluctance.[2] Was this sheer partisan politics? Were western congressmen disregarding instructions and the will of their constituents? Or was there something

---

[1] *Cincinnatus* in *Indiana Farmer*, vii (May, 1858), p. 49.

[2] Most writers have maintained that the Agricultural College Act was peculiarly a western measure. Professor Earle D. Ross mentions western opposition to the Act in *Democracy's College: The Land-Grant Movement in the Formative Stage* (Ames, Iowa, 1942), pp. 57 ff.

inherently wrong with the bill which impelled them to oppose it?

One of the most striking facts about the development of the American frontier is that in pioneer communities, where one would expect every moment of the settler's time to have been absorbed by the struggle for survival, cultural interests survived and were cherished. Newspapers were published in every little hamlet, local and state historical societies were organized, and numerous denominational colleges and state universities were founded. Not all these developments could be supported locally; newspapers were maintained by government advertising, the historical societies were not the heavily endowed and well financed organizations of today, the denominational colleges were largely supported by donations from the East, and the state universities were begun only with the benefit of Federal aid.

Early in the nineteenth century there developed in the United States a demand for vocational education in agriculture and mechanical arts.[3] When the Smithson bequest came to the nation it was proposed to use it for endowing a national agricultural university in Washington which should train scientific farmers, but nothing came of the suggestion.[4] Several attempts were made to establish schools of agriculture, but these small experiments were not particularly successful. Failing to obtain either private aid or sufficient support from indi-

[3] Arthur Charles True, *History of Agricultural Education in the United States, 1785–1925* (Washington, 1929), 45, *passim; House Reports of Committees,* 35 Congress, 1 Session (1857–58), No. 261, pp. 8–10.

[4] See the views of Henry L. Ellsworth, Commissioner of Patents, *Annual Reports,* 1837, p. 5, and 1842, p. 2; also memorial of Charles Lewis Fleischmann, December 8, 1838, in *House Documents,* 25 Cong., 3 Sess. (1838–1839), No. 70. Fleischmann stated that he had previously memorialized Congress for aid to establish an agricultural college in Washington but had later doubted the power of Congress to grant such aid. Silas Wright, former governor of New York, commented in 1847 upon government neglect of agriculture as follows: "It is universally conceded that agriculture has shared but lightly in the fostering care and government patronage which have been liberally extended to commerce and industry . . ." (*Albany Cultivator,* iv [new series; October, 1847], p. 318). Wright's speech was also published in the *Western Farmer and Gardener,* iii (September, 1847), p. 119. In a memorial of the Minnesota legislature of January 29, 1858 (*Laws of Minnesota,* 1 Sess., 1858, pp. 351–352), asking for land grants for agricultural colleges, it was pointed out that "large appropriations have been made for Naval and Custom House establishments, and for Military Academies and Colleges, and extensive grants of land have been made for the improvement of rivers and harbors, for railroad purposes, and the like, yet but little or nothing has been done to aid the farmers and promote the interests of agriculture, and for the practical and industrial education of the people."

vidual states, agricultural leaders turned to the Federal Government for assistance. They argued that while industry and commerce had been aided in numerous ways, for example by tariffs, patent laws, ship subsidies, river and harbor appropriations, and canal grants, little or nothing had been done for agriculture. The demand for Federal aid for vocational or agricultural schools was fostered by agricultural societies, farm journals, labor organizations, and social reformers. By 1857 the movement had gained such wide support that Justin Smith Morrill, Representative from Vermont, was persuaded to introduce in the House a bill to provide for grants of land to the states to aid them in financing farmers' and laborers' colleges.[5]

The first Morrill bill specified that for the purpose of establishing such colleges each state would be given 20,000 acres of public land for each senator and representative it had in Congress. In those western states where there still existed public land the selection could be made by the state or by officials of the college to which the grant was given. Such states would be privileged to sell their land at once or to withhold it from market until it would bring a higher price. States in which there was no public domain were to receive scrip for the acreage to which they were entitled. They were not to enter land with the scrip but were required to sell it to assignees who could use it to enter "any of the unappropriated lands of the United States subject to sale at private entry at one dollar and twenty-five cents, or less, per acre." [6] The congressional debates on the Morrill bill brought out clearly the conflict of philosophies over land policy. Support for the measure

[5] *Congressional Globe*, 35 Cong., 1 Sess. (1857–1858), December 14, 1857, p. 33, and April 20, 1858, p. 1697; *House Reports of Committees*, 35 Cong., 1 Sess., No. 261.

[6] Much controversial writing has been devoted to the question of the authorship of the Agricultural-College Act. Professor Earle D. Ross has reviewed the controversy in an article which is a model of historical investigation and restraint, "The 'Father' of the Land-Grant College," *Agricultural History*, xii (April, 1938), pp. 151–186. To the student of land policy the controversy appears to be of little importance, since practically all the features of the Act of 1862 were carried over from earlier measures. Agricultural colleges were not new in 1862. Land grants had been given to endow universities in the colonial and early national period, and every public-land state had received a donation for the endowment of a university or "seminary of learning." The actual method of aiding the proposed colleges was borrowed from the Dix bill of 1854, which is described below. So far as the land donation policy is concerned, the Morrill Act contains not one feature which had not been discussed for years prior to 1857.

came from the older states of the Northeast, and opposition came from the South and the new states and territories of the West.

Since 1789 the South had clung tenaciously to a narrow interpretation of the Constitution. Its attitude was based on fear lest an aggressive majority in the North, if not shackled by constitutional limitations, adopt measures which might place the South permanently in bondage to its more powerful rival. The constitutional susceptibilities of the South were especially keen in the matter of disposing of the public lands. Southerners maintained that free homesteads to settlers, free grants to railroads, and donations to agricultural and mechanical colleges were all contrary to the spirit and letter of the Constitution. Some of the classic statements uttered during the debate on the Morrill bill by southern states-rights advocates are instructive. Said Senator James M. Mason of Virginia: "It is one of the most extraordinary engines of mischief," it is "misusing the property of the country," it is "an unconstitutional robbing of the Treasury for the purpose of bribing the States." [7] Senator Clement C. Clay, of Alabama, denounced the measure as being "most delusive and seductive," a "magnificent bribe to the States," a "long step toward the overthrow of this truly Federal . . . Government. . . . It extorts the consent of the States by a sort of moral duress. You tempt them to their own self-abasement and self-destruction. . . ." [8] He called it "one of the most monstrous, iniquitous and dangerous measures which have ever been submitted to Congress." [9] George E. Pugh, Senator from Ohio, who held similar constitutional views, said that the object of the measure was "to displace the control of the State governments over the most important of all the pursuits of our citizens. . . ." He declared that the measure involved "as atrocious a violation of the organic law as if it were the act of an armed usurper." [10]

It is the opposition of another group, however, which is the more important because it looked into the future, rather than backward to

---

[7] *Cong. Globe*, 35 Cong., 2 Sess. (1858–59), February 1, 1859, p. 718.
[8] *Id.*, February 7, 1859, p. 852.
[9] *Id.*, February 3, 1859, p. 786.
[10] *Id.*, February 1, 1859, p. 715.

the Constitution, to test the wisdom of the agricultural-college measure. Many critics of the American land system directed their severest strictures not at the revenue provisions but at the wide-open character of the land laws which permitted capitalists and incorporated companies to purchase unlimited amounts of public land anywhere in the West. Since the first settlement in America, capitalists and land companies had been buying land in extensive quantities and when settlers reached the areas so acquired they found no land available except at speculators' prices. Despite the growing liberality of the land laws, speculators continued to forestall the settlers and prevented the development of a democratic land system in many areas. The Bloomington, Illinois, *Pantagraph*, arguing for a free homestead law to check speculation, said:

> It is the demon of *land speculation* that is to be throttled by the homestead law; land speculation that seizes the choice spots of the country in advance of the emigrant's arrival, separates the settlers' cabins by wide tracts of unreclaimed wilderness, and encircles every embryo town and populous city with leagues of waste land as absolutely wild as when the deer and the Indian were its only inhabitants.[11]

A resident of Wisconsin observed:

> All the lands immediately on the banks [of the Rock River near Janesville] were already taken up & held at high prices. One half the county in which Janesville was situated was already bought up by speculators & held at high prices. From these facts I was satisfied that the county would settle slowly, that neighborhoods would be scattered & extended & not sufficiently compact for society & schools & that on the whole I should never be fully pleased with my situation if I should locate there.[12]

A Nebraska writer was equally critical of speculators' holdings:

> Four miles from the city [Salt Creek] we strike the Speculators' Reservation, and for TWELVE miles we travel this lonely waste, with scarcely an object to vary the monotony of the rolling prairie and teeming grass To the North, to South, or perhaps to the West, along some tardy stream, amid a

---

[11] *Pantagraph*, March 8, 1859.

[12] C. M. Baker, Geneva, Walworth County, Wisconsin, January 13, 1839, to George W. and James Baker, Bridgeport, Addison County, Vermont, in Edward Larrabee Baker, editor, *Charles Minton Baker and the Pioneer Trail* (Chicago, 1928), pp. 213–214.

patch of timber, a tenant's cabin heaves in sight. . . . This land for beauty or utility is unsurpassed in the world, yet it is as useless to the actual settler as if it was as barren as the desert of Sahara.[13]

The legislature of Iowa, frightened by the concentration of land ownership in the hands of speculators, memorialized Congress in 1858, urging that all remaining public lands be reserved for actual settlers:

> The sale of public lands to other than actual settlers [argued the memorial] has materially retarded the growth and prosperity of our State; that many large tracts of our best lands have been purchased by speculators, and placed beyond the reach of the great mass of emigrants who are seeking new homes within our borders, and thus sacrificing the interests of thousands of the enterprising and industrious poor for the benefit of a few nonproducers.
> Your memorialists will not attempt to enumerate the many evils which have resulted from this system, nor will they endeavor to portray the incalculable benefits that would accrue to the newer States and Territories from the proposed change.[14]

The speculators' holdings not only retarded local development but forced the wide dispersal of population, made necessary the extension of highways and railroads into thinly populated areas, and raised the costs of local government. Furthermore, it was difficult to collect taxes from absentee owners and as a result the resident proprietors had to bear an unfair share of the tax burden. Speculators frequently found it desirable to place tenants upon their lands to protect them from being plundered and to begin improving them, and the West deeply resented the intrusion of an institution it felt to be un-American and undemocratic. More than anything else the westerners disliked the fact that it was the improvements made by settlers in the vicinity of land owned by speculators which gave value to the speculators' holdings. The speculators' profits, whether from rents or sales, were drained off to the East and contributed nothing to western development. "What the land speculator makes upon the rise of his land is

---

[13] *Peoples Press* (Nebraska City), August 21, 1862.
[14] *House Miscellaneous Documents*, 35 Cong., 1 Sess., No. 89. The memorial is dated February 20, 1858.

wrung from the hard labor and incessant toil of the honest but poor settlers," is the way a Senator from Minnesota described it.[15]

Thoughtful westerners, no matter how much they wanted agricultural colleges, could not bring themselves to support a measure which would further land monopoly by giving speculators the chance to acquire nine or ten million acres of public land at substantially less than the government minimum price. They had before them the experience of the country with the military-bounty land warrants granted to the veterans of the Mexican War and of various Indian engagements. These warrants, to the amount of 61,228,110 acres,[16] had promptly depreciated to as low as 50 cents an acre, although they generally ranged in price from 62 cents to $1.10 per acre.[17] They quickly passed into the hands of dealers who advertised them for sale and by far the largest proportion were purchased by speculators who entered tracts ranging from 5,000 to 100,000 acres in the states of the upper Mississippi Valley.[18] The scrip granted by the agricultural college measure to the eastern states would, it was feared, go into the same hands as had the military land warrants and would make possible further large scale speculation in public lands.

These western critics argued that it was inconsistent of Congress to promise free homesteads to actual settlers while at the same time facilitating land monopolization by granting scrip to the eastern states. They pointed out that the proposed bill continued the old paradox of liberalizing the land laws without terminating policies which produced land monopoly. Senator Morton S. Wilkinson of Minnesota said:

The scrip . . . will pass into the hands of speculators, a remorseless class of vampires, who care little for the common prosperity, and still less for the

[15] *Cong. Globe,* 37 Cong., 2 Sess. (1861–1862), May 28, 1862, p. 2395.
[16] Benjamin H. Hibbard, *History of the Public Land Policies* (New York, 1924), 132.
[17] W. W. Corcoran, Washington, April 4, 1849, to Sidney Breese, Corcoran MSS, Library of Congress; *New York Tribune,* February 5, 17, March 11, 29, 1852; *Freeport* (Illinois) *Journal,* May 23, 1856; Leavenworth (Kansas), *Daily Conservative,* January 8, 1862. The warrants were regularly quoted in the financial columns of the New York papers.
[18] The abstracts of warrant entries of the numerous land offices in Illinois, Indiana, Iowa, Wisconsin, Michigan, Minnesota, Missouri, and Kansas reveal that a large proportion of these warrants were used by speculators. The abstract volumes are in the National Archives, Washington, D. C.

cause of education. . . . The practical effects of this measure would be to negative or counteract the salutary result which we all hope will grow out of the passage of the homestead bill.[19]

"Jim" Lane, of Kansas, a state which already had seen much of its best land bought up by speculators, thundered at the Morrill bill, predicting that it would bring to his troubled land a far greater concentration of absentee ownership, comparable only to that which prevailed in Iowa.[20] No bill, he said, had ever been introduced in Congress which was

> more iniquitous so far as the western States were concerned. . . . In it is contained the ruin of the State that I . . . represent. In it is a contradiction of the homestead proposition. My understanding has been that the wealth of the locality is to educate the children of the locality. By the provision of this bill . . . you say to the laboring white man who has no land, "you can have the land, but before you get it you must establish and maintain an agricultural college." [21]

Henry M. Rice of Minnesota, as practical a politician as sat in the Senate, predicted that agents of non-residents would cull out the choicest lands, "blighting, like the locusts every region which may attract them. . . ."[22] With Senator James T. Shields of Minnesota, he endeavored to amend the bill to prevent speculators from entering lands in his state with the scrip.[23] Trusten Polk of Missouri tried to protect his state in the same way, while Samuel C. Pomeroy of Kansas proposed that no person be permitted to acquire more than 640 acres with the scrip. All these amendments, which would have made the scrip less attractive to speculators, were defeated.[24] James S. Green of Missouri, William M. Gwin of California, and George E. Pugh of Ohio shared the fears of their western colleagues. Pugh predicted

---

[19] *Cong. Globe*, 37 Cong., 2 Sess., May 28, 1862, p. 2395.

[20] In no state, save Illinois, was there a greater amount of land owned by non-residents than in Iowa, a fact of which Senator James W. Grimes was somewhat sensitive. He attempted to challenge Lane's statement but the latter in reply turned the tables on Grimes by calling attention to his well known propensity for land speculation. Lane had good reason to fear the speculators' influence in parts of his own state which were already blighted by absentee ownership. (*Cong. Globe*, 37 Cong., 2 Sess., May 22, 1862, p. 2276.)

[21] *Id.*, p. 2275. The speaker was James H. Lane, formerly of Indiana.

[22] *Cong. Globe*, 35 Cong., 2 Sess., February 1, 1859, p. 717.

[23] *Id.*, February 4, 1859, p. 785.

[24] *Cong. Globe*, 37 Cong., 2 Sess., June 10, 1862, pp. 2626–2627.

that the states would sell their scrip for nominal prices and that speculators would purchase and locate it "by empires on your public domain."[25] He maintained that the military bounty acts had put the "States of Iowa and Wisconsin, and perhaps Minnesota and others, into the hands of non-resident proprietors," a fate from which he wanted to save the newer states and territories.[26]

Another fundamental objection to the Morrill bill was that it would benefit the older states at the expense of the newer ones. As the grants would not be based on actual need but on population, the densely settled and wealthiest states would receive the largest grants and the poorest, the least developed and the most needy would receive the smallest grants. California and Rhode Island would receive grants of the same size, while other eastern states in which farming was relatively unimportant would receive grants greater than would be given to Minnesota, Kansas, or Nebraska.

All these arguments might well have led the advocates of the measure to consider the counter proposal made by Timothy O. Howe of Wisconsin. Senator Howe urged that Congress grant to the states out of the land revenues the sum of $30,000, instead of 30,000 acres of land, for each congressional representative and senator to which they were entitled.[27] Unfortunately, Congress was as yet unable to bring itself to make financial grants for education and consequently resorted to the long standing custom of using the public lands, regardless of the direful predictions of the western representatives.

Western opposition to and eastern support of the agricultural-college bill may be attributed chiefly to the fact that it included a new principle of land distribution: land in one state was to be given for the benefit of another. In the past the Federal Government had made grants to states and territories of land within their borders for educa-

---

[25] *Cong. Globe,* 35 Cong., 2 Sess., February 1, 1859, p. 715.
[26] *Id.,* 716. A writer in the *New York Tribune* who signed himself "Free West" urged the editor to oppose the measure to grant lands for the aid of agricultural colleges because it was a "nefarious outrage on the West," calculated "to loot" that section of the public lands promised to actual settlers under the Homestead Act. He condemned the "sinister designs" of those supporting the measure. (*New York Tribune,* May 27, 1862.)
[27] *Cong. Globe,* 37 Cong., 2 Sess., June 10, 1862, p. 2632.

tion and local improvements. Had the agricultural-college bill followed precedent by providing for grants of land only to those states in which there was still public land available, it would have received the unqualified support of all westerners. But this would have deprived the East of any direct benefit from the measure and eastern Representatives were insistent that, through the use of scrip, land grants should be given to all states, regardless of the effect such a policy would have on the land system.

Representatives of the eastern and non-public land states had early advocated donations of public land to aid various enterprises within their boundaries but without notable success.[28] In the fifties, when prejudices against the liberal donation of land for worthy purposes seemed to be breaking down, Congress was asked to make grants to aid the states in caring for the indigent insane. This measure came close to enactment in 1854. Dorothea Dix, one of that remarkable coterie of women reformers who did so much to arouse Americans to the existence of major social abuses in their midst, created so strong a sentiment for Federal aid for the care of the insane that members of Congress dared not resist it, regardless of their doubts about the constitutionality of such a measure. A bill to grant to the states 10,000,000 acres of public land to be apportioned "in the compound ratio of geographic area and representation . . . in the House of Representatives" [29] passed both houses by large majorities. Many ardent states-rights advocates refrained from voting, so fearful were they of the scorn of the reformers under the leadership of Miss Dix. In effect, they "passed the buck" to President Franklin Pierce, who had the courage of his convictions and vetoed the measure.[30] The veto message is disappointing, for it is a résumé of the views of those who

[28] In 1819 the Connecticut asylum for the education and instruction of deaf and dumb persons was granted a township of public lands, or 23,040 acres, to be located in some western state or territory. Similarly, in 1826, the Kentucky asylum for teaching deaf and dumb persons was given a township, less the sixteenth section, or 22,400 acres, to be located somewhere on the surveyed portion of the public domain (*6 United States Statutes-at-Large*, 229, 339).

[29] *Senate Journal*, 33 Cong., 1 Sess., May 4, 1854, pp. 372–374.

[30] The vote in the House was 81 to 53 and in the Senate 25 to 12. On the move to pass the measure over the president's veto fourteen additional senators plucked up sufficient

sought to shackle Federal power to protect minority interests and it does not consider the wisdom of the measure from the point of view of land policy.[31] Pierce's veto served to stiffen the attitude of the strict constructionists who had previously dodged the vote on the measure and it was sustained by a vote of 21 to 26, whereas the bill originally passed the Senate by 25 to 12.[32]

The Dix bill, however laudable its purpose, threatened serious damage to the land system and to the west. Although it was defeated on this occasion, the principle of granting land in the West for the benefit of improvements or institutions in the East bobbed up again in measures to grant four million acres in Michigan, Wisconsin, and Minnesota to subsidize a canal around Niagara Falls,[33] and to aid the public schools of the District of Columbia by a donation of another

---

courage to vote no and it was defeated 21 to 26. (*Cong. Globe*, 33 Cong., 1 Sess., March 8, 1854, p. 572, and April 19, 1854, p. 954; *Senate Journal*, 33 Cong., 1 Sess., p. 479.)

[31] *Senate Journal*, 33 Cong., 1 Sess., May 3, 1854, pp. 361–369.

[32] The successful campaign of Dorothea Dix to induce Congress to adopt her measure is positively amazing when one considers the obstacles she had to overcome such as inertia, disinterestedness, constitutional opposition, and dislike of the West for a measure which obviously would make easier large-scale acquisitions by speculators and land companies. Williamson R. W. Cobb, member of Congress from Alabama, and a strict constructionist, gives an inkling of her methods and success in a speech of expiation in 1858: "I have a . . . difficult job before me, and that is to reconcile the vote which I shall give in relation to this bill [agricultural college] with the vote which I gave upon another bill. And I cannot perform it without simply coming down and acknowledging frankly that I was wrong in the vote which I gave, when the impulse of this heart, whether good or bad, prompted me to act in behalf of a proposition to grant lands for the establishment of insane asylums in the States—a proposition gotten up by Miss Dix. . . . She is a meritorious, generous, and noble-minded woman. She went down into my State, and her charms had such an extraordinary effect upon the people of that portion of the country that the Legislature of my State adopted a joint memorial to the Congress of the United States, without a dissenting voice, requesting their Representatives and instructing their Senators to vote for that bill. Then it was, sir, that I gave way to my better feelings, and voted for that bill" (*Cong. Globe*, 35 Cong., 1 Sess., April 22, 1858, p. 1742). Similar explanations were made by others. Additional information on the remarkable ability of Miss Dix to stir up sentiment for a measure whose object was highly laudable but whose means of attaining that object threatened serious damage to the land system may be found in Francis Tiffany, *Life of Dorothea Lynde Dix* (Boston and New York, 1892), especially chapter xv, "The Five Million Acre Bill," chapter xvi, "The 12,225,000 Acre Bill," chapter xvii, "Again the 12,225,000 Acre Bill," and chapter xviii, "The Presidential Veto."

[33] It was natural for the New York legislature to memorialize Congress in support of the bill to grant land for the construction of a canal around the Falls of the Niagara River, but one is somewhat surprised to find the Wisconsin legislature adopting a similar resolution. (*Senate Miscellaneous Documents*, 35 Cong., 1 Sess., No. 261; *House Miscellaneous Documents*, 35 Cong., 1 Sess., No. 131.)

million acres.³⁴ These measures which had no Dorothea Dix behind them were not acted upon by Congress.

The agricultural-college bill was actually more unpalatable to the West than the Dix bill. The former provided for grants of land to the states solely on the basis of population while the latter provided for grants according to the area and the population of the states. Under the Dix bill the western states, because of their greater size, would have received a fair share of the lands it was proposed to grant, but under the Morrill bill the East's share would be disproportionately large. Efforts to substitute the donation ratio of the Dix bill for that of the Morrill bill failed.³⁵

The conflict of ideas between those who supported land grants for western institutions and those who favored reserving the public lands for actual settlers was never settled. Opposition to grants for *absentee* institutions, such as were provided for in the Dix and Morrill bills, was especially strong in the West, and the bars were let down only once—in 1862. There was also developing in the West before the Civil War a feeling that the railroad land-grant policy had gone too far, as is evidenced by a memorial of the Nebraska legislature of 1857, in which it is argued that the Pacific Railroad bill then before Congress should not be passed because it would further land monopoly and harm settlers' interests. Although railroad land grants continued to be made until 1871, there were many people in the West who had grave doubts as to the wisdom of the policy.

By 1857 the West was coming to question the wisdom of the entire public land system, based as it was on the revenue concept. Revenue meant sale to settlers or speculators, and when settlers lacked funds they had to depend on loan sharks or speculators to buy for them. The pre-emption law had not been of any assistance to penniless fron-

---

³⁴ *Cong. Globe,* 35 Cong., 2 Sess., December 23, 1858, p. 186, and February 1, 1859, p. 717.

³⁵ As President Buchanan pointed out in his veto message, the Morrill bill provided for the donation of some 580,000 acres to the states in which there was public land, while the non-land states would receive almost ten times as much, or 5,480,000 acres. The move to substitute the more liberal feature of the Dix bill was defeated in the Senate, 25–28. *Cong. Globe,* 35 Cong., 2 Sess., February 1, 1859, p. 713, and February 4, 1859, p. 785. Another amendment to make the grants proportional to the area of tillable land in each state was also defeated. *Id.,* p. 785.

tiersmen unable to buy their claims; neither had the claim associations been able to protect the squatter beyond the opening of the land sale. The result was, according to contemporary estimates, that between a third and a half of the farms in the West were mortgaged.[36] To relieve the embattled squatters, when it seemed that a free-homestead measure could not be passed because of southern opposition, the West suggested that no further lands be opened to sale. The next step it took was to demand that all public lands be closed to entry save by settlers.[37] Such steps were too advanced for the East and South but, if adopted, they would have made the agricultural-college scrip of little or no value. It is clear that the West wanted no more land to pass into eastern control, whether it was individual or institutional.

The strongest support for the Morrill bill naturally came from the eastern states which were to receive the largest grants under it. This section had always maintained that the public lands belonged to the nation and should be used for the general welfare rather than for the benefit of the particular states in which they lay. The income from the sale of lands went into the Federal treasury, from which the eastern states derived benefit, and they were naturally reluctant to countenance any reduction in land revenues. Opposition to land reform, consequently, had been strong in the East prior to 1850, but thereafter it subsided as this section saw the advantages which would come to it from a rapidly developing West. Many easterners were now ready to support free homesteads and liberal land grants to railroads in exchange for support for high tariffs, favorable immigration laws, a national banking system, and ship subsidies. They also demanded as a *quid pro quo* a direct share in the public lands of the West for charitable purposes, railroads, canals, and agricultural colleges. In the Morrill bill the East hoped to secure a part of the public lands and

---

[36] *New York Tribune*, January 23, 1860.

[37] Memorial of the legislative assembly of the Territory of Minnesota to the President, March 10, 1857, *Laws of the Territory of Minnesota*, 8 Sess., 1857, pp. 298–299; memorials of the legislature of Minnesota, January 11, 1858, January 22, 1858, January 29, 1858, August 12, 1858, *Laws of Minnesota*, 1 Sess., 1858, pp. 351–354, 371–373; memorial of the legislature of Iowa, February 20, 1858, *House Misc. Doc.*, 35 Cong., 1 Sess., No. 89.

also to pay off its obligation to the farmers for their support of the major legislation of the Lincoln administration.

Perhaps the ablest critic of land policy in America was Horace Greeley. He detested speculation in land and was forever condemning measures which made easy acquisition of land by non-residents. His travels through the West had given him a realistic picture of the problems of that area and a deep sympathy for the debt-ridden farmers who were desperately striving to secure title to their claims. No man dealt harder blows in the campaign for the adoption of the free-homestead policy. But his zeal for agricultural colleges overcame his realistic understanding of the land system. He called the agricultural-college measure "a very moderate concession to the Old States," and chided the West for not being willing to give the East this act in return for free homesteads and railroad land grants.[38] The Homestead Act, he thought, would virtually end land speculation; he failed to see that the agricultural-college measure provided another opportunity for speculators, and he was blind to the obvious conflict between the principles of the two measures.[39]

Representative Morrill undertook to answer the arguments of the opposition. He paid his respects to the members of the states-rights school as follows: "I know very well that when there is a lack of arguments to be brought against the merits of a measure, the Constitution is fled to as an inexhaustible arsenal of supply." [40] Less satisfactory was his reply to the arguments of the western representatives. He was convinced that the scrip "will go into the hands of *bona fide* settlers, because such will be the only purchasers to be found, unless at a depreciation of price, and these will be obtained by the several States disposing of their scrip on a credit and retaining the lien on the land. Such an arrangement will not certainly be to the disadvantage of the land States."[41] From this muddled statement one can see how misinformed the Vermont Representative was con-

[38] *New York Tribune,* June 21, 1862.
[39] *Id.,* February 28, 1859, February 1, 1862.
[40] *Cong. Globe,* 35 Cong., 1 Sess., April 20, 1858, p. 1692.
[41] *Cong. Globe,* 37 Cong., 2 Sess., June 6, 1862, Appendix, p. 257.

cerning the operation of the Federal land system. If one thing was clear it was that the scrip would be used chiefly by speculators.

Jacob Collamer, Senator from Vermont, and John Bell, Senator from Tennessee, agreed with Morrill in deploring the grudging illiberality of the land states toward the East.[42] When the bill for a grant of land to aid in the construction of the Mobile and Chicago Railroad was being considered in 1850, Bell had tried to have part of the Federal land grant—which lay in Illinois, Mississippi, and Alabama—applied to the construction of that portion of the line extending through Kentucky and Tennessee. His failure still rankled nine years later when he was again contending for the "equitable distribution of the public domain among all the states. . . ."[43]

The same feeling of resentment against the West for insisting that the public land be used only for public institutions and improvements in that section may be seen in actions taken by the legislature of New York and the Vermont State Agricultural Society. In the midst of the discussion on the Morrill bill, when the West was voicing its opposition, the legislature of New York adopted a joint resolution urging the New York representatives and senators "not to vote any further special appropriations of the public lands to the new states, until some just general provisions be made by which the original states shall receive their equitable proportion of said lands, or the proceeds thereof."[44]

The resolutions of the Vermont State Agricultural Society illustrate the eastern attitude even better:

> Whereas, the public domain has been achieved by the united valor and common treasure of the country, and of right belongs to all—to the people of the old States as well as to those of the new—and as the agriculture of our country is the foundation of our national prosperity, and is of vital importance to all other interests, and the education and intelligence of those devoted to its pursuits are of a paramount consideration . . . therefore,

---

[42] *Cong. Globe*, 35 Cong., 2 Sess., February 1, 1859, p. 722.
[43] *Id.*, February 7, 1859, p. 856.
[44] *Laws of New York*, 81 Sess., 1858, p. 667. An observer in Washington, in 1857, is quoted as saying: "Incredible as it may seem there is actually a prospect that the old States are going to share in the distribution of public lands." *American Farmers' Magazine* (January, 1858), xii, 12.

Resolved, by the Vermont State Ag[ricultural] Society . . . that some portion of this widely extended domain should be set apart and appropriated for the purposes of education, equally among all the States of the Union, in proportion to the ratio of Representatives in Congress . . . while our public lands are being squandered and frittered away, why should not the people lay claim to some of the benefits accruing therefrom? [45]

Dorothea Dix had taught the country much about lobbying and her methods were effectively copied by the advocates of the agricultural college bill.[46] Like Miss Dix, they went to the state legislatures to get joint resolutions adopted urging the senators and representatives of those states to support the bill. This was no difficult task in the eastern states where sentiment for sharing in the proceeds of the public lands was strong. The legislatures of Rhode Island, New Jersey, and Maine each adopted such a resolution.[47] Western legislatures could be moved less easily, but sufficient pressure was exerted to get favorable action from Illinois, California,[48] and Ohio.[49] The Illinois resolution—a project of Jonathan Baldwin Turner—asked for grants of land for each state worth not less than $500,000.[50] The resolution of the Ohio legislature was adopted "without due consideration, and in an unguarded moment." The legislature subsequently made a complete reversal, declared strongly against the land grant method of the Morrill bill, and urged that public lands be granted only to actual settlers.[51] Four other western states—Michigan,[52] Iowa,[53] Wisconsin,[54] and Minnesota—in which the desire for agricultural colleges was in conflict with the prevailing distrust of the method of subsidizing them contained in the Morrill bill—memorialized Congress to

---

[45] *Country Gentleman* (February 4, 1858), xi, 81.
[46] Earle D. Ross, *Agricultural History*, xii, 169 ff., and Arthur C. True, *op. cit.*, 103, mention the actual lobbyists who were working in Washington to get the bill through Congress.
[47] *Senate Misc. Doc.*, 35 Cong., 1 Sess., docs. 183, 184, 224.
[48] *Id.*, doc. 259.
[49] *Laws of Ohio*, 53 Assembly, 1 Sess., 1858, p. 194.
[50] *House Misc. Doc.*, 33 Cong., 1 Sess., doc. 31.
[51] *Laws of Ohio*, 53 Assembly, 2 Sess., 308. Ben Wade professed ignorance of these resolutions when they were called to his attention by his colleague. (*Cong. Globe*, 35 Cong., 2 Sess., February 1, 1859, p. 714.)
[52] *House Misc. Doc.*, 35 Cong., 1 Sess., doc. 57.
[53] *Senate Misc. Doc.*, 35 Cong., 1 Sess., doc. 202.
[54] *Senate Misc. Doc.*, 35 Cong., 2 Sess., doc. 46.

grant lands to them individually, but did not endorse the Morrill bill. Wisconsin, in 1858, asked for a grant of 500,000 acres [55] and in 1859 it asked for "an adequate amount of public lands" for an agricultural college.[56] The action of the legislature of Minnesota is enlightening. In a joint resolution of January 29, 1858, the legislature condemned land speculation as being detrimental to the interests of the people, stated that it was the duty of Congress to protect settlers against land monopoly, declared for a free homestead policy, and urged that a "liberal grant of land may be made to this state, and to others similarly situated," for an agricultural college.[57] Four days later a second resolution was adopted calling for a land grant for a Minnesota agricultural college.[58] The Indiana house of representatives adopted a resolution urging the enactment of a measure to grant lands for agricultural colleges, but the state senate did not act upon the matter.[59]

A combination unique in American history was brought together to support the agricultural-college bill. It included the agricultural societies, farm and rural journals,[60] organized labor, the brilliant but erratic Horace Greeley and the highly influential *New York Tribune*, the leaders in the movement for vocational education, and many members of Congress commonly identified with the commercial and industrial interests. If state vocational schools must come, the latter interests certainly preferred to have them subsidized from the proceeds of western land sales instead of by taxation. There was also support for the measure from some western members of Congress who were more interested in the establishment of agricultural colleges than they were fearful of furthering land speculation. The combination was irresistible. In the sessions of 1858 and 1859 Justin Smith Morrill in the House and Ben Wade in the Senate—despite the in-

---

[55] *Laws of Wisconsin* (1858), pp. 241–242.
[56] *Laws of Wisconsin* (1859), p. 254.
[57] *Laws of Minnesota*, 1 Sess. (1858), pp. 351–352.
[58] *Id.*, 358.
[59] *Indiana House Journal*, 40 Sess. (1859), pp. 229–230.
[60] Most of the farm journals supported the movement for agricultural colleges, but some, like the *Ohio Cultivator*, were skeptical about it. This journal held that it would "build up the most stupendous literary hospital for political invalids and sap-rotted theorists that the world ever saw." Quoted in Eugene H. Roseboom and Francis P. Weisenburger, *History of Ohio* (New York, 1934), p. 312.

structions he received from the Ohio legislature—drove the measure through Congress.[61]

The sectional lineup in both branches of Congress shows that the bill received the solid support of New England, strong aid from the Middle Atlantic States, and scattered votes from the border states and the Old Northwest. The public-land states gave 35 votes for the measure and 58 in opposition. (See Table 1, p. 20.)

If the archaic views of the strict constructionists were losing their hold upon the North, they were still cherished by James Buchanan. He agreed with Mason and Clay that the agricultural-college bill would destroy the old balance of power between the states and the Federal Government, and he therefore stood squarely with the South in unalterable opposition to the measure. But Buchanan was a Democrat and the Democratic party had always depended for much of its support upon the frontier West. He therefore embodied in his veto message the view earlier stated so forcibly by Pugh of Ohio, Rice of Minnesota, and Green of Missouri that

This bill . . . will operate greatly to the injury of the new States. . . . Nothing could be more prejudicial to their interests than for wealthy individuals to acquire large tracts of the public land and hold them for speculative purposes. The low price to which this land scrip will probably be reduced will tempt speculators to buy it in large amounts, and locate it on the best lands belonging to the Government. The eventual consequence must be that the men who desire to cultivate the soil will be compelled to purchase these very lands at rates much higher than the price at which they could be obtained from the Government.[62]

Buchanan also expressed the fear that the measure would further reduce revenues derived from the public lands at a time when government expenditures exceeded revenue. His veto was sustained, but an aggressive North did not accept the decision as final.[63]

---

[61] The House passed the bill on April 22, 1858, and the Senate on February 7, 1859. (*Cong. Globe*, 35 Cong., 1 Sess., p. 1742 and *id.*, 35 Cong., 2 Sess., p. 857.)

[62] *Id.*, February 26, 1859, pp. 1412, 1414.

[63] Horace Greeley took Buchanan to task in his most biting language for the presidential veto. He argued that the states would retain their lands instead of selling them to speculators as Buchanan and others had predicted; he denied that the measure would be of aid to speculators and maintained that the revenue feature was not important. But worse still, he practically said that the votes of western Democrats were given

TABLE 1

Vote on the Agricultural-College Bill of 1858–59 *

	HOUSE		SENATE	
	For	Against	For	Against
Maine	6	0	2	0
New Hampshire	3	0	2	0
Vermont	3	0	1	0
Massachusetts	11	0	1	0
Connecticut	3	0	1 (1)	0
Rhode Island	2	0	2	0
NEW ENGLAND	28	0	9	0
New York	23	7	2	0
Pennsylvania	10	9	1 (1)	0
New Jersey	5	0	1 (1)	0
MIDDLE STATES	38	16	4	0
Delaware	1	0	0	1
Maryland	4	1	1	0
Kentucky	2	8	2	0
Tennessee	3	6	1	0 (1)
Virginia	0	9	0	2
North Carolina	0	7	0	2
South Carolina	0	4	0	2
Georgia	2	6	0	0 (1)
OLD SOUTH	12	41	4	7
Ohio	9	9	1	1
Indiana	6	5	0	0 (1)
Illinois	4	3	1 (1)	0
OLD PUBLIC-LAND STATES	19	17	2	1
Michigan	4	0	1 (1)	0
Wisconsin	0	2	2	0
Minnesota	0	0	0	1
Iowa	2	0	1	1
Missouri	1	6	0	2
California †	1	1	2	0
NEW PUBLIC-LAND STATES (WEST)	8	9	6	4
Alabama	0	7	0	2
Arkansas	0	2	0	2
Louisiana	0	3	0	1 (1)
Mississippi ‡	0	3	0	2
Texas	0	2	0	2
Florida	0	0	0	1 (1)
NEW PUBLIC-LAND STATES (SOUTH)	0	17	0	10
Total vote	105	100	25	22

* The numbers in parenthesis represent those paired for or against the bill.

† Senator William M. Gwin voted for the measure because he was so instructed by the legislature of California, though he had doubts as to the wisdom of his action. (*Cong. Globe*, 35 Cong., 2 Sess., February 7, 1859, pp. 854–855, and February 13, 1859, p. 784.)

‡ Senator Albert G. Brown voted against the bill because of instructions from the Mississippi legislature. (*Id.*, February 7, 1859, p. 856.)

In 1862 the agricultural-college bill was introduced in Congress again, this time with the amount of land to be granted to each state increased to 30,000 acres for each representative and senator in Congress. Again the Northeast, which stood to gain so much from it, overwhelmingly supported it. Southern opposition was now silenced, but the outcry from the frontier states was still shrill. Many westerners, more of them than in 1858 and 1859, when the issue was involved in the North-South controversy, were torn between their desire to support a democratic system of higher education for the farmers and workers and their fears that the measure would contribute further to land speculation and land engrossment. They made a last desperate effort to amend the bill to limit the amount of land individuals could acquire with the scrip to 640 acres. The Senate adopted the amendment by the close vote of 20–19,[64] but promptly reversed itself.[65] The two votes taken on the amendment reveal solid support by Illinois, Indiana, Iowa, Kansas, and Oregon, and one vote each from Minnesota and Wisconsin. Lacking southern assistance, the West was overwhelmed by the aggressive East, now firmly in the saddle. The measure passed the Senate, June 10,[66] the House, June 17, 1862, and was signed by President Lincoln.[67] The latter's views on land policy, despite his frontier connections, were closer to those of Henry Clay than to those of Jefferson. It was also true that he, like others, regarded the Agricultural-College Act as less a land and more an educational measure. Only the most consistent land reformers kept up their opposition to the bitter end. The combined House-Senate vote on the measure shows that the landless states voted 93 to 5 for it and that the public-land states voted 30 to 27 for it. (See Table 2, p. 22.)

It is not difficult to account for the opposition of the members of Congress from Indiana and Illinois to the Agricultural-College Act.

because of their subservience to the "Slave Power." This is scarcely fair to those who were sincerely opposed to the measure, but it shows how much Greeley permitted his hatred of slavery to becloud his judgment. (*New York Tribune*, February 28, 1859.)

[64] *Cong. Globe*, 37 Cong., 2 Sess., June 10, 1862, p. 2627.
[65] *Id.*, 2629. The vote on reconsideration was 25–15.
[66] *Id.*, 2634.
[67] *Id.*, 2770; *U. S. Stat.*, xii, 503.

TABLE 2

Vote on the Agricultural-College Act of 1862

	HOUSE		SENATE	
	For	*Against*	*For*	*Against*
Maine	1	0	2	0
New Hampshire	2	0	2	0
Vermont	2	0	2	0
Massachusetts	8	0	2	0
Connecticut	3	0	2	0
Rhode Island	1	1	2	0
NEW ENGLAND	17	1	12	0
New York	17	3	2	0
Pennsylvania	17	0	1	0
New Jersey	3	0	1	0
MIDDLE STATES	37	3	4	0
Delaware	1	0	0	1
Maryland	3	0	1	0
West Virginia	4	0	2	0
Kentucky	9	0	1	0
Tennessee	2	0	0	0
OLD SOUTH	19	0	4	1
Ohio	12	3	1	0
Indiana	1	7	0	1
Illinois	2	4	2	0
OLD PUBLIC-LAND STATES	15	14	3	1
Michigan	2	2	2	0
Wisconsin	0	1	0	2
Minnesota	0	2	1	1
Iowa	0	1	1	1
Missouri	1	0	0	0
Kansas	0	0	1	1
Oregon	0	0	2	0
California	0	1	2	0
NEW PUBLIC-LAND STATES	3	7	9	5
Total vote	91	25	32	7

These states had nothing to fear from the further acquisition of land by speculators through the use of scrip, since their public lands were practically gone. Moreover, they were to receive generous subsidies compared with the newer public-land states. However, their representatives had not as yet assimilated the eastern attitude sufficiently to make them forget their frontier prejudices. In these two states were great tracts of land owned by resident and non-resident speculators whose unimproved holdings and opposition to expenditures for roads, schools, bridges, and other public works retarded the development of some of the richest counties. In Indiana the Ellsworths, the "Yale Crowd," the "cattle kings," [68] in Illinois the Scullys, the Funks, the Vandeveers, all great landed proprietors, still possessed estates which would put to shame many principalities and duchies abroad. Some of these great estates were only slightly developed; on others dwelt tenants in wretched hovels.[69] Absentee ownership blighted great areas of fertile land, prevented the development of an independent proprietor class, introduced what many considered an un-American system —tenancy—led to the abuse of the land and early depletion of the soil, and fed the fires of sectional hatred and social discontent.[70]

At the very time the agricultural-college bill was being considered in Congress, there was beginning in the Indiana legislature [71] a fight—which was to last for a full generation—over a bill to facilitate the collection of rents by giving landlords a lien on the crops of tenants. Believers in the democratic way of life were shocked at the introduction of such a measure and succeeded in defeating its enactment until 1881. Until then, the issue cropped up in almost every session, producing many acrimonious debates between those legislators who seemed to represent the interests of the landlords and those who were sympathetic to the increasing tenant class.[72]

George W. Julian and William S. Holman, sturdy Hoosier representatives of the underprivileged, out of the experience of their own state became leaders in the movement for land reform.[73] Staunch sup-

---

[68] Paul Wallace Gates, "Land Policy and Tenancy in the Prairie Counties of Indiana," *Indiana Magazine of History* (March, 1939), xxxv, pp. 1–26.

[69] Wm. Goodwin Moody, *Land and Labor in the United States* (New York, 1883), p. 79.

[70] Mention should be made of the Granger, Greenback and Populist movements, the causes of which may be traced to the breakdown of the democratic land system.

[71] The session of 1857 was marked by numerous arguments over the measure. *Indiana House Journal*, 39 Sess., 1857, pp. 998–999, 1155; *Indianapolis State Sentinel*, January 13, 14, 23, 1857.

[72] *Brevier Legislative Reports*, 40 Sess., 1859, p. 79; *Brevier Legislative Reports*, 41 Sess., 1861, p. 76.

[73] Since 1845 Holman had acted as agent for Allen Hamilton in renting a farm in Dearborn County for which, because there were no good public lands in the vicinity,

porters of a free-homestead policy and of all measures designed to curb land speculators by assuring settlers the sole right of acquiring land from the Federal Government, Holman and Julian conducted a notable crusade in Congress and in the popular journals of the day to carry out Jefferson's ideal of creating a nation of landowners through a democratically functioning land system.[74] None could say they opposed vocational education for farmers and workers. Yet they voted with a majority of the Indiana delegation against the Morrill bill, basing their opposition on the unfortunate effects of unbridled speculation and land accumulation which the measure would facilitate.

Senator Joseph A. Wright of Indiana, a real son of the soil, had a better understanding of western farm problems than any other member of Congress. He spoke from experience when he observed: "Nothing is so disadvantageous to a new State as to have a large amount of its land held by non-residents prior to its settlement." [75] He deplored tenancy,[76] and frequently condemned unsound farm practices which were already becoming associated with tenant operation of land.[77] Neglect of crop rotation, too much dependence upon corn for the major crop, and failure to keep cattle and to manure the land called forth his scathing denunciation. Education, he believed, would lead to better farm practices. In 1851, when governor of Indiana, he urged the establishment of agricultural schools where experimental farming could be carried on and training could be given in modern methods of agriculture.[78] The same year he asked the legislature to establish a

---

there was always a ready supply of tenants. Letters of Holman to Hamilton, March 29, 1845, February 15, 1848, March 24, 1849, January 23, 1850, September 5, 1850, December 16, 1855, December 20, 1856, December 3, 1858, April 13, 1861, Hamilton MSS, Indiana State Library.

[74] Paul Wallace Gates, "The Homestead Law in an Incongruous Land System," *American Historical Review* (July, 1936), xlii, 677 ff. This article contains some material on the connection of Browning and Harlan with the sale of the Cherokee Neutral Tract.

[75] *Cong. Globe*, 37 Cong., 2 Sess., May 30, 1862, pp. 2441–2442.

[76] *Address of Governor Joseph A. Wright Delivered before the Wayne County Agricultural Fair, 1851* (Indianapolis, 1851), p. 6.

[77] *Id.*, 7; *Address of His Excellency, Jos. A. Wright, Governor of the State of Indiana, Pronounced at the New York Agricultural State Fair, Elmira, Oct. 5, 1855* (Indianapolis, 1855), p. 11.

[78] *Address of Governor Wright to the Citizens of Cannelton, Indiana, on Saturday,*

state board of agriculture to which should be appropriated money sufficient to provide for state and local agricultural societies and for numerous agricultural fairs.[79] In 1858, when minister to Prussia, he visited a famous agricultural school at Hohenheim, about which he wrote glowing descriptions to the *Ohio Farmer*.[80] He early advocated a free-homestead law which would, he hoped, create a large class of owner-operators independent of land speculators and landlords.[81] In 1862, when he was at the peak of his political power and was regarded by President Lincoln as "the most potent man in the State . . ."[82] Wright could not bring himself to vote for the Morrill bill, which, he was convinced, would further land speculation.

Three other prairie politicians who, because of the exigencies of party politics had been led to support the agricultural-college bill in 1858 and 1859, reversed themselves in 1862. Schuyler Colfax of a northern Indiana constituency, Owen Lovejoy of the Alton district of Illinois, and James R. Doolittle of Wisconsin lived in areas where the heavy hand of the land speculator was everywhere felt. When they could no longer count upon a presidential veto, they felt themselves obliged to join in the fight against the measure.

Prairie politicians who supported the effort to restrict the amount of land that individuals could acquire with the scrip, but who voted for the bill in the end, were Browning and Trumbull of Illinois, Harlan of Iowa and Pomeroy of Kansas. Orville H. Browning, whose extensive legal practice had brought him into intimate contact with James F. Joy, the rising railroad king; James F. Harlan, a timeserving politician; and Lyman Trumbull, a conservative Illinois Senator whose sense of ethics was surprisingly high for the "Gilded Age," were all close friends of Lincoln. Samuel C. Pomeroy, the "Senator Dillworthy" of *The Gilded Age*, rarely showed regard for settlers' inter-

May 5, 1851, p. 4. In 1857 Wright urged that certain funds be used to endow an "Agricultural Professorship" at the State University (*Wabash Weekly Intelligencer*, January 21, 1857).

[79] *Monticello Prairie Chieftain*, January 14, 1851.

[80] *American Farmers' Magazine* (November, 1858), xii, 666–671.

[81] *Address of Governor Joseph A. Wright Delivered before the Wayne County Agricultural Fair*, pp. 6–7.

[82] J. W. Usher, Washington, July 25, 1862, to R. W. Thompson, Thompson MSS, Indiana State Library.

ests. Henry M. Rice, Senator from Minnesota, himself an able and successful speculator, condemned the measure strongly in 1859 and again in 1862; nevertheless, in the latter year he voted for it.[83] A few other relatively unknown congressmen from the public-land states, including Albert S. White, of Indiana, supported the measure. White, a lawyer, railroad president, and "conservative," [84] lacked the sympathetic understanding of the settler's problems possessed in such abundant measure by Julian and Holman. He was the only member of the Indiana delegation who voted for the Agricultural-College Act in 1862.

Unlike the long series of land reforms which had been adopted since 1800, the Agricultural-College Act cannot be considered a western product. It was one of the few land bills of the middle of the nineteenth century which was forced on the West by a combination of older states having no Federal lands. The West won its demand for homesteads, in part, but suffered defeat on the Agricultural-College Act.

[83] *Cong. Globe*, 35 Cong., 2 Sess., February 1, 1859, p. 718, February 4, 1859, p. 785, February 7, 1859, p. 857; *Cong. Globe*, 37 Cong., 2 Sess., June 10, 1862, p. 2634.
[84] *Dictionary of American Biography*, xx, 84–85.

CHAPTER TWO

The States Dispose of Their Land Scrip

§ 1. SPECULATORS CONTROL THE MARKET

OVER a long period of years the Federal Government had devised a land system which, imperfect though it was, yet worked fairly satisfactorily in the physical details of surveying, advertising, selling, and patenting land. Complaints were directed at the methods, the inefficiency, and the dishonesty of many of the employees of the General Land Office, but despite all, its record was fairly clear of major scandals. This could not be said of state land departments by the most charitable critic. Large quantities of public land had already been granted to the states for education, canals and railroads, and the draining of swamps, and the administration of these lands was notoriously fraudulent and wasteful. The new principle embodied in the Agricultural-College Act of granting to the older states land scrip which could be located only in the West made it necessary for twenty-seven states to provide for its management and sale.

Political morality had reached such a low level in the 1860's that the possession of millions of acres of scrip by the states seemed to call forth a concerted effort by spoilsmen to make use of it for their personal benefit. The story of the disposal of the agricultural-college scrip is one of neglect, carelessness, incapacity, and something closely akin to corruption.[1] The result was that in a number of instances the proceeds from the sale of the scrip were disappointingly small.

---

[1] A writer in the *American Farmers' Magazine* (December, 1858), xii, 705–706, foretold the story of the disposal of the scrip, as follows: "Some of the land would be fooled away, and nobody would know exactly where the avails had lodged. Some of the money would stick to the troughs, instead of flowing into the central reservoir. Politicians would swallow large juncks [sic], and you could not get it out of their maws. . . . There would be sad doings with the land and the money. Some of it would

Under the terms of the Agricultural-College Act only the interest upon the endowment derived from the sale of the scrip could be used by the states for the support of the agricultural colleges they were expected to establish. Consequently they had a strong incentive to turn their scrip into cash quickly. From the outset the opponents of the Act had contended that the measure was designed to make easier the accumulation of land by eastern speculators and that the forced sale of the scrip would depress the price to such low levels that small benefit would accrue to the newly established colleges. Unlike the military land warrants previously referred to, the agricultural-college scrip could not be used by pre-emptors to secure their small claims. This restriction made it of no use to a large class of settlers and depressed its price. Moreover, the scrip had to compete with free homesteads, which further reduced the demand for it. When, therefore, the northern states began to sell their scrip in 1864 and 1865 they found they were selling in a buyers' market and that the chief demand came from speculators. But, so pressing were the needs of the new agricultural colleges that in most cases the states could not wait, and they dumped their scrip in the market in such quantities that its price fell to a low of 42 cents an acre. The Rhode Island scrip was sold at this price; North Carolina and Kentucky sold their scrip for 50 cents an acre; New Hampshire and Ohio sold theirs for 53 cents an acre, and Indiana sold its for 54 cents an acre. Other states—including New York and Illinois, whose sales are described below—did somewhat better by selling their scrip at a later date.

Some of the states sold their scrip by methods not altogether fair and aboveboard. A block of Maine scrip was purchased in this way by Cyrus and George Woodman, extensive dealers in land and scrip. In March, 1866, Cyrus Woodman stated that he had found the governor of Maine and a member of his council friendly to him and through them had learned the bids of all competitors. Woodman was permitted to submit a late bid after the others had been opened and, as a result, secured 60,000 acres at 52½ cents an acre, which was the

go to erect piles of buildings, that would not be worth a tithe of the cost. . . . Some would pay very unworthy professors for doing nothing. Scamps would in some cases get the control, instead of honest men."

lowest price Maine received for any of its scrip.[2] In July, 1866, Woodman was negotiating for the New Hampshire scrip and urged his brother to go to Concord and consult with the state treasurer. That the same tactics were to be used in the negotiations is shown by the following statement: "It may be safe & expedient to offer him say $250 to let us know, (in case of competition) what bid from us will secure the scrip." [3] The Woodmans failed in New Hampshire because they lacked the influence which they enjoyed in their native state of Maine. They noted, however, that other agents were successful in using the same tactics they had used in Maine.[4] The Woodmans were offered 360,000 acres of Massachusetts scrip provided they would give a share of the profits derived from the business to a number of state officers, including the attorney general.[5] From Vermont they acquired scrip to the amount of 60,000 acres.

The large amount of military land warrants issued to ex-soldiers between 1847 and 1855 had prevented any dealer in warrants or any combination of such dealers from controlling the market and pegging the price. The warrants were issued to soldiers in all parts of the country and, in most cases, were sold to agents, banks, or land dealers. They were bought and sold on a small margin by brokers, and their price was regularly quoted in the large dailies. In contrast, the agricultural-college scrip was issued to twenty-seven states which preferred to sell their entire allotment in one deal. Bids for small quantities were not encouraged, but the broker who could take the full issue, even though on time, was favored. The result was that most of the scrip was acquired by a small number of dealers, and by 1866 one man had come to control the market.

[2] Cyrus Woodman, Boston, March 2, 21, 1866, to George Woodman; George Woodman, New York, March 3, 26, 1866, to Cyrus Woodman, Woodman MSS, Wisconsin Historical Society. Numerous complaints of fraud in connection with the disposal of the agricultural-college scrip of Maine led, in 1876, to the creation of a legislative committee to examine the matter. The investigation induced five members to believe that wrong had been done, while the other five members were convinced that the officials should be exonerated. (*Report of the Evidences and Conclusions of the Committee to Investigate the Sale of the Agricultural College Scrip*, made to the 55th Legislature, State of Maine, Augusta, 1876.)
[3] George Woodman, New York, July 10, 1866, to Cyrus Woodman.
[4] *Id.* to *id.*, New York, January 25, 1867.
[5] *Id.* to *id.*, New York, June 7, 8, 1864.

Gleason F. Lewis of Cleveland, acting for himself and as agent for David Preston of Detroit, outdistanced all rivals in securing scrip. Lewis described himself as a "land warrant broker who cashed government vouchers, bought and sold land warrants, collected pensions, dealt in agricultural college scrip and edited the 'Old Soldiers Advocate.'"[6] In 1867 he advertised that he had bought all the scrip of Kentucky, Indiana, Maryland, North Carolina, and New Hampshire, and part of that of Pennsylvania, Ohio, Massachusetts, and some other states. At this time his purchases amounted to more than 3,000,000 acres and subsequently he acquired nearly 2,000,000 acres additional.[7] These deals gave him a practical monopoly of the scrip, and it was but natural that other states should turn to him to dispose of their holdings.

§ 2. SPECULATIVE SCRAMBLE FOR LANDS

The land boom of the post-war years was stimulated by the sale of the agricultural-college scrip, which made possible the entry of large tracts of land at a relatively low cost. It was in the timbered sections of northern Michigan, of Wisconsin, and of Minnesota that the greatest boom occurred. Within two or three years the rush for land threatened to exceed the 1,000,000-acre maximum to which the Morrill Act limited scrip entries in each of the public land states. To secure the scrip entries that they wanted before the maximum was reached, lumbermen and eastern speculators frantically pushed their land-hunting expeditions and rushed their selections to the land offices for entry. In 1867 the maximum was reached in Michigan and Minnesota and in 1868 it was reached in Wisconsin and Nebraska. When the totals of entries for the various districts were compiled it was found that in these four states the maximum had been exceeded by as little as 78,000 acres in Nebraska and by as much as 397,000 acres in Michigan.

---

[6] G. F. Lewis, Cleveland, Ohio, March 16, 1865, to J. M. Edmunds, G File, General Land Office, Department of the Interior, Washington.

[7] George W. Julian refers to the advertisement in a speech in Congress of March 6, 1868, *Cong. Record*, 40 Cong., 2 Sess. (1867–1868), p. 1715; Bureau of Corporations, *The Lumber Industry* (4 parts, Washington, 1913–1914), Part I, p. 253.

Those making the late entries now sought relief from Congress and joined with another group which wanted certain restrictions upon the use of scrip removed. In 1870 a pliant Congress legalized these entries in excess of 1,000,000 acres.[8]

Congressional anti-monopolists were aroused to great indignation when they learned of the large quantities of scrip entered in the western states during 1866–1869. They pointed out that Lewis had come to control the market for the scrip and that huge tracts were being entered by speculators who had no intention of improving the land but were merely holding it for a rise in value.[9] Had they examined the entry books of some of the land offices, they would have found ammunition for the battle against monopolists. As the opponents of the Agricultural-College Act had predicted, the issuance of 7,830,000 scrip-acres had had the effect of reducing the cost of land to speculators. Homesteaders had no need for the scrip, pre-emptors were denied the right to use it, but capitalists who were looking for large tracts of land found the scrip a great boon, for it enabled them to get nearly double the amount of land that they could buy with cash. The land-office abstracts of the three lake states and of Kansas, Nebraska, and California show that most of the scrip was used by speculators to acquire timber and farm lands. Among the prominent persons whose names appear on the entry books are Henry Ward Beecher, Simon Cameron, Samuel J. Tilden, John Sherman, and Amos A. Lawrence. The following list includes only a few of the largest holdings secured by means of agricultural-college scrip: [10]

Name	Located in	Acreage
Chapman, William S.	California	210,000
Cornell, Ezra	Wisconsin	499,000
Crothers, John P.	Nebraska	29,000
Dodge, Satterlee & Mason	Michigan	85,000

[8] 16 *U. S. Stat.*, 186.
[9] See the speeches of Oliver P. Morton of Indiana, Alexander Ramsey of Minnesota, and Timothy O. Howe of Wisconsin in the *Cong. Record*, 40 Cong., 1 Sess. (1867), March 26, 1867, pp. 346–347, and of George W. Julian, *Cong. Record*, 40 Cong., 2 Sess., March 6, 1868, pp. 1712–1716.
[10] Compiled from the abstracts of entries made with agricultural-college scrip, National Archives, Washington, D. C.

Name	Located in	Acreage
Friedlander, Isaac	California	192,000
Frost, Geo. E.	Michigan	34,000
Hansell, B., Trustee	Michigan	72,000
Harper, Rice (Jay Cooke et al.)	Minnesota	45,000
Howe, Calvin	Minnesota	89,000
Lawrence, Amos A.	Kansas	62,000
Miller & Lux	California	79,000
Mitchell, John W.	California	32,000
Palms & Driggs	Michigan	103,000

Dozens of other lumbermen, speculators, and mining groups entered from 5,000 to 50,000 acres in the same way.

Such engrossment of the public lands led the anti-monopolists to introduce a bill in Congress in 1868 to restrict to three the number of sections which might be acquired with scrip in any township. The measure slipped through easily and became a law on July 27, 1868.[11] As usual, the General Land Office was slow in transmitting notices of it to the local land officers, but speculators were not so slow. After the passage of the bill, but before news of it reached the Stockton and Visalia offices in California, 66,720 acres were entered in solid tracts. In Nebraska, Minnesota, and Iowa there was also unusual activity at the land offices, caused by people seeking to enter solid tracts with the scrip before the new measure went into effect.[12]

The Act of 1868 naturally depreciated the value of the scrip, and this led representatives of the eastern states to demand its repeal. Ezra Cornell, who, as is to be shown in the following chapter, was still holding 100,000 scrip-acres, journeyed to Washington and induced Senator Roscoe Conkling to support repeal. In behalf of Cornell University and two or three other colleges which still held their scrip, Conkling argued against the Act of 1868, pointing out that the restrictions on the scrip had depreciated its value from $1 to 60 cents an acre. Cornell and Conkling won converts for repeal, but when they tackled Thomas A. Hendricks of Indiana they aroused him to fiery opposi-

[11] 15 *U. S. Stat.*, 227.
[12] Letter of January 19, 1869, of Jos. S. Wilson, Commissioner of the General Land Office, in *Cong. Record*, 40 Cong., 3 Sess., February 4, 1869, p. 874.

tion. Hendricks countered with a typical anti-monopoly speech in Congress opposing repeal, wherein he said:

As I understand, . . . the purpose of Mr. Cornell is to hold this scrip until he makes the locations himself, selecting good lands, and to hold the lands until they shall go up in value. So far as he may locate the scrip upon pine lands in the timber region of country, there is no serious objection to that; but when the proposition is distinctly made to locate large bodies of the public lands for the benefit of a college or for the benefit of any other institution, and let them be held thus in dead hands, if I may so express it, until the farmers go in and improve the surrounding country, make farms, schoolhouses, churches, and roads, and give a value to this land that is held in large bodies, so that there may be a speculation to the holder growing out of the enterprise of the farmers, I shall not approve upon any proposition whatever. I think that is the purpose, and I think the purpose is not right in view of the interests of the settler.[13]

Cornell's visit to Washington was unsuccessful, but in the following year the restrictions on the use of the scrip were somewhat lightened.[14]

In the early seventies those southern states which previously had been denied their share of scrip finally received it. In practically all cases they sold the scrip to Lewis, who paid 90 cents an acre for it. This was nearly twice the price obtained by such northern states as New Hampshire, New Jersey, Pennsylvania, Indiana, and Maine. Radical reconstructionists may have delayed the establishment of southern agricultural colleges, but they did the South a service in withholding the scrip from sale for a time. But none of the states receiving scrip, except New York, could feel that Congress had adopted a system of endowing the colleges which was adequate.

Most of the western states which received lands instead of scrip managed their possessions as badly as the eastern states did their scrip

---

[13] *Id.*, 874–875.
[14] The Act of July 1, 1870, authorized the use of scrip by actual settlers in the same way that military warrants could be used in entering pre-emption claims (16 *U. S. Stat.*, 186). Previously only speculators could use the scrip. As interpreted by the Commissioner of the General Land Office in instructions to the local land officers, July 22, 1870, the Act of 1870 did not remove the three-section limitation upon entries in a township, nor did it remove the million-acre maximum, except that pre-emption claims entered with scrip were not to be counted toward the maximum (Circular: "Application of Agricultural College Scrip to Pre-emptions," copy in Cornell University Library).

and consequently had little to show for the generosity of Congress. Exceptions are Minnesota, California, and Kansas.

§ 3. SMALL RETURNS FOR MANY COLLEGES

The meager returns obtained from land or scrip were discouraging, and supporters of vocational education came to regret that the states had not been given a cash subsidy for their agricultural colleges in place of the land or scrip donations. The endowments were quite inadequate, and in consequence the early history of many of the colleges is marked by promising beginnings, followed by quick retrenchments. Except for small appropriations for buildings, the states were not able to support the struggling institutions, and additional Federal assistance was sought. In 1872 the National Agricultural Convention, representing the land-grant colleges as well as agricultural societies, met in Washington for the purpose of securing a further donation from Congress. There was some controversy as to the best proposal to urge upon Congress; some members, like William W. Folwell of Minnesota, favored equal donations of land or scrip to all states regardless of population; others favored an additional donation based on population, as in the Morrill Act. Few—whether westerners or easterners—were satisfied with the grants of land or scrip the states had received. The western states, it was pointed out, had received little land, although some of them had obtained high prices for their tracts by withholding them from sale for a few years, while the eastern states had received large scrip-acreages but had been forced to sell at low prices. The members pressed hard for a cash subsidy or for an additional grant of land, but were unsuccessful.[15]

The framers of the Agricultural-College Act clearly intended that the scrip should not be used by the eastern states to acquire land in the West but that it should "be sold by the said States." To make doubly certain, they included this provision in the Act:

---

[15] "Proceedings of the National Agricultural Convention," February 15–17, 1872, *Sen. Misc. Doc.*, 42 Cong., 2 Sess. (1871–1872), pp. 3–84; Illinois Industrial University, Board of Trustees, *Fifth Annual Report* (1871–1872), p. 71; *id., Sixth Annual Report* (1872–1873), p. 74.

In no case shall any State to which land scrip may thus be issued be allowed to locate the same within the limits of any other State, or of any territory of the United States, but their assignees may locate said land scrip upon any of the unappropriated lands of the United States subject to sale at private entry at one dollar and twenty-five cents, or less, per acre. . . .[16]

These two restrictions would seem both to preclude the states from entering land with the scrip and from assigning it to state institutions which would do so. But a number of states, which saw an opportunity of sharing in the land boom that accompanied the return of prosperity after 1862, did not accept this interpretation.

Senator Morrill's own state of Vermont was one of the first to accept the Government's bounty. Its act of December 1, 1862, named two agents to receive the scrip, and directed them to examine the public lands subject to private entry and to procure information which "will be useful in the disposal and location of the Scrip." These agents were also authorized to sell or assign any part of the scrip and to invest all "moneys derived from the sale of lands or scrip."[17] On April 21, 1863, Massachusetts authorized the appointment of a commissioner "to locate, without unnecessary delay, all the land scrip . . . and to sell the same from time to time. . . ."[18] Subsequently, both states decided not to acquire land and sold their scrip at relatively low prices. Whether or not the reversal of policy was brought about by doubts as to the legality of the state's acquiring land with the scrip is not clear. One cannot help wondering whether Senator Morrill's own section was led by him to consider locating the scrip, or at least was influenced by a private interpretation he may have given to the Agricultural-College Act.

Rhode Island and Illinois were more determined than Vermont and Massachusetts to create a substantial endowment for their agricultural colleges by speculating in western lands. They did not permit the doubts—which some members of their legislatures may have had—to prevent them from undertaking large ventures in western land. A third state, New York, sold its scrip to one of its prominent residents

[16] 7 *U. S. Stat.*, 503.
[17] *Vermont Statutes*, 1862, pp. 38–39.
[18] *Massachusetts Private and Special Statutes, 1860–1865*, p. 419.

who agreed to use it to enter lands for the benefit of an agricultural college. Senator Henry M. Rice's prediction was in this way partly fulfilled. In the course of debate on the Morrill bill he had said:

> Their agents [eastern states] will locate the land. . . . The States will issue it [scrip] to their own agents, and they will locate the lands; they will follow along the border of our settlements, they will follow on the line of our railroads, and they will take every acre of the land that is worth anything, and there let it lie as an incubus on our prosperity, until it shall be worth five, ten, twenty, or fifty dollars an acre, and that value added to it by the labor of the citizens of the State.[19]

§ 4. BROWN UNIVERSITY'S MISFORTUNE

Rhode Island assigned its interest in scrip to Brown University on condition that it establish a college or department of agriculture.[20] The university was required "to locate, without unnecessary delay, and at their best discretion, the said scrip upon some of the public lands of the United States, properly open to be located upon, and from time to time sell and dispose of the lands . . . so that the largest price can be obtained for the same." [21] These provisions may have been included on the recommendation of two prominent Providence merchants and land dealers, Robert H. Ives and John Carter Brown, who were trustees of the university. Before the Civil War Ives and Brown had entered 162,000 acres in Illinois and Iowa, and subsequently they acquired 56,000 acres in Kansas, Nebraska, Missouri, and Minnesota. The experience and the profits which they had derived from their western lands may have led them to favor using the 120,000 acres of scrip which the state had received to locate land in the West.

The trustees of Brown University determined to locate their scrip in Kansas, and "within 2 hours after the passage of the resolution of assignments" they undertook to press the General Land Office to issue the scrip promptly.[22] Congress was then engaged in making lavish

---

[19] *Cong. Globe*, 25 Cong., 2 Sess., February 1, 1859, p. 718.
[20] *Providence Journal*, January 15, 28, 1863.
[21] *Rhode Island Statutes*, 1863, p. 214; *Providence Journal*, January 15, 1863.
[22] New York, *Senate Documents*, 97 Session, 1874, No. 103, p. 389; *Providence Journal*, January 28, 1863.

donations of public land to railroads, and the trustees apparently planned to anticipate railroad selections; hence their haste. Although no scrip entries could be made before July 2, 1863, on several occasions prior to this date the trustees sent an agent to Washington, accompanied by the Rhode Island Secretary of State, to urge that the scrip be issued promptly. Bureaucratic red tape delayed action, and the trustees, alarmed lest their plans be frustrated by the representatives of the railroads, sent their agent, Horace Love, and President Barnas Sears to Kansas in May, 1863, to make selections and have them withheld from entry until the scrip could be forwarded from Washington.[23]

Love spent over a month in Kansas inspecting land and making selections,[24] and when President Sears arrived in the latter part of June he was ready to make the formal entries. Promptly, at nine o'clock on the morning of July 2, the first day on which entries could be made with agricultural-college scrip, they attended the land office at Atchison and filed application for the entry of 26,080 acres. Four days later they applied to enter an additional 13,920 acres. The local land officers, impressed by President Sears's explanation that the scrip had been delayed by the General Land Office, agreed to reserve the land for him. The tracts thus reserved were in the vicinity of the projected Atchison & Pikes Peak Railroad, which had been given a land grant by Congress the previous year. It was good business to locate land near a railroad route, since its value would rise sharply once the line was constructed, and there was nothing improper in anticipating the railroad's selections. But the Atchison & Pikes Peak Railroad and its promoter and president, Samuel C. Pomeroy, Senator from Kansas, were no mean adversaries to encounter.

Senator Pomeroy had early settled at Atchison and he labored mightily to transform the little town into a busy metropolis. His first

[23] Love had formerly been engaged jointly by Waterville (now Colby) College and Brown University to secure additions to their endowments (Walter C. Bronson, *History of Brown University, 1764–1914* [Providence, 1914], p. 332). It was stated that he was put in charge of the land business "as well for his intelligence and interest . . . as for his experience in the business of Public Land Offices" (*Rhode Island Public Documents,* 1864, No. 12, p. 4).

[24] While in Kansas in 1863 Love took advantage of the opportunity to make a homestead entry which in the following year he sought to commute (Horace T. Love, Washington, December 24, 1864, to J. M. Edmunds, G File, General Land Office).

success was in getting the land office located at Atchison. What was more important, he brought railroads to it. The Atchison, Topeka & Santa Fe Railroad, destined to become one of the transcontinentals, the Atchison & Nebraska, the Atchison & Pikes Peak, and a number of other lines were induced to make Atchison their terminus, and for a time it looked as if Pomeroy's town might become an important railroad center and forge ahead of Kansas City and the numerous smaller cities of the Missouri Valley.[25] To the Atchison & Pikes Peak Railroad was given the same subsidy—$16,000 and 12,800 acres of public lands for each mile of railroad constructed—as was given to the Kansas Pacific and the Union Pacific. True, the subsidy and land grant were to apply for only 100 miles, but through Pomeroy's influence the railroad secured another juicy plum, the right to buy 123,000 acres of much desired Kickapoo Indian lands at $1.25 an acre.[26] Pomeroy was an active member of the so-called land and Indian "rings" which were rapidly acquiring some of the best lands and highly lucrative Indian contracts in Kansas, and it was the misfortune of Brown University that its agents crossed swords with Pomeroy and his friends.

When the promoters of the Atchison & Pikes Peak Railroad learned what lands had been selected for Brown University they were galvanized into action. After making a "flying survey" of the line, they rushed their report to Washington to prevent the confirmation of the selections made by Love and Sears. The Commissioner of the General Land Office, J. M. Edmunds, ruled that the register and receiver of the Atchison land office had acted improperly and illegally in reserving land for Brown University. He also denied that there had been any delay in issuing the scrip, saying that the Agricultural-College Act interdicted the location of the scrip before July 2, 1863, and that within "a month and five days of that time, and as soon as the printed forms and records were furnished us" the scrip was sent to the states.

[25] Draft of letter of the Acting Commissioner of the General Land Office, September 18, 1865, to Secretary of Interior, Commissioners' File, Interior Department; *Freedom's Champion* (Atchison), September 11, 1858; *Lawrence Republican*, September 2, 1858; *Council Grove Press*, November 30, 1863.
[26] 13 *U. S. Stat.*, 623.

Edmunds ordered the local officers to reopen the reserved lands to entry and to accept the first legal entries for them. The Commissioner also took occasion to remind the local land officers that the Agricultural-College Act "requires 'said scrip to be sold' " by the states, which makes one wonder whether he was questioning the right of the State of Rhode Island to assign its scrip to Brown University and the right of the latter to enter land with it.[27]

Not discouraged, Brown University sought the assistance of the Rhode Island delegation in Congress to induce the Commissioner to reverse his decision and to confirm the selections. Further selections were also made which it was planned to enter "as required." [28] Love, Sears, and the Rhode Island delegation put up a strong fight and eventually triumphed over the powerful opposition of the railroad forces. In 1864 there was added to the Union Pacific Railroad bill of that year a section which stated that all lands "which were located, or selected to be located" under the Agricultural-College Act of 1862 should be excluded from the land grant of the lines which were to join the Union Pacific. Two years later the Secretary of the Interior reversed the decision of Commissioner Edmunds and removed the suspension which had been placed on the entries of Love and Sears.[29] Some of their selections did not conform to technical quarter-sections required by the law, but the university was permitted to make substitutions so that practically all the original selections—or lands equivalent in value to them—were acquired. Altogether some 46,200 acres were entered in Marshall and Nemaha Counties. Meantime, the construction of railroads into the area brought in its wake a large immigration, and, as the government land in the vicinity was quickly snapped up, a demand for the land held by speculators was soon created. Foresighted investors now had the opportunity of reaping a harvest of profits, but, unfortunately, Brown University was not to collect its share.

---

[27] J. M. Edmunds's letter is in New York, *Senate Documents*, 97 Session, 1874, No. 103, pp. 391–392.
[28] *Loc. cit.*, 394.
[29] Horace T. Love, Windsor, Vermont, October 25, 1866, to J. S. Wilson, G File, General Land Office.

It appears that early in January, 1865, the university had decided to dispose of its lands and unlocated scrip, regardless of the price.[30] When the details of the sale were divulged it was found that the land and scrip had been sold on credit, without interest, for $50,000.[31] This was at the rate of 42 cents an acre, the lowest price received by any state for its scrip. The official historian of Brown University has explained the sudden abandonment of the land business as resulting from the heavy "cost of locating the lands, paying taxes, negotiating sales, and defending some of the titles." [32] It is true that the legislature had required the university to pay all the expenses of locating, managing, and selling the lands and also to pay the taxes thereon, a charge which, the board of trustees reported, was "a draft upon the limited income of the university, which it cannot afford." These expenses were certain to be large for some time and the university could not reimburse itself from sales of land for several years. There was then good reason for its officials contemplating the land investment with misgivings, but these difficulties should have been foreseen. Belated recognition of the obligations they had incurred is no justification for the panicky sale made by the trustees.

Somehow an injustice had been done to the university, for the price received was scandalously low. Much time and money had been expended in making the selections which, within a short time, were to be confirmed. They had been well located in a rich agricultural area, and when the Atchison & Pikes Peak Railroad was constructed it ran through the center of them. Within a short time the land would easily have brought from $5 to $10 an acre.[33] Equally scandalous

---

[30] New York, *Senate Documents*, 97 Session, 1874, No. 103, p. 395.

[31] *Loc. cit.*, 396; *Providence Journal*, January 13, 1866. Most scrip sales of any quantity were made on credit but with interest.

[32] Bronson, *op. cit.*, p. 334.

[33] In 1868 the Kansas State Agricultural College offered for sale 90,000 acres of choice land in Marshall, Washington, Riley, and Dickinson Counties, of which it sold 16,000 acres in Marshall County in 1869 for $64,000 (compiled from Marshall County Deed Records and *Kansas Farmer*, v [May, 1868], p. 80). The Union Pacific Railroad, Central Branch, successor of the Atchison & Pikes Peak Railroad, in 1868, advertised 152,000 acres of land in Atchison, Brown, and Jackson Counties, Kansas, for sale at prices ranging from $2.50 to $15 an acre. The Union Pacific Railway advertised in the same year 2,000,000 acres in Kansas for sale at from $1 to $5 an acre. The Union Pacific Railway, Southern Branch, offered 1,300,000 acres in Kansas in 1869 at from

was the sale of the scrip for substantially less than other states were receiving at the time. For example, Ohio, which received 629,920 acres of scrip, sold 27,000 acres in small lots between August, 1865, and August, 1866, for prices ranging from 75 to 82 cents an acre. Then, in September and October, the remainder of the scrip was dumped on the market and the price fell to 53 cents, or 13 cents more than the Rhode Island scrip brought.[34] The correspondence of George and Cyrus Woodman reveals even better the going price for the scrip. On January 4, 1866, just a few days before the Brown lands and scrip were sold, George instructed his brother to sell scrip for 65 cents an acre. On February 17, 1866, George wrote that the bid price for scrip was 55 and on February 20, George offered to take 80,000 acres of scrip at 52½ cents. In March, 1866, George and Cyrus bought 60,000 acres of Maine scrip at the bottom price of 52½ cents while other purchasers paid from 53 to 57½ cents.[35]

The Brown lands and scrip were sold to Horace T. Love, who had been in charge of making the selections, and he in turn sold the land in 1866 and 1867 to Stebbins & Porter of Kansas for an average of 93 cents an acre.[36] They also acquired part of the scrip and with it entered 54,000 acres in Kansas and Nebraska. These acquisitions made the firm one of the largest landowners in the two states. Meantime, Love offered the remainder of the scrip he had acquired from Brown for 19 cents an acre more than he had paid for it.[37] That the sale to Love should arouse "sharp criticism" was to be expected.[38]

$2 to $8 an acre, and the firm of Van Doren & Havens of Leavenworth, Kansas, offered for sale 200,000 acres of Kansas land at from $3 to $10 an acre (*Kansas Farmer*, v [January, March, 1868], pp. 14, 47; vi [October, November, 1869], pp. 173, 192).

[34] Thomas C. Mendenhall, editor, *History of the Ohio State University* (3 vols., Columbus, Ohio, 1920), vol. i (1870–1910, by Alexis Cope), pp. 11–12.

[35] New York, *Senate Documents*, 97 Session, 1874, No. 103, p. 372.

[36] Horace T. Love, Windsor, Vermont, December 8, 1866, to J. S. Wilson, and Love (for Stebbins & Porter), Washington, D. C., January 27, 1867, to J. S. Wilson, G File, General Land Office; Nemaha County Deed Records, D, 145, E, 446.

[37] Horace T. Love, New York, March 21, 1866, to Francis Palms (Palms MSS, Burton Historical Collections, Detroit Public Library).

[38] Bronson, *op. cit.*, p. 334.

§ 5. GOOD MANAGEMENT IN ILLINOIS

The Illinois scrip was managed in a way that reflects credit upon the state and the officials of the new university. Unlike the neighboring states of Indiana, Michigan, Wisconsin, and Iowa, Illinois had failed to establish a state university before the adoption of the Act of 1862. It was also somewhat slower than neighboring states in utilizing its scrip, which amounted to 480,000 acres. Delay was caused by the rivalry of a number of Illinois towns that were competing for the location of the university. After a spirited struggle from which Champaign-Urbana emerged victorious, the legislature in February, 1867, incorporated the Illinois Industrial University—now the University of Illinois—and to it assigned the scrip.[39]

Apparently the legislators of Illinois, like those of Rhode Island, entertained no doubt that it was legal for a state-incorporated institution to enter the scrip despite the restrictions embodied in the Act of 1862. However, they authorized the trustees of the new university either to enter the scrip or to sell it. Their reason for doing so probably was that the Illinois university, unlike Brown, was in immediate need of funds, since its only source of revenue, except the promised land-grant fund, was a $450,000 subsidy of Champaign County, from which only a small income could be expected because it was not all in interest-bearing securities.

The trustees organized on March 12, 1867, but took no action on the disposal of the scrip until May 8, when they authorized the sale of 180,000 acres of scrip at not less than 54 cents an acre. This was approximately the market price at the time, and there was little hope of securing a higher price for any but scattered lots until the bulk of the scrip still remaining in the hands of the states had been sold. The trustees could not wait, and had to accept the prevailing price. Satisfied with this transaction, they authorized the sale of an additional 100,000 acres of scrip, which brought 58 cents an acre. By this time the scrip was rising in value, and when, on November 26, 1867, the board received from G. F. Lewis an offer to buy 100,000 acres for 85

[39] Act of February 28, 1867, *Public Laws of Illinois*, 25 General Assembly, 1867, p. 123.

cents an acre, some of the trustees felt that the previous sale had been ill-advised. Lewis, who was now attempting to control the market, finally bought the 100,000 acres at 90 cents.[40] Thus 380,000 acres of scrip had been sold for $250,192, or at an average price of 66 cents. Illinois's delay in accepting the Federal grant and turning the scrip over to the university had made possible an advance in price, over that received by Indiana and Ohio, of 12 cents an acre. But Illinois was to do even better.

Although the university needed to sell the bulk of its scrip early in order to have a fund earning interest as soon as possible, the trustees intended from the outset to invest a substantial amount of the scrip in lands. However, they had doubts about their right to use the scrip in this way and they urged the senators and representatives of Illinois to secure an amendment to the Agricultural-College Act "to enable the Trustees of the Industrial University . . . to locate the lands, or any part of them . . . at their discretion, instead of selling the scrip."[41] As no such amendment was adopted, it would seem that the doubt of the trustees subsequently disappeared, for on May 8, 1867, they instructed their officers to "ascertain the practicability of obtaining desirable lands and to locate 100,000 acres if, in their judgment, judicious selections could be made."[42]

After making "extensive enquiries" concerning opportunities for land investments in Minnesota, Iowa, Kansas, and Nebraska, the Regent, John M. Gregory, and one of the trustees, Moore C. Goltra, went to west-central Minnesota, where they entered 15,972 acres in Pope, Kandiyohi, and Renville Counties. Subsequently, Goltra visited Gage County, Nebraska, just north of where the Brown University scrip had been entered, and located 9,340 acres.[43] Goltra was of the

---

[40] Illinois Industrial University, Board of Trustees, *First Annual Report*, pp. 37, 43, 67, 95; *id., Second Annual Report*, pp. 56–57; Ezra Cornell, New York, December 6, 1867, to William A. Woodward.

[41] Illinois Industrial University, Board of Trustees, *First Annual Report*, 1868, p. 28.

[42] *Id.*, p. 37.

[43] Some 56,000 acres of Gage County land was acquired by speculators with agricultural-college scrip—more than one-tenth of the total area of the county. This concentration of speculator ownership retarded settlement and had other unfortunate effects upon the development of the county which called forth a scorching indictment of the Act of 1862 by Hugh J. Dobbs, in his *History of Gage County, Nebraska* (Lincoln,

opinion in November, 1867, that at least 30,000 acres additional could be entered and that the entire amount of 100,000 acres might be obtained with an extension of time. He stated that the selections already made would within a few years be worth from $3 to $5 an acre. Numerous difficulties in making selections intervened, however, and on June 12, 1868, Goltra abandoned hope of entering the entire 100,000 acres and moved that 50,000 acres of scrip be sold at not less than $1.10 an acre.[44] The trustees still planned to enter the remaining 25,000 acres of scrip, and in 1869 Goltra made another search for suitable land.[45] In 1871 Regent Gregory, while admitting that all efforts to locate the remaining scrip had thus far been unsuccessful, expressed the hope that when additional land in southern Kansas was surveyed it would be possible to complete the selections.[46] In 1872 the remainder of the scrip, 24,480 acres, was sold for $1 an acre. A total of $319,172 had thus far been received for the 454,480 acres of scrip, or 70 cents an acre. This sum, invested in county bonds bearing 10 per cent interest, brought in a larger return than any other state received from its land scrip fund.[47]

Gregory, Goltra, and the other trustees of the university followed a conservative policy in selecting land. Pine land they avoided because the risks were greater in dealing in it than in prairie or farming land and because it required more careful management. Unlike many eastern speculators they refused to make entries "sight unseen" but insisted on examining the land personally before they would risk the scrip. When in 1869 and 1870 they were unable to find first-class selections, the more attractive lands having already been selected or claimed by homesteaders, they were not rushed into taking inferior land. Finally, as subsequent examinations were to show, their selections were wisely made.

Burt Powell, whose *History of the University of Illinois* is an able piece of historical research, has pointed to the brilliant success of

1918), pp. 59–62. Cf. Robert Diller, *Farm Ownership, Tenancy and Land Use in a Nebraska Community* (Chicago, 1941).
[44] *Second Annual Report*, p. 73.
[45] *Id.*, p. 73; *Third Annual Report*, pp. 88, 92.
[46] *Fourth Annual Report*, pp. 64, 107.
[47] *Sixth Annual Report*, p. 112.

Cornell University in locating its scrip and managing its lands, and has expressed regret that the trustees of Illinois did not enter the entire 480,000 acres of scrip in western land instead of the paltry 25,000 acres. The fault was not with the trustees, however; they had to sell the larger part of the scrip in order to provide revenue for immediate needs. Furthermore, both Illinois and Cornell found it necessary to carry their lands until the eighties and nineties before prices could be obtained which covered costs and a fair return on the investment. Had there been forced liquidation prior to 1880, neither institution could have escaped without losses. From the vantage point of the twentieth century one can see that investments in good prairie or pine lands, if properly managed and held through the periods of depression, brought in large profits, but there were long periods when land prices were low, and many holders lost confidence and sold out. Whether the State of Illinois could have paid taxes on 480,000 acres of unproductive land for fifteen or twenty-five years is not clear. One might also question whether it would have been expedient for the university to locate such an amount of land in Kansas or Nebraska at a time when agrarianism was growing so rapidly. Cornell University managed its land and scrip differently from Illinois and was somewhat less subject to attacks by grangers. Wisconsin, it should be noted, proved to be a safer state for absentee owners to have investments in than Kansas or Nebraska during the critical years 1870–1900.

The records of the land business of the University of Illinois, so far as they are available, do not reveal the numerous complications which Cornell University encountered in the administration of its Wisconsin land. There was little to steal from the prairie sections Illinois had selected; squatters upon prairie lands might cut down the few trees for fencing, pasture their stock on the grasslands or remove the hay, break small patches for cultivation, and sometimes enclose entire areas illegally, but they did no irreparable or even serious damage to the land. It was not necessary to employ agents to protect the land, attorneys to oust squatters and to attempt to recover damages for stolen timber, or log-drivers to run the illegally cut timber to market. The Illinois officials did not find the taxes on their land unbearable, they seemed satisfied with the rise in land values, and they certainly could have no cause for complaint at the prices they ultimately received.

The University of Illinois, in common with most holders of prairie land, was forced to wait longer than it had anticipated for the expected rise in land values. In 1867 the finance committee thought that the lands might bring from $3 to $8 an acre "within a few years."[48] Five years later agents were sent to Nebraska and Minnesota to inspect the land and prepare estimates of its value with a view to early sale. The Nebraska land was found to be in an area that was rapidly being settled and was estimated to be worth from $4 to $7 an acre, but the Minnesota land, still remote from railroads and receiving little attention from settlers, was valued at only $2 to $5 an acre. In 1874 another agent reported additional improvements in the vicinity of the Nebraska land, but the panic of 1873 and resulting depression brought to a halt the demand for land for a decade.[49]

Meantime the University of Illinois was being called upon to meet an increasing burden of taxes upon its land. Fortunately the state legislature, although niggardly in its early appropriations for the university, was willing after 1873 to grant money for the taxes. Altogether $63,200 was appropriated by the state from 1873 to 1901 for this purpose. This was no great sum, but if all the 480,000 acres of scrip had been entered, the tax burden, at the same rates, would have amounted to well over a million dollars. Such a sum, one can well imagine, would have seemed too great to members of the legislature, and there would doubtless have been demands for early sales, possibly premature sales, which would have been disastrous. Cornell University, it may be pointed out, after the first fruitless years was able to meet the taxes upon its land from sales.

Gage County, Nebraska, developed rapidly between 1870 and 1890, its population increasing from 3,359 to 36,344.[50] Such a rapid influx

---

[48] *First Annual Report*, p. 67.

[49] *Fifth Report*, pp. 157–158; *Sixth Report*, p. 73; *Seventh Report*, pp. 117–118.

[50] The growth of the county was somewhat retarded by the existence within it of the Otoe Indian Reserve, a part of which was opened for sale in 1878 (Addison E.

of settlers assured enquiries for the university land. In 1882 bids were received offering $4 to $6 an acre, but they did not tempt officials to sell.[51] In 1883 another examination showed that the university land was almost completely surrounded by well developed farms and was parcelled out among a number of cattlemen and sheepmen, chiefly non-residents from Missouri and Kansas, who were pasturing 10,000 or 12,000 head of stock on it.[52] The examiners recommended that the land be offered for sale at $12.50 to $15 an acre; if it were decided not to sell even at these prices, they urged that the land be leased.

Much of Nebraska was still relatively undeveloped, partly because the state and federal land systems had been so rigged to favor speculators that they had easily acquired large amounts of land, thus here, as elsewhere, retarding settlement. When these speculators could not get the price they demanded they found it possible to rent their land to tenants who could not find satisfactory homesteads. The census of 1880 revealed that 18 per cent of the Nebraska farms were operated by tenants, and that Gage County, in which William Scully and other proprietors held substantial holdings, had 24 per cent of its farms tenant-operated.[53] The University of Illinois was already leasing a number of farms in Illinois to tenants and it naturally decided, in the absence of satisfactory bids, to lease its Nebraska land.[54] In 1884 it rented 29 quarter sections for $596.[55] The unleased land was used by cattlemen, but it was difficult to make them pay rent. Unlike the Scullys, the university had no intention of keeping its rented land permanently, and the policy of leasing was adopted only as a temporary means of making the land pay, in part, its cost of maintenance.

By 1884 the price of land in Gage County had reached such levels

Sheldon, "Land Systems and Land Policies in Nebraska," *Publications,* Nebraska State Historical Society, xxii [Lincoln, 1936], 207, 332).

[51] An offer of Major J. W. Pearman, of Nebraska, to buy all the Gage County land was rejected. *Twelfth Report,* pp. 166, 173–174.

[52] *Id.,* p. 209.

[53] Jacob Shoff entered 23,000 acres in Gage County in 1869 and 1870. Scully's land was acquired from dealers in the eighties (Sheldon, *op. cit.,* p. 321).

[54] In 1869 the University of Illinois leased 400 acres to six persons at rents ranging from $2.80 to $5 an acre (*Third Report,* p. 115).

[55] *Twelfth Report,* p. 236.

that the university was enabled to make sales at the valuation it had set. The 9,340 acres were sold between 1884 and 1889 for an average of $13.01 an acre.[56]

The Minnesota land was sold more slowly. It was remote from settlement and from railroads, and until well into the seventies there was unsold government land in its vicinity. The trustees watched the Minnesota land carefully, frequently sending examiners to report on the price of surrounding land and on improvements and other factors which might affect land values. Rents were collected from some tracts, and in the nineties it became possible to sell them at the price set upon them. The 16,099 acres brought an average of $12.90 and grossed $207,878.

For the 25,440 acres it entered in Nebraska and Minnesota, the University of Illinois received a total of $329,518, which is an average of $12.95 an acre. This was more than the entire 454,480 acres of scrip had brought, and it is not surprising that the officials deplored the failure to enter more of the scrip. The entire business of managing the scrip sales, scrip entries, rentals, and land sales had been conducted with caution and wisdom, a record in sharp contrast to that of Rhode Island and numerous other states.[57]

[56] *Fifteenth Report*, pp. 66–70. The descriptions of the land, the names of purchasers, and the prices and payments are all given.

[57] The summary of sales is taken from a manuscript prepared by C. P. Slater, "History of the Endowment Fund of the University of Illinois," March 5, 1934. It is impossible to determine the net profits derived from the sale of the Nebraska and Minnesota land because the minutes of the Trustees' meetings contain no analysis or summary of costs. It has been seen that the State of Illinois appropriated $63,200 for taxes. There were few expenses aside from those incurred by the land examiners, the costs of advertising and of publishing circulars, and agents' fees, all of which were small items. It is probable that the university made a profit of about $10 an acre over what it would have received from the sale of the scrip.

CHAPTER THREE

Ezra Cornell Founds a University

NEW YORK STATE and the college which it chartered to teach "agriculture and the mechanic arts" managed the New York land scrip with unparalleled success. The disposal of this scrip and the entrance of Cornell University into one of the largest and ultimately most successful land speculations in American history is important as illustrating the functioning of government land policies.

Since it had the largest representation in Congress, New York received a greater amount of scrip than any other state, 989,920 acres. At prices prevailing in 1864 and 1865 this quantity would have sold for a half-million dollars, which would have yielded at least $30,000 annually. Few colleges in the United States had so large an income, and in New York State only Columbia College could boast such riches.[1] New York had its share of denominational colleges, most of which had only a small income from fees, little or no endowment, and few students, and it was to be expected that these small colleges would cast longing eyes at the Federal grant.

There were two institutions in New York, both chartered in 1853, which had real claims upon the Federal grant. They were the New York State College of Agriculture, at Ovid, on Seneca Lake, and the People's College at Havana, near Montour Falls, twenty-five miles south of Ovid. The charters of these institutions had been obtained as a result of a decade of agitation by numerous workingmen's associations and agricultural societies, ably supported by such men as Harri-

[1] The total income from fees, investments, and rents, in 1864, of each of the principal colleges of New York was as follows: Columbia, $166,116; Elmira, $28,838; Genesee, $6,828; Hamilton, $15,592; Madison (now Colgate University), $10,405; New York University, $14,313; Rochester, $8,542; Union, $20,691 (*Seventy-eighth Annual Report of the Regents of the University of the State of New York, 1865* [*Senate Documents,* 88 Session, 1865, No. 55]).

son Howard [2] of Lockport, D. C. McCallum of New York, and Horace Greeley, editor of the *New York Tribune*. Both colleges were founded with similar purposes: to provide higher education for farmers and mechanics in agricultural and mechanical arts, fields which were quite neglected by existing colleges. Unfortunately private support for non-sectarian colleges was not forthcoming, and the state was called upon for assistance.

In 1856 New York agreed to loan the State College of Agriculture $40,000 for buildings when it could show that an additional $40,000 had been subscribed privately.[3] The loan gave encouragement to local interests around Ovid, who raised $40,000 in pledges to secure the location of the institution in their midst. A tract of 750 acres bordering on Seneca Lake was acquired and a "pretentious edifice" was constructed on this property.[4] In 1860 the college was opened with an enrollment of twenty-seven students, among whom were two sons of Ezra Cornell.[5] Unfortunately, the institution was in difficulties from the outset because of inadequate financial support, interest on a debt it had incurred in financing construction, the outbreak of the Civil War, the withdrawal of its president for war duties, and, finally, the enlistment of many of its students. Faced with an emergency, the trustees sought further aid from the state but none was forthcoming. Finally, in December, 1861, the college was forced to close its doors. Its trustees did not give up hope, however, that aid would still be provided, and when the Agricultural-College Act was passed the big chance seemed to have come.[6]

[2] In the library of Cornell University there is a manuscript "Sketch of the Origin of the 'Mechanics Mutual Protection' organization and of the establishment of the People's College," prepared by Harrison Howard, Ithaca, New York, January 1, 1886, in which is traced the movement for a college of mechanical arts in New York State. There is also a scrapbook kept by Howard, containing newspaper clippings of numerous meetings at Buffalo, Lockport, Seneca Falls, Elmira, and elsewhere, called for the purpose of arousing interest in People's College.

[3] Act of March 31, 1856, *Laws of New York*, 79 Session, 1856, p. 96.

[4] New York, *Assembly Documents*, 76 Session, No. 36, February 18, 1853; *id.*, 78 Session, No. 64, February 16, 1855; *id.*, 82 Session, No. 118, March 3, 1859; *id.*, 83 Session, No. 27, January 10, 1860.

[5] Benjamin Cornell, Agricultural College, Ovid, December 15, 1860, to his grandfather, Elijah Cornell (Cornell MSS, De Witt Historical Society).

[6] Annual report of the New York State College of Agriculture, January, 1861 (New York, *Assembly Documents*, 84 Session, 1861, No. 20); report of John A. King, Chair-

People's College, of which Horace Greeley was an enthusiastic trustee, likewise was meagerly supported and seemed to be just another of the numerous educational experiments which had not "caught on." Charles Cook, a former contractor on the Chemung Canal and the Erie Railroad, provided funds for the construction of a large building and donated an extensive site for the institution at Havana, a town which he was promoting. He also offered to purchase Elmira Female College and to consolidate it with his institution but his offer was rejected.[7] Cook's liberality did not meet expectations and the college languished until 1862, when Cook became a member of the State Senate, where he sought a public appropriation for the college. Adroit manoeuvring secured the enactment of a measure which provided that when People's College could show that it had engaged seven professors and was prepared to receive students it would be granted $10,000 annually for two years, the money to be applied toward the payment of salaries and the enlargement of the library.[8]

Emboldened by this success, the advocates of People's College came back to the legislature in 1863 to ask that the land grant be given to it. The promised subsidy was not sufficient to enable the college to open, and the State Comptroller reported that People's College had been in existence for eleven years but had never had a student nor a professor.[9] Nevertheless, the trustees made a vigorous fight for the land grant and their efforts prevailed over those of the advocates of the State Agricultural College.[10] They secured an act which provided that the income from the sale of the land scrip was to be given to People's College if it could show within three years that it owned buildings, grounds, library facilities, and laboratory apparatus suffi-

man of the Board of Trustees of the New York State College of Agriculture, March 2, 1864 (New York, *Senate Documents*, 87 Session, 1864, No. 87).

[7] *New York Tribune*, March 2, 1859. There is a sketch of Cook in the *History of Tioga, Chemung, Tompkins and Schuyler Counties, New York* (Philadelphia, 1879), pp. 657–658.

[8] Act of April 24, 1862, *Laws of New York*, 85 Session, 1862, pp. 868–869.

[9] Annual Report of the Comptroller, January 5, 1864 (New York, *Assembly Documents*, 87 Session, 1864, doc. 4, p. 28).

[10] Ezra Cornell, Albany, February 6, 1866, to George F. Wheeler (Cornell MSS, Cornell University). Act of May 14, 1863, *Laws of New York*, 86 Session, 1863, pp. 884–887. Manuscripts cited in this study, unless otherwise indicated, are found in the rich collection at Cornell University.

cient to accommodate 250 students, possessed a farm of 250 acres with sheds, buildings, tools and other farm implements, and had a faculty of ten competent professors. The Act of 1863 was loosely framed, especially that section which provided that if there should be a surplus in the income from the land-scrip fund over and above the needs of People's College it should be divided among other colleges which could comply with the conditions of the Morrill Act.

It was not long before the trustees of People's College realized that the requirements of the Act of 1863 could be met, if at all, only with the greatest difficulty. They therefore asked for an extension of time in which they might continue their efforts to raise the necessary funds. Encouraged by the apparent failure of People's College, the rival institution at Ovid resumed agitation for a share of the income from the land scrip.[11] Furthermore, numerous religious colleges with small incomes and few students but great ambitions joined in the scramble for a share of the government's bounty. Andrew D. White, a member of the Senate in 1865, many years later wrote his recollections of this contest in which he said:

> Hamilton College was represented at various times by the president who I think was Dr. Fisher, the treasurer, Mr. Williams, and the agent, Dr. Goertner. Genesee College was represented somewhat later by a very powerful body of leading men from its neighborhood and by its chief speaker Professor Bennett afterwards of Syracuse. Rochester University was perhaps the most vigorous of all in its action upon the Legislature through the public press. Dr. Anderson became very bitter and Pursell the leading democratic editor kept up a series of most malignant attacks against Mr. Cornell, and all connected with him up [to] the time of Mr. Cornell's death.
>
> As to Hobart and Madison Universities my impression is that they were represented at some of the hearings before the committee, but their main activity was in the newspapers.
>
> The influence of Union against us was felt strongly at Albany in a general way but Columbia did not, so far as I remember, take any part in the struggle against us.[12]

---

[11] Report of John A. King, Chairman of the Board of Trustees, New York State College of Agriculture, 1864 (New York, *Senate Documents*, 87 Session, 1864, doc. 55, pp. 1–5).

[12] Andrew D. White, Ithaca, New York, October 29, 1895, to W. T. Hewett (White MSS). See also the Albany *Atlas and Argus*, March 11, 1865. Carl Becker has called

Into this turbulent scene Ezra Cornell was forced by his own enthusiasm for vocational education for farmers and mechanics.

Ezra Cornell was a self-made man whose fortune was acquired more by good luck than good management, for the simple fact is that he was not a good business man. In 1828 he settled in Ithaca, where he was successively employed as mechanic, millwright, general manager of a factory, and contractor. In 1841 he undertook to market a newly perfected plow in Maine, where he had exclusive rights to its sale. An inventor in his own right, he devised a machine for laying telegraph lines underground which might have made him money had not the overhead system of lines proved more feasible. Cornell's inventive genius and the quickness with which he grasped the problems of the new telegraph industry brought him to the attention of its leaders. His talents were immediately employed by them, and for the next twelve years he was engaged in constructing telegraph lines, persuading people to invest in the growing industry, and promoting and managing new companies. Over-construction and too much competition, combined with serious errors in managing his own companies and in making contracts with others, brought Ezra Cornell to the point of bankruptcy, from which he was saved by the fortuitous organization of the Western Union Telegraph Company and the opportunity it gave him of exchanging his shaky investment for one which was shortly to bring him wealth. The rise in the market value of Western Union securities left Cornell with a comfortable fortune estimated by his son at two million dollars.[18]

Gradual withdrawal from active participation in the telegraph industry left Cornell with time to engage in other enterprises. He served six years in the state legislature, where he gave special attention to problems of agriculture. But his chief interests were centered

---

my attention to an error in White's statement. It was not William Pursell, editor of the *Union and Advertiser*, but Robert Carter, editor of the *Rochester Democrat*, who led the attack upon the bill to charter Cornell University. In the Cornell MSS, De Witt Historical Society, there are 46 petitions, numerously signed, asking the legislature to provide for the division of one-half the income from the land scrip among colleges other than People's College, or asking that $50,000 of the fund be granted to Genesee College and Genesee Wesleyan Seminary at Lima.

[18] Alonzo B. Cornell, *Biography of Ezra Cornell, Founder of Cornell University* (New York, 1884), p. 118.

in Ithaca. If the city was to hold its own against rival communities in central New York it had to be given railroad connections. Cornell's funds were poured lavishly into lines to connect Ithaca with Geneva, Elmira, and Utica. The panic of 1873 wrought havoc with these enterprises and seriously depleted his capital.

Cornell was keenly interested in the welfare of workingmen and farmers. Their lot, he felt, could be improved by education. The Cornell Library of Ithaca, to which he gave $100,000, was designed to provide reading opportunities for those people who could not afford to buy the best literature in technical and cultural fields. On his farm of 300 acres, on East Hill overlooking Ithaca, he kept the best breeds of cattle, sheep, and swine and hoped that through them he could improve the livestock of his section. He was active in the State Agricultural Society, of which he became president in 1862. The numerous addresses he gave on agriculture breathe a liberal desire to aid the farmers by improving agricultural practices. He became an early advocate of technical training for young farmers and mechanics, and yearned to aid them by providing educational opportunities for them. He was a warm friend and trustee of the State Agricultural College, to which he sent two of his sons. When the land scrip issue came before the legislature his first thought was that the income should be given to the State Agricultural College, but later he came to support a plan to divide the income between it and People's College. To the former he contemplated giving $300,000 as an endowment,[14] but his heart was not in that enterprise as much as it would have been had the college been located at Ithaca. When Andrew D. White, a prominent member of the New York Senate, protested against dividing the land scrip on the ground that the returns from it would be inadequate for more than one institution, Cornell agreed with him and gradually came to the decision to establish a new college at Ithaca. Here was Cornell's great opportunity. With an endowment of more than a million dollars—to be derived from a gift he was prepared to make and from the proceeds of the land scrip—such an institution could provide technical training for many young men of the working class. This

[14] Andrew Dickson White, *Autobiography* (New York, 1905), i, 295.

was the purpose closest to his heart, and for the remainder of his life it was his principal interest.

By 1865 it was apparent that there was little financial support to be had for either People's College or the State Agricultural College. It is true that each institution had a considerable estate in land and buildings, and to many it may have seemed best to select one of the two and grant it the entire endowment. But White and Cornell were now thinking of a new institution, and each of them was ambitious to locate it in his own community, the one in Syracuse and the other in Ithaca. By promising to endow the new university with $500,000, Cornell won White over to the Ithaca location. White made a fighting speech in the senate in support of a new institution, in the course of which he condemned the Agricultural College as being bankrupt and People's College as totally unable to meet the minimum requirements established by the State.[15] But White did more than merely speak for the Ithaca location; he won the support of Senator Charles J. Folger by agreeing to join with him in a move to have the State locate a proposed insane asylum on the site of the Agricultural College.[16] By clever tactics White induced the New York Central Railroad lobby, then engaged in a campaign to secure the repeal of an act limiting passenger rates to two cents a mile, to aid in getting the Cornell bill reported out of committee, where it seemed to be buried, to the Senate floor.[17] Despite these moves the advocates of People's College were still sufficiently strong to secure a three-month extension of the period which that institution might have to conform with the requirements of the Act of 1863.[18] If at the end of that time the college had failed, the income from the land scrip was to become available to

[15] Undated document, perhaps a draft of a speech, prepared by Ezra Cornell, 1865, Cornell University; pamphlet, *The Cornell University: Speech of Hon. Andrew D. White, in Senate, March, 1865*.

[16] Folger had argued that the State Agricultural College should be continued by the state as a seminary offering instruction in agriculture and engineering on the freshman level (*Atlas and Argus*, March 11, 1865).

[17] *Utica Herald and Gazette*, April, 1865; *Atlas and Argus* (Albany), March 29, 1865, quoting the *Rochester Democrat;* Andrew D. White, Helsingfors, Finland, September 8, 1893, to George L. Burr, Cornell University.

[18] Statement signed by A. H. Bailey, James A. Bell, and Andrew D. White (Cornell MSS).

Cornell University. A final compromise was the inclusion within the act chartering Cornell University of a provision which required Ezra Cornell to pay to Genesee College, a small Methodist institution, the sum of $25,000. These vote-swapping and logrolling arrangements made possible the chartering of Cornell University and the conditional grant to it of the income of the land-scrip fund.

Meantime, the State had authorized its Comptroller, Lucius Robinson, to offer the land scrip for sale and to invest the proceeds. After consulting with other state officers the Comptroller set a price of 85 cents an acre on the scrip and advertised it for sale in 1864. The bulk of the scrip of other states had not as yet been thrown on the market, and it was possible to sell 76,000 acres at this price before the market weakened. Thereafter, Robinson did not feel justified in selling at 50 or 60 cents, which was all that the scrip was bringing, and in January, 1865, he suggested that "the land be held until sales can be made at fair rates." [19]

After securing the charter for the university Ezra Cornell took a keen interest in the management of the land scrip, which he hoped would provide a large income for salaries and expenses. The charter provided that the scrip should be sold by the Comptroller and that the income only should be paid to the trustees of the new institution. Although there was good ground for urging haste in selling the scrip to meet the financial needs of the university, Cornell proposed a plan which would have prevented, possibly for years, income being derived from the government's bounty. The plan was for the State to entrust the scrip to Cornell, who would use it to acquire land in the West for the benefit of the university. When the State Comptroller refused to agree to this plan, Cornell tried to interest the trustees of the new university in buying the scrip and making entries with it, but again he failed. As a last resort he undertook, with his own resources, to buy the scrip, enter the lands, and manage them until they could be sold profitably. All returns above cost, and seven per cent interest for the

---

[19] *Reports* of the Comptroller, 1864, p. 28; 1865, pp. 29–30. The net proceeds from the sale of the scrip were $64,440, as a rebate of two cents an acre was allowed on 8000 acres "in consideration of certain advantages offered in the matter of advertising in the Northwestern States."

use of his capital, he agreed to donate to Cornell University. To this plan the Comptroller assented.

The first step was taken in October, 1865, when Cornell bought 100,000 acres of scrip at 50 cents an acre. This price was slightly less than scrip was bringing in the market at the time, but in view of the purpose for which it was being acquired it was accepted. The next year Cornell made a new contract with the State for the purchase of the remainder of the scrip, as fast as he could use it, at 60 cents an acre, one-half of which was to be paid in "good seven per cent bonds" and the other half—secured by good collateral or by the titles to the land acquired with the scrip—was to be paid when the returns from the land business in which Cornell was engaging for the university permitted. In both contracts Cornell agreed to pay into the Cornell Endowment Fund the net proceeds of the land business. Two distinct funds were thus provided for, namely, the Land Scrip Fund, which came from the sale of the scrip by the State and which was to be used for the support of the program of education authorized in the Morrill Act, and the Cornell Endowment Fund, which was to serve as a general endowment.

The 989,920 acres of land scrip which New York State received were all purchased by Ezra Cornell except for the 76,000 acres previously sold by the Comptroller. Of this amount 521,120 acres of scrip were used by Cornell to enter land in Wisconsin, Kansas, and Minnesota. Selecting the land was no small task and merits a chapter in itself. There were numerous agents of eastern capitalists looking for land at the same time with the depreciated land scrip, and the maximum of 1,000,000 acres which could be entered was soon exhausted in the important states. By 1868 it was becoming increasingly difficult to acquire land with agricultural-college scrip, since the quotas had been exhausted in Michigan, Wisconsin, Minnesota, and Nebraska, and the quality of the land elsewhere available was not attractive. Furthermore, the trustees of Cornell University were pressing Ezra Cornell to sell a portion of the scrip which remained in his possession and for which—under the terms of the second contract—he had not paid cash, in order that there might be a larger income immediately available for instruction. Before the demands of a united board of trustees Cornell gave way and agreed to sell the remaining scrip.

Prior to 1867 scrip sales had brought about 53 or 55 cents an acre, but Cornell hoped to manipulate the market to raise the price to a dollar or more.[20] In combination with G. F. Lewis, Cornell urged the governors of those states which had not sold their scrip to hold it until the price should rise. To his gratification, within "a few weeks" after operations were begun the price did rise and he was able to sell 100,000 acres at 90 cents and 180,000 at $1 an acre. This success encouraged him to refuse offers for $1 for smaller lots and to hold the remaining scrip for $1.15. The market turned downward, however, and the last 101,920 acres were sold to Lewis at 86 cents.[21] Like the southern states, Cornell was fortunate in offering the scrip for sale when it was bringing a relatively high price.[22] It should, perhaps, be pointed out that the additional price received for the New York land scrip over what Ezra Cornell paid to the State Comptroller was not added either to the Land Scrip Fund or to the Cornell Endowment Fund.

Cornell did not plunge into the western land business without first asking advice from many quarters and weighing well the risks in-

---

[20] The following sales of scrip at prices above 55 cents were made before 1867: Ohio, 12,800 acres at 80¢, 13,760 at 75¢ and 320 at 56¢; West Virginia, 320 at 65¢, 3,200 at 62¢, 320 at 61¢, and 5,280 at 60¢; Indiana, 2,560 at 60¢; Maine, 7,680 at 57½¢; New York, 76,000 at 85¢; Pennsylvania, 22,400 at 81¢. (New York, *Senate Documents*, 97 Session, 1874, No. 103, pp. 363–381; Asa E. Martin, "Pennsylvania's Land Grant Under the Morrill Act of 1862," *Pennsylvania History*, ix [April, 1942], pp. 105 ff.).

[21] Cornell explained his efforts to raise the price of scrip in his testimony given before the Supreme Court in Orange County in the case of Woodward against Cornell (*Woodward vs. Cornell*, 1871, 2 vols., ii, 864 ff.; this record is cited hereafter as *Woodward vs. Cornell*). An earlier effort at a combination of scrip holders to control the price was made by Governor John A. Andrew of Massachusetts, who suggested a "concert of action between the states with regard to the sale" of the scrip. This suggestion was characterized by the Maine legislature as a "wise and prudent measure," and the Governor was authorized to act in concert with the officials of other states in selling the scrip (*Maine Acts and Resolves*, 1864, Act of March 24, 1864). In 1865 or 1866 there was held a scripholders' convention for the purpose of raising the price of scrip (Horace Love, New York, March 21, 1866, to Francis Palms [Palms MSS, Burton Historical Collections, Detroit Public Library]).

[22] G. F. Lewis afterwards stated that Cornell had succeeded in so raising the price of scrip that other states received some $5,000,000 more than they would have obtained without his aid (G. F. Lewis, Cleveland, Ohio, May 17, 1873, to Ezra Cornell [Cornell MSS, Cornell University]). The letter was edited and published in the *Ithaca Journal* and from there reprinted in Albert W. Smith, *Ezra Cornell* [Ithaca, New York, 1934], pp. 163–164). There is no basis for the $5,000,000 figure.

volved. The first person he called upon for help was William A. Woodward, a friend and a former resident of Ithaca.[23] From March, 1865, when Cornell first approached Woodward, until 1871, when the two broke off relations as a result of a misunderstanding over the compensation which the latter was to receive for his services, Woodward had an important part in locating and administering the Cornell lands.

Woodward, who described himself as a "merchant's counsellor," [24] had been in the land and warrant brokerage business for a number of years. In 1848, having acquired a considerable quantity of military land warrants on a falling market, he went west to dispose of them. There he found prices substantially higher than in New York and he was able to rid himself of the warrants at a profit. While on this western trip he learned of a method of securing quick, almost fabulous, returns upon money.[25]

Pioneer settlers on the frontier frequently preceded the surveyor or land officer, squatted upon the public lands before they were open to sale, constructed rude improvements, and, when the public sales were announced, made frantic efforts to raise sufficient money to buy their claims. Since they had no title to mortgage it was practically impossible for them to raise the $200 needed to buy their quarter-section claim unless they were fortunate enough to be able to borrow from relatives or friends in the East. In desperation, the luckless squatters went to the "loan sharks" who frequented the government land offices, their pockets bulging with gold to be loaned at extortionate rates. In some cases the squatters agreed to deed one-half of their improved claim if the loan shark would enter the land for them.[26] More frequently, the squatter agreed to permit the loan shark to enter his claim, take title, and draw up a contract of sale which each party signed. According to the contract, the squatter was to buy his claim for $230 and to make payments in one or two years, with interest at 12 per cent. The loan shark would enter the land with a

---

[23] *Woodward vs. Cornell*, pp. 2 ff.
[24] Woodward, Vail's Gate, New York, August 10, 1865, to Ezra Cornell.
[25] *Id.*, May, 1865, to Victor M. Rice.
[26] John Catlin, Madison, Wisconsin, August 2, 1838, to Moses Strong (Strong MSS, Wisconsin Historical Society).

military warrant which cost perhaps 90 cents an acre. His profit upon the transaction, if payments were completed in two years, would be $141.20 on an investment of $144, or approximately 48 per cent a year. In case the negotiation was arranged through a local agent he would, of course, receive a commission or share in the profits. The records of numerous investors from the East, the Middle West, and the South, who loaned large sums through western agents, indicate that the profits from the "time entry" business, as it was called, were more than substantial.[27]

Many contracts thus entered into by squatters were never fulfilled, and the loan shark would find the land on his hands with taxes and interest costs accumulating. If he were caught with heavy commitments just before a financial crash, such as that of 1857, he might have extreme difficulty in carrying through his operations to a better time when he could unload. Speaking from experience, Woodward warned Cornell that an investor in western lands must be prepared for such contingencies and should retain a sufficient reserve to enable him to carry his lands through a period of depression and to keep up tax payments until they were sold.[28]

Woodward himself financed the entry of more than 40,000 acres of land for settlers in Wisconsin on the time entry basis. From these investments he secured a good return. He also bought and sold prairie and hard-wood lands which were suitable for farming. He first worked through Catlin & Williamson of Madison, but by 1860 he had changed to Henry C. Putnam of Eau Claire. As a result of his operations in Wisconsin Woodward had acquired considerable familiarity with the state, its land, tax, and registry laws, the districts preferred by settlers,

[27] The figures in the text are taken from the contracts made by William A. Woodward through his Wisconsin agents, Catlin & Williamson of Madison. The contracts are dated from 1848 to 1853 and are in the papers of Catlin & Williamson, Wisconsin Historical Society. These prices are somewhat lower than were charged by agents in Iowa and Illinois and by other agents in Wisconsin. Washburn & Woodman of Mineral Point charged $240 for each quarter section instead of $230 (Washburn & Woodman, Mineral Point, Wisconsin, April 9, 1853, to D. K. Noyes, Baraboo, Wisconsin [Washburn & Woodman Letter Book, 1853, Wisconsin Historical Society]). There the profits ran as high as 75 per cent a year. I have described the operations of two of the largest southern operators in western lands in "Southern Investments in Northern Lands before the Civil War," *Journal of Southern History*, v (May, 1939), pp. 161–163.

[28] Woodward, Vail's Gate, New York, August 10, 1865, to Ezra Cornell.

and the opportunities for speculating in Wisconsin land. More important, perhaps, he had engaged as his western agent one of the shrewdest land dealers in Wisconsin if not in the entire upper Mississippi Valley.[29]

Cornell wrote frequently to Woodward in 1865 concerning the western land business, about which he was seeking as much information as he could get. Woodward was familiar only with Wisconsin, and he recommended that state unreservedly to Cornell, assuring the latter that if the scrip were entrusted to him he could locate it on land that would within a few years sell for ten to twenty times its cost. Woodward proposed to use some scrip to enter land for squatters at frontier interest rates and other scrip to acquire farm land. He felt certain that there would be immediate returns from these operations sufficient to carry a larger investment in pine land until expected prices could be obtained. Woodward felt himself to be on safe ground in making these rosy promises because he planned to employ H. C. Putnam as his agent in selecting the land. As will be explained more fully later, Putnam was in a position to control the selection of the best pine land on the upper Mississippi, and he assured Woodward that with the 900,000 acres of Cornell land scrip he could acquire practically a monopoly of the upper-Mississippi pine for the University.

Although getting along in years like Cornell himself, Woodward was willing to enter a new enterprise provided he could be assured of profitable returns. He was doubtless stirred by Cornell's vision of a new university, but his letters clearly show a motive of self-interest. Woodward's worst trait was his facile way of speaking or writing as one who was thoroughly familiar with the farming, the land, and the lumber business of Wisconsin. The success he had attained in his ventures and his ingratiating manner enabled him to win the confidence of Cornell who, for a time, relied heavily upon him, although, as events were to show, there was little basis for that reliance. The simple fact is that Woodward had been fortunate in his land business

[29] The details of Woodward's land business may be worked out from the records in the Catlin & Williamson MSS, Wisconsin Historical Society, and the Putnam-Woodward correspondence, Cornell University. Woodward's own description of his operations may be found in his testimony in *Woodward vs: Cornell.*

and had made a considerable profit from it, but lacked the knowledge necessary for successful large-scale operation in western lands. Furthermore, Woodward desired to fill a position for which there was no real justification, that is, to act as a middleman between Ezra Cornell and the actual agent in Wisconsin who was to have charge of selecting the land, paying taxes upon it, and selling it. Woodward's chief and only important part in the Cornell land business was in encouraging Ezra Cornell to make his entries in Wisconsin and in introducing him to a more able, more shrewd, and more experienced land dealer, Henry C. Putnam.

Cornell considered other states besides Wisconsin for his land operations. Woodward told him that "excellent selections" could also be made in Missouri "to great advantage, either for purposes of speculation, or for settlers." [30] He also reported favorably on the "fine rolling prairies" of Kansas and Nebraska. Cornell sought information on Kansas from Elijah C. Chase, a nephew who had settled somewhat earlier at Shawnee. Chase replied that taxes were high in Kansas, a factor which discouraged many speculators from investing there, that the homesteaders were rapidly taking up the best land in the valleys, and that regions back from the streams on the higher sections were not as attractive. Chase stated that there was still good land in his state and expressed a willingness to enter it for Cornell.[31] Upon his recommendation 4,000 acres were acquired in Kansas, but Cornell was not sufficiently impressed with that state to risk a great amount of scrip in it. Apparently no further consideration was given to Kansas and Nebraska prairie land. Minnesota interested Cornell and he made efforts to secure information concerning opportunities for land investments there, but the descriptions provided him did not make the state appeal to him as Wisconsin did. Consequently, he entered only 7,968 acres there.[32]

Cornell had a distant relative living in Chippewa Falls, Wisconsin, with whom he corresponded about pine lands on the Chippewa. W. J.

---

[30] Woodward, Vail's Gate, New York, January 27, 1866, to Ezra Cornell.

[31] Elijah C. Chase, Shawnee, Kansas, December 9, 1865, to Ezra Cornell.

[32] Stephen Miller, St. Paul, Minnesota, July 9, 1866, to Ezra Cornell; Cornell, Albany, February 12, 1866, to John E. Bell, Minneapolis, Minnesota.

Cornell was a well-known timber cruiser, logger, and contractor who fared well in the various enterprises in which he engaged. He was well respected, apparently knew the pineries thoroughly, and might have been of considerable assistance to Ezra Cornell.[33] W. J. Cornell stated that he had 50,000 acres of good pine lands already selected which he would be glad to enter for Ezra Cornell for one-fourth of the land.[34] Had the offer been accepted it might have saved Cornell and the university a great deal of trouble and expense. But there was one principal difficulty in the way and that was Henry C. Putnam, who had such complete control of the Eau Claire land office, where all entries in the Chippewa Valley had to be made, that no rival could secure land that Putnam wanted for himself or for his clients. W. J. Cornell could not promise his kinsman that by using the land scrip they could secure a monopoly of the pine on the Chippewa, as Woodward could.

Cornell also corresponded with an old friend who lived in Waupaca County, Wisconsin, about the possibility of locating some of the scrip on the Green Bay watershed. Cornell asked his friend whether lands owned by non-residents were taxed more heavily than those owned locally and what would be the prospect for entering and selling within a comparatively short time from 10,000 to 100,000 acres in northeastern Wisconsin.[35] These and other enquiries brought him a good deal of information about the Wisconsin pineland business.

On the first board of trustess of the university was a man who doubtless had much to say to Cornell about investments in the pine lands of the lake states. John McGraw had by 1865 accumulated more than his share of wealth in the lumber industry. During the

---

[33] In 1860 W. J. Cornell advertised that he had thoroughly explored 20,000 acres of pine land in the Chippewa Valley and was prepared to locate for others (*Eau Claire Free Press*, May 24, 1860). In 1873 he was engaged to construct a wagon road for a distance of 30 miles in the wilderness south of La Pointe which, it was later reported, was "very thoroughly" built (*Ashland Press*, November 1, 1873, January 10, 1874; *Chippewa Herald*, January 23, 1874).

[34] W. J. Cornell, Chippewa Falls, Wisconsin, March 31, April 2, 1866, to Ezra Cornell; E. Cornell, Albany, April 11, 1866, to W. J. Cornell.

[35] Cornell's letters to Ira Millard of New London, Wisconsin, are dated March 5, 22, April 3, 8, December 18, 1865, and February 6, 1866.

Civil War years he and Henry W. Sage had acquired some choice pine land in the Saginaw Valley of Michigan. At Bay City, which they had a share in establishing, McGraw constructed a "mammoth saw mill" described as "unquestionably the champion of the world in the way of fast cutting," and Sage's mill was only slightly smaller.[36] McGraw alone and with others owned lumber yards at Tonawanda and Rochester, New York; Portsmouth, Michigan; and Indianapolis, Indiana. Subsequently he acquired an interest in some of the largest mills on the Mississippi and the St. Lawrence and he and his associates bought many thousands of acres of pine in Wisconsin, Minnesota, and other states. McGraw's widespread interests did not lead him to forget his home community of Ithaca, in which he took great pride. He owned a large block of real estate in the city. He was a charter trustee of Cornell University and was the first person to provide a permanent building on the campus. His wealth was to be given liberally to the university and he served it well from 1866 to the time of his death in 1877. Ezra Cornell came to lean upon McGraw in land matters, and McGraw's confidence in pineland values may well have confirmed the favorable opinion of Wisconsin pine lands that he had got from Woodward.

It was upon the advice of such men that Ezra Cornell undertook one of the largest land speculations in American history.

[36] *Lumberman's Gazette,* June 13, 1874, p. 1; speech of John F. Driggs, *Congressional Globe,* May 7, 1868, p. 2381.

CHAPTER FOUR

Hazards of Land Speculation in Wisconsin

To WHAT extent and to whom had the public domain in Wisconsin been alienated, the state in which Ezra Cornell proposed to invest a million dollars? Ever since 1834, when Wisconsin lands were first opened to sale and settlement, speculators and "loan sharks" had been attracted there. Quantities of eastern and southern capital had been invested in lands and mortgages, and from the beginning the territory had been under heavy obligations to absentee capitalists. In the thirties it was the mineral lands of the lead district around Mineral Point, the prairie and hard-wood lands in southern Wisconsin, and town lots in ambitious communities such as Belmont, Platteville, Madison, Milwaukee, and Green Bay which attracted attention. Many of the large purchasers entered land for settlers on the time-entry basis, as Woodward did at a later date. A partial list of the larger entries made by non-residents in the thirties will give an indication of the extent of the speculation and of the areas from which the investors came (see Table 3, on the next page).

The panic of 1837 was followed in Wisconsin by a long period during which prices were low, speculation in land was almost dormant, little new capital was available for investment, and immigration declined. In the late forties the tide began to turn, and for a decade men and money flowed into the state at a rapid rate. By 1850 there were 305,000 people in Wisconsin, most of whom had recently arrived, and during the next decade the population increased by 470,000. The state developed most rapidly between 1846 and 1857, when land entries were made at the rate of 1,000,000 acres a year on the average, or more than three times as rapidly as in the post-panic years.

TABLE 3

LARGE ENTRIES IN WISCONSIN BY NON-RESIDENTS, 1834–1839 [1]

Name	Residence	Acres
Baker, L.	New York City	8,420
Biddle, E. S. & T.	Philadelphia, Pennsylvania	8,100
Bronson, F., et al.	New York City	24,464
Carroll, C. H. & W. T.	Livingston County, New York	11,230
Comstock, Merle	Jo Daviess County, Illinois	15,151
Denniston, G. V.	Albany, New York	5,209
Hale, E	Ontario County, New York	8,517
Hall & Olcott	Charlestown, New Hampshire	6,426
Healey & Kercheval	Detroit, Michigan	21,145
Hubbard, G. S.	Chicago, Illinois	6,694
Hubbard, H., et al.	Charlestown, New Hampshire	5,191
Jones, D.	Detroit, Michigan	16,233
Lyon, L.	Kalamazoo County, Michigan	23,433
Murray, C. A.	London, England	20,000
Newberry, W. L.	Chicago, Illinois	8,170
Newkirk, M.	Philadelphia, Pennsylvania	11,355
Russell, W. S.	Boston, Massachusetts	26,830
Smith, G.	Chicago, Illinois	21,663
Wadsworth & Dyer	Chicago, Illinois	9,875
Walker, M. O.	Rensselaer County, New York	14,909
Watson, J. T.	New York City	10,283

In many instances this period of pseudo-prosperity bore hard on squatters on the public lands. Caught unprepared by the announcement of the government land sales, as squatters always were, they were hard pressed to raise the funds to purchase their claims. Again, the loan shark or his agent appeared to take advantage of their poverty by loaning them funds at extortionate rates of interest. This was the period when William A. Woodward of New York, Cyrus Woodman and Cadwallader Washburn of Mineral Point, Wisconsin, Miles White of Baltimore, Maryland, Easley & Willingham of Halifax Court House, Virginia, and numerous other eastern and southern capitalists loaned millions of dollars on western land, much of it in Wisconsin, to desperate squatters.

After 1846, too, eastern capitalists once more undertook to enter raw prairie or wooded land in advance of settlers in the hope of

[1] The information on entries of Federal lands throughout this study has been compiled from cash, warrant, and scrip abstracts of land entries, National Archives.

TABLE 4

Large Land Entries in Wisconsin by Residents, 1846–1857

Name	Residence	Acres
Ansley, Thomas	Iowa County	25,360
Cheyney, Hazen	Rock County	14,560
Eaton, Parley	Iowa County	11,200
Eldred, Anson, et al.	Milwaukee	12,000
Field, George B.	Rock County	48,000
Fitzgerald, John	Brown County	45,480
Gray, Hamilton H.		13,680
Guggenheim, Mark	Brown County	38,880
Jervis, William B., et al.	Dane County	23,230
Knapp, Stout & Co.	Menomonie	15,000
Legate, Charles F.	Iowa County	18,740
Scheffer, Louis		29,000
Trowbridge, Benjamin	Sheboygan County	14,120
Trowbridge, William S.	Milwaukee	23,560
Washburn & Woodman	Mineral Point	130,220

gaining the fabulous profits which the loan sharks were making. Local speculators also felt their confidence restored and began to buy land in large quantities. Tables 4 and 5 show the larger entries made by residents and by non-residents of the state respectively dur-

TABLE 5

Large Land Entries in Wisconsin by Non-Residents, 1846–1857

Name	Residence	Acres
Beebe, Thomas H.	Chicago, Illinois	27,420
Bradley, Daniel W.	Bangor, Maine	11,000
Buckingham, Alvah	Zanesville, Ohio	11,840
Corwith, N. & H.	Galena, Illinois	11,000
Gardiner, Freeland B.	Cook County, Illinois	12,470
Jewett, Samuel A.	Ramsay County, Minnesota	12,000
McCrea, Augustus	Washington, D. C.	46,080
Mansfield, John W.	New Haven, Connecticut	14,080
Mitchell, Charles J.	Charleston, South Carolina	10,540
Morrison, Dorilus	Bangor, Maine	18,244
Ogden, William B.	Chicago, Illinois	14,600
Pairo, Charles W.	Washington, D. C.	13,080
Riggs, Slidell, et al.	Washington, D. C.	18,160
Weston, Samuel F.	Henry County, Illinois	27,000
Woodward, William A., et al.	New York City	35,000

ing the years 1846–1857. These figures include land entered on the time-entry basis for settlers.

Absentee land owners and loan sharks were both feared and hated on the frontier. True, most influential westerners, including legislators, editors, bankers, and government officials, were themselves speculating in land, and many of them must have had their tongues in their cheeks when they condemned absentee ownership. However, westerners carefully distinguished between resident and absentee speculators. The former paid their taxes more regularly, made some improvements perhaps, and used their profits for the development of the community, whereas the latter took their profits elsewhere and did nothing for the community. The local man often placed tenants upon his land to protect and improve it and pay the taxes, but the absentee, unless he had an able and honest agent, was not able to give his land the attention it needed and the result was that it was pillaged and plundered, particularly if it was timbered, and farmers could not then be induced to settle upon it. Idle and unimproved land yielded little in taxes, contributed nothing to the aid of railroads, drainage, or other local improvement schemes, and sometimes, by its very existence, blighted the reputation and future prospects of an area. Compact and orderly settlement was impossible where settlers were forced to scatter widely in their search for government land, and scattered settlement made it difficult and expensive to secure roads and schools.

Some of the more notable purchasers and absentee speculators came to be frequently excoriated by the press and by politicians. In Illinois it was the Scully estate and in Wisconsin it was the estate of Sir Charles Augustus Murray which were condemned. Senator George W. Jones of Iowa commented, in 1851, on the 20,000-acre estate of Murray as follows:

In Wisconsin, near where I now reside, an English capitalist did buy at the Government land office for that district a large tract of the most fertile and valuable land, for which he paid the minimum price in money. . . . That single case . . . had the most deleterious effect on the settlement and improvement of that part of the country. I know the country well, for I resided in it for some seventeen years, and know that it is one of the richest counties in America for fertility of soil, mineral resources, water power, timber, etc., and yet it has been kept back in population and wealth because of this monopoly, whilst less fertile and desirable districts, where no such obstruction existed, have become thickly settled. These lands were entered in 1836-7 and are still held by the original purchaser, who many years ago . . . refused $5 per acre, and would not sell now for less than . . . ten or fifteen dollars. The consequence is that the emigrant has to push on still further to the westward, at the loss of time, and money, and health, to get inferior land and a less desirable home.[2]

The *Eau Claire Telegraph* also made disparaging remarks about the "Lords of England" who had sought to monopolize Wisconsin lands by buying thousands of acres "through a hireling" as Murray had done in Grant County.[3] Horace Greeley, America's most noted agrarian philosopher and a severe critic of land policies, visited Wisconsin in 1855, and wrote some illuminating paragraphs about the damage done to the state by speculators:

Between Beloit and Janesville, on Rock River, two thirds of the land is yet wild; and on inquiring the price of a portion of it, I was answered "Thirty dollars per acre." To break up and fence this, dig the necessary wells, put up decent buildings, etc., would increase the cost of a hundred acre farm to at last $6,000; which would nearly buy as good a farm in New Jersey. Why should monopoly be permitted?

I fell in with a humble man near Madison, Wisc., who . . . told me that he removed to that section twenty years ago, and took up 80 acres of land—all he wanted—expecting soon to be surrounded by neighbors and friends. Unhappily, the great Land speculation of 1835-6 engulfed him. Every adjacent tract was snatched up and held for high prices, *as it still is;* "and so," said my informant, "my children have grown up unschooled, and I am still without neighbors, and very poorly accommodated with mills, roads, postoffices, etc." Such are the influences that are daily crowding off thousands to Kansas, Nebraska, Minnesota, etc., seeking some spot of earth uncursed by the grasp of the forestaller.[4]

At the end of the second boom period no small part of the southern half of Wisconsin was either owned by or mortgaged to absentees.

---

[2] *Cong. Globe*, 31 Cong., 2 Sess., 1850–1851, February 5, 1851, p. 442. Joseph Schafer has studied in detail the land investment of Charles Augustus Murray in "Lands Across the Sea," *Wisconsin Magazine of History*, xiii (June, 1930), pp. 417–429.

[3] Quoted in *Omaha Nebraskian*, January 22, 1857.

[4] *Waukesha Plain Dealer*, May 9, 1855.

Speculators had bought here and there, acquiring many hundreds of thousands of acres of prairie and hard-wood lands. They had also been attracted to the pineries of the Red Cedar, the Black, the Wisconsin, and the Chippewa Rivers, in which they had entered vast tracts of virgin timber.

The panic of 1857 halted immigration, town promotion, and land speculation, but during the Civil War conditions improved. There followed another great assault upon the public domain in Wisconsin, and again huge blocks of land, now mostly pine land in northern Wisconsin, were acquired by eastern and local capitalists. The panic of 1873 put an end to this large-scale land purchasing for a time, but it was renewed in the eighties, and speculators and lumbermen then engaged in a bitter struggle for possession of the last stands of pine in public hands (see Table 6, p. 71).

The government's pine-land policy was as unsatisfactory as its farm-land policy. When lumbering first began on the Wisconsin, the Black, the St. Croix, and the Green Bay pineries, loggers had gone on land closest to rivers and had cut the timber regardless of ownership. Unauthorized timber cutting on the public domain had occurred throughout American history and the situation in Wisconsin was nothing new, but it developed in an aggravated way that eventually forced government action. Reports came to the General Land Office in Washington in the late forties that not only was there a good deal of promiscuous cutting by small operators but that large companies were being formed to lumber on the St. Croix, the Wisconsin, and the Green Bay pineries. Alexander Montgomery of Beaver Dam wrote on July 7, 1846, to the General Land Office: "A most destructive wasteful slashing of timber has been going on in this region for the last year. Section after section has been stripped of all the timber which could be worked into rails or boards, the tops are left to rot on the land and will most effectually prevent occupancy." Caleb Cushing, whose interests in the town of St. Croix were substantial, wrote on December 13, 1846, complaining of the amount of timber stealing which was taking place in the St. Croix Valley and recommending that the lands be offered for sale. Harry F. Brown, Register of the Green Bay land

TABLE 6

Some Wisconsin Land Entries, 1865–1888

Name	Residence	Acres
Bennett, Russell H.	St. Paul, Minnesota	15,040
Burnham, George	Milwaukee	16,549
Burrows, George B.	Madison	10,400
Corwith, Henry	Galena, Illinois	28,000
Darling & Wright	Detroit, Michigan	22,640
Dodge, William E.	New York City	10,360
Eau Claire Lumber Company	Eau Claire	58,600
Ebert, Rudolph	Fond du Lac	19,400
Farnsworth, George	Oconto County	11,400
Gilmore, Charles D.	Washington, D. C.	72,356
Hewitt, Henry, Jr.	Menasha	11,673
Jackson, M. E. & E. G.	Winnebago County	35,180
Jenkins, James	Winnebago County	39,351
Knapp, Stout & Co.	Menomonie	120,000
Lovejoy, Allen P.	Janesville	18,850
Luddington, Stephenson & Co.	Marinette	40,000
Lyman, George N.	Fond du Lac	15,000
McGraw & Dwight	Ithaca, New York	34,627
Miller, Wilmot H.	Winneconne	22,800
Palms, Francis	Detroit, Michigan	112,567
Patrick, William S., et al.	Detroit, Michigan	48,800
Pillsbury, Oliver P.	Milwaukee	24,513
Pound, Halbert & Co.	Chippewa Falls	27,113
Preston, David	Detroit, Michigan	12,240
Putnam, Henry C.	Eau Claire	18,500
Rust, William A.	Saginaw County, Michigan	37,400
Sage & McGraw	Ithaca, New York	45,049
Sawyer, Philetus	Oshkosh	11,500
Schulenberg, Frederick, et al.	Stillwater, Minnesota	19,687
Scott, Thomas B.	Wood County	25,210
Smith & Buffington	Eau Claire	11,380
Staples, Isaac	Stillwater, Minnesota	35,655
Starr, William	Fond du Lac	22,486
Thorp & Chapman	Eau Claire	16,000
Tyson, Pierce & Weil	Milwaukee	18,544
Ward, David	Oakland County, Michigan	10,440
Washburn, Cadwallader	La Crosse	10,160
Wilson, Walter C.	Chicago, Illinois	11,480
Woodman, Cyrus	Mineral Point	11,400

office, on October 24, 1849, called attention to the "extensive depredations" being made upon the timber lands in his district. He said that "upwards of 15,000,000 feet of pine lumber" was being manufactured annually on the Green Bay watershed, "every foot of which is plundered off the public lands." He added: "The lumbering season is now approaching and the lumbermen are making extensive preparations for wider and deeper depredations." [5]

In an attempt to prevent organized plundering of the pine lands, the government appointed a number of special timber agents to enforce the laws against timber stealing from the public lands.[6] These agents were instructed to investigate carefully the areas where large-scale logging was under way, to ascertain whether any cutting was being done on public lands, and if so to seize the logs and hold them until the operators would enter the despoiled lands or, in the event of their refusal to do so, to sell the logs for the government. The subsequent investigations revealed that practically every lumberman in Wisconsin was cutting illegally on public lands.[7]

Influential lumbermen whose logs were seized and against whom suits were instituted for violating the law complained to their representatives in Congress and demanded that the agents be dismissed. Their appeals aroused the sympathy of Henry M. Rice of Minnesota, "Long John" Wentworth and Stephen A. Douglas of Illinois, and Ben C. Eastman, Henry M. Dodge, and Isaac P. Walker of Wisconsin, who protested against the vigor of the enforcement agents and urged their dismissal.[8] Such pressure was not easily resisted, and in 1856 the lumbermen had their way: the agents were dismissed; John W. Wilson, Commissioner of the General Land Office, who was responsible for the vigorous prosecution of the timber plunderers, was dropped from the government service, and the suits against the accused were discontinued.[9] Thereafter the task of enforcing the regulations against

[5] See also letters of William Coxe Dusenbery, February 19, 1849, to D. D. Bright, and of W. D. Viele, May 10, 1849, to George W. Jones, General Land Office, Washington.

[6] In 1852 there were four timber agents to protect the government lands in the Lake States (annotation on letter of Alexander H. H. Stuart, June 3, 1852, to Wm. E. Eskridge, Secretary's File, Department of the Interior).

[7] The letters of Herman M. Cady, James B. Estes, and Ike Willard, timber agents, in the Secretary's File, Department of the Interior, throw a flood of light on the large-scale stealing of timber in Michigan and Wisconsin.

[8] There are numerous letters from these members of Congress, protesting against the enforcement activities of the timber agents, in the files of the Interior Department, now in the National Archives.

[9] R. McClelland, Secretary of the Interior, November 24, 1855, to Commissioner of the General Land Office (Letter Book No. 3, Secretary's Files); Thos. A. Hendricks,

timber stealing was left to the registers and receivers of the land offices. In an office ordinarily busy these men were already overworked and they had little time to devote to the matter. Furthermore they were, in numerous instances, friendly to the very lumbermen who were violating the law and such a relationship was not one to ensure vigorous enforcement. Consequently, illegal logging continued in all the major pineries. In 1865 it was reported that from "one-third to one-half of the best pine timber on the Chippewa" had been cut off by trespassers wherever it was most accessible.[10]

So long as the General Land Office looked with its blind eye upon illegal cutting on the public lands the lumbermen had no incentive to buy the land, and sales dragged slowly at the pinery offices. When complaining in 1849 of the large amount of timber stealing that was going on almost unhampered in his district, the register of the Green Bay office said: "No one will buy, of course, so long as he can steal with impunity. . . ."[11] The situation changed, however, when the pine-land speculators appeared at the land offices in the mid-fifties. From Michigan, Maine, and New York, from southern Wisconsin and from Illinois they came, drawn by the rising prices of lumber and the stories they had heard of the rich pineries of northern Wisconsin. From 1853 to 1857 they entered great tracts of pine land at the Menasha, Mineral Point, Stevens Point, and St. Croix land offices, to the wrath of the local lumbermen.

The bitterest feeling against the government for permitting unrestricted speculation in pine land was aroused in the lumbering towns of Stevens Point, Eau Claire, and Chippewa Falls. Here were large sawmills whose owners had just freed themselves from the activities of the special timber agents and who now found themselves faced

December 31, 1855, to Geo. E. Hand, District Attorney, Detroit, Michigan (Miscellaneous Letters, vol. 42, General Land Office).

[10] General Land Office, *Annual Report*, 1865, p. 75.

[11] Harry F. Brown, October 24, 1849, to Justin Butterfield, General Land Office. It was not uncommon for representations to be made to the General Land Office that if lands were brought into market and offered for sale they would be purchased and the depredations would cease. See letters of A. Van Vorhes, Register, and N. Greene Wilcox, Receiver, Stillwater Land Office, Minnesota, July 24, 1852, to the General Land Office; Caleb Cushing, December 13, 1846, to Jas. H. Piper; Robert Smith, Alton, Illinois, May 24, 1849, to R. M. Young, and the numerous petitions from the Willow River and Mineral Point districts in 1850–1851, General Land Office.

with the competition of absentee capitalists seeking to wrest control of the government pine lands from them. The *Eau Claire Free Press*, which represented the rising lumber industry on the Chippewa, battled valiantly against the invasion of non-resident capital. In 1860 it expressed the hope that the valuable pine lands of the Chippewa would be acquired by people who would "manufacture the lumber here at home where it legitimately belongs." The Stevens Point *Wisconsin State Register* condemned the activities of the pine-land speculators and the policy of the Federal Government which permitted them in the following editorial of May 29, 1861:

> The land policy of the general government has been a mistaken policy, always. One of the great injuries done to the Lumbermen of the Pineries, has been done by the selling of land to speculators. This never should have been done, either in the pineries or the agricultural lands. The selling of land ought always to have been confined to the actual settler. A few years back, a great land speculation rage possessed the whole country. On this river [Wisconsin] and tributaries, vast outlays of money and labor had been expended in opening the lumber region to improvement and settlement. These men ought to have been encouraged by the government. But, instead of this, a set of speculators, that never do anything for the development of the productive industry for the country, were let in upon those who had invested . . . and were likely to take up all the unoccupied pine land.

The West, although reluctant to abandon its traditional individualism, cast about for some means of restraining the activities of speculators and checking the rate at which land was being engrossed by absentees. In Wisconsin the *Eau Claire Telegraph* favored the establishment of claims clubs to prevent the "Lords of England" from "monopolizing" land as Murray had done in Grant County.[12] The *Eau Claire Free Press* urged the mill men to enter the best pine land before "Foreign Speculators" took it up.[13] Other papers advocated ending the practice of making cash sales and in future reserving the public lands for entry only by homesteaders and pre-emptors.[14] At the same time there was organized in the East a committee of workers

[12] Quoted in *Omaha Nebraskian*, January 22, 1857.
[13] May 14, 1863.
[14] *Monticello Spectator*, Monticello, Indiana, August 1, 1860; *Nebraska Advertiser*, Brownville, Nebraska, July 23, 1857; *Desoto Pilot*, Desoto, Nebraska, May 18, 1858.

called the New York Committee of Land Reformers, which urged not only the withdrawal of all lands from cash purchase, but the establishment of a maximum of 160 acres for farms, and limitations upon the right of alienation.[15] Horace Greeley took up these demands and labored valiantly for them in the *New York Tribune*. He and other radical land reformers sought to have these provisions to check large-scale purchasing and land engrossment included in the various drafts of a free homestead measure then under consideration.

Holders of lands in Wisconsin watched with anxiety the tortuous progress of the homestead measure through Congress. Restrictions on cash sales would not necessarily harm them, but free grants would, they feared, reduce land values and speculators' profits.[16] Representative Ben C. Eastman of Wisconsin, himself a speculator in the lands of his home state, became frantic as he watched the support which the homestead measure attracted and he wrote to his associate in land deals, Cyrus Woodman: "Hell is broken loose and I know not how to chain the devil. Will not this system of disposing of the lands ruin us who own lands in the States?"[17] The loan sharks also were troubled at the prospect of a free-grant measure, for they feared it would end their profitable business.[18] When President Buchanan vetoed the homestead bill in 1860, speculators breathed a sigh of relief; they could feel safe for at least two years. Their relief was reflected in the "considerable rise" in the price of land warrants after the veto message was delivered.[19] But they had obtained only a respite, and doubtless many speculators in western lands agreed with Pinckney W. Ellsworth of Hartford, Connecticut, a partner of Moses W. Strong in an investment in 1200 acres of land in Wisconsin, who wrote: "Greeley's notion, which he has impudently stuck into the Republi-

[15] John Wind, New York City, July 14, 1856, to John C. Breckinridge (Breckinridge MSS, Library of Congress).

[16] Easley & Willingham, Halifax Court House, Virginia, July 26, 1854, to Hoyt Sherman (Easley & Willingham MSS, University of Virginia).

[17] Ben C. Eastman, Washington, March 19, 1852, to Cyrus Woodman (Woodman MSS, Wisconsin Historical Society).

[18] Easley & Willingham, Halifax Court House, Virginia, March 20, 1854, to Johnson & Casady (Easley & Willingham MSS, University of Virginia).

[19] James S. Easley, Halifax Court House, Virginia, July 6, 1860, to George Weare (*loc. cit.*).

can platform & to be acted upon when they get the power viz, 'Land to the landless;' it bodes no good to present holders." [20]

The Homestead Act, as it finally passed Congress, was no longer Greeley's thoroughgoing reform measure. It had been shorn of many of its important provisions and emerged a compromise, unsatisfactory to land reformers and distasteful to land speculators. Land sales were not restricted, no limitations upon the right of alienation were included, and settlers who wanted to get an early title to their land in order to borrow on it had still to go to loan sharks for the necessary $200. The principle of free grants was a victory for the West, but only a partial victory; the old evils of large-scale purchasing, speculators' deserts, and usurious loans remained. Not only that, for Congress, at the time of the adoption of the Homestead Act, was planning to abstract millions of acres from the public domain for subsidies of one kind or another, of which the nine or ten million acres granted to the states for agricultural colleges was but one.

In Wisconsin the *Eau Claire Free Press* took up the cudgels in opposition to the "Agricultural College Humbug," the friends of which, it held, were casting about "preparatory to lighting upon the most valuable government lands in . . . this and other States. . . . In our opinion the Agricultural College Bill is not only a humbug, but a great outrage upon the newly and sparsely settled States and Territories, from which the land is to be selected." It urged homesteaders and others intending to develop the area to anticipate the speculators and enter the best remaining lands. "We hope that every choice location in this region of country will be taken by an actual settler, so that, the Agricultural College Sharks will have to accept the bluffs or barrens, or go where they will not deprive the best portions of the State of the anxious labor necessary to improve them." In June, 1862, the *Free Press* deplored the enactment of the agricultural-college measure, and again urged settlers to forestall the speculators by selecting and pre-empting their locations promptly.[21] In the following year the *Free Press* expressed regret that the agent of the State of Wisconsin

---

[20] Pinckney M. Ellsworth, Hartford, Connecticut, June 30, 1860, to M. M. Strong (Strong MSS, Wisconsin Historical Society).

[21] *Eau Claire Free Press*, June 26, 1862.

had appeared in Eau Claire to "gobble up" lands for the agricultural college, and once more urged settlers to hasten the location of their lands.[22] That the state agent found the local feeling very strong is seen by the comment he made to the governor:

> There is a wide spread [sic] hostility among the people of our State, not to the Ag. & Mechanical College in the abstract, but to the location of the lands in their vicinity; this feeling against the withdrawal of the public domain from entry under the Homestead law is very natural, but at the same time exceedingly embarrassing to your commissioners as it renders it difficult to determine what localities to visit. . . .[23]

It was in the Chippewa Valley that the largest amount of agricultural-college scrip was to be located by absentee interests during the sixties, and this valley expressed in numerous ways its dislike of these speculators. As late as 1876 the agent in charge of the Cornell lands in Wisconsin described this animosity as follows:

> The Law *giving* the scrip is *looked* upon as a *fraud* upon the Nation & the people in as much as it was conceived in the minds of a few Land Sharks & some Members of Congress in the Eastern States who found they could make use of popular ideas which seemed to favor the Cause of Education & thus get this Scrip afloat in such quantities that it would sell for a Song & thus enable these Sharks to buy up the immense tracts of prairie & other Lands which today is retarding the settlement of the country.[24]

Wisconsin, though it ardently wanted an agricultural college, did not favor the Morrill Act, and its residents watched with keen disfavor the accumulation of lands by non-residents.

In the sixties agrarianism reared its head in the upper Mississippi Valley. Among the states principally affected was Wisconsin. Some of the causes were the large grants to railroads, the high freight rates charged by these corruptly managed companies on whom public assistance had been lavished, the rapid accumulation of farm and pine lands by absentee and resident speculators, the high prices by which these speculators made it difficult for a poor immigrant to acquire a

---

[22] *Id.*, May 7, 14, 21, 1863.
[23] William N. Reed, Alma, Buffalo County, August 24, 1863, to Governor Saloman (Governor's Letters, Wisconsin Historical Society).
[24] H. C. Putnam, Eau Claire, November 23, 1876, to J. W. Williams, Cornell University. *Eau Claire Free Press*, May 30, 1869; July 18, 1874.

farm, the high interest rates charged on the frontier, and finally the appearance of tenancy. Amorphous in its character, the agrarian movement was not to come to a head under the leadership of the Grange until the seventies, but one sees many manifestations of it during the Civil War decade: continued agitation for the cessation of cash sales and of the policy of granting land subsidies to railroads, the fight of settlers to prevent the foreclosure of their railroad farm mortgages, and the ever-recurring hostility displayed toward absentee owners. Wisconsin scarcely seemed the safest state for an eastern capitalist to choose for a large investment in land.

Every boom period in the nineteenth century saw extensive purchases made of Wisconsin land, but despite the recurrence of this practice many have doubted that profits were made in the business. So frequently was the unprofitable nature of land speculation discoursed upon by contemporary newspapers and by speculators themselves that historians have come to accept their gloomy views without examining them with sufficient care. For example, two of Wisconsin's ablest historians have expressed such an opinion. Frederick Jackson Turner observed: "Increasing facilities of transportation, and increasing security of the squatter rights through preemption, made the speculators' profits more than doubtful in many cases." [25] Dr. Joseph Schafer, who has made minute studies of the settlement of Wisconsin, states: "In their expectation of profit from holding farm lands speculators were often disappointed." [26]

It cannot be denied that there is evidence to support the views of Professors Turner and Schafer. Every boom period has been followed by the inevitable cycle of lean years during which there was little demand for land and even less ability on the part of settlers to pay for it. Speculators who had invested heavily in land just before the crash and who did not have sufficient funds to carry their holdings for ten or twenty years might not be able to recover their original investment, to say nothing of making any profits. Such was the situation of many

[25] *The United States, 1830–1850* (New York, 1935), pp. 292–293.
[26] Joseph Schafer, *Wisconsin Domesday Book, Town Studies*, vol. i (*Publications*, Wisconsin Historical Society [Madison, 1924], p. 10).

investors in Wisconsin after the panic of 1837, and their lamentations have led historians astray.

In this period Cyrus Woodman came to Wisconsin to manage the estate of the Boston & Western Land Company, which consisted of 27,375 acres in Wisconsin, 21,625 acres in Illinois, and property in a number of towns. Woodman had not been long in the West before he began transmitting to his employers gloomy letters not calculated to encourage them to think highly of their investment. In 1840 he concluded that the stockholders "will never make anything by their investment in this country." He argued, "The day of speculation in Western lands has gone by." After he had examined the company's lands in Grant, Iowa, Marathon, and Dane Counties, he expressed his disappointment at their poor quality, declaring that several hundred acres were scarcely worth paying taxes on and that the remainder could not be expected to sell for more than $1.25 or $1.50 an acre.[27] Such pessimistic remarks discouraged the investors, who agreed to sell most of their land to Woodman for a small sum. Woodman's employers lost heavily, but Woodman was to receive large returns from his investment.

Woodman's letters were no more gloomy than the pessimistic statements which appeared during 1839 to 1843 in western papers concerning prospects for land speculation. For example, in 1839 the *Galena Gazette* commented upon the privately owned lands in southwestern Wisconsin which were available for sale at 62½ cents to $1.25 an acre, heavy taxes having forced the non-resident owners to sell out.[28] Two years later the *Peoria Register* predicted that Illinois lands would be offered by non-residents as low as 37½ cents an acre.[29] After the crash of 1857 the *Grant County Herald* of Wisconsin made similar observations:

The holders of large bodies of Western lands on speculation are a sickly set of fellows. The chances are that large portions of the late Iowa, Minnesota,

---

[27] Cyrus Woodman, Winslow, Illinois, April 1, 1840, February 10, 1843, to Rice, Sewall, and Hubbard, Trustees (Woodman MSS).
[28] Quoted in *Chicago American*, October 1, 1839.
[29] *Peoria Register and Northwestern Gazetteer*, November 12, 1841.

Northwestern Wisconsin entries will be in second hand market far below Government prices. Their air-castles, built on land monopoly, are having their foundations washed away by a crashing crisis of their own begetting, for it is conceded that the present bank crisis is caused by letting so much money out to land speculators. We have always held, upon a basis of calculation that must stand, that the losses far overbalance the profits on Western land speculations when such speculations are attempted by non-residents. That there are some accidental profits to a few non-resident land holders we admit, but in a large majority of cases there are heavy losses. All that is good, and great, and wise join in perpetual conspiracy against non-resident land monopolists. This is a great secret never taken into account by the poor deluded victim who offers his money in sacrifice and himself to disappointment.[30]

These gloomy predictions were not fulfilled in Woodman's case. He cleared a substantial fortune by buying and selling Wisconsin farm and pine land, making usurious loans to settlers and acting as agent for eastern capitalists. His purchases, which exceeded 100,000 acres, were made chiefly in boom periods and he was caught with large holdings after the panics of 1857 and 1873. His correspondence during the dull years is full of gloomy comments on the unprofitable nature of the business, the difficulty of making sales and collections, high taxes, and timber depredations upon his land. In 1864, in remarking that he was abandoning some lands which were entered twenty-six years previously, he said:

By unjust taxes or in some other way people are trying to rob me all the while. I should be glad if I can sell out my lands in the West, and get my property into New England among a civilized people. I want to die and be buried in that land and not in this great Western Mudhole.[31]

Three weeks later he wrote that he had been land-poor for years and that his judgment told him to sell out his lands but that the habit of investing in lands was so strong that he would probably always keep himself in the "same situation." [32] He concluded that "most of the speculations in western lands by non-residents are failures. Many

---

[30] Quoted in the *National Intelligencer,* September 26, 1857.

[31] Cyrus Woodman, Detroit, Michigan, April 2, 1864, to Chas. L. Stephenson (Woodman MSS).

[32] Woodman, Detroit, Michigan, April 26, 1864, to Governor Fairbanks (*loc. cit.*).

years often elapse when it is impossible to effect sales. . . ." Woodman managed his land business with a minimum of dependence on agents, kept after the timber thieves, was not forced to sell during poor years, and prospered despite the pessimistic tone that pervades his letters. Being a resident, he was not harmed as much as non-residents by timber thieves, squatters, unjust assessments, and tax sales.

Charles Mason, Federal Commissioner of Patents and subsequently patent attorney in Washington, and one of the important dealers in real estate in Iowa, was less fortunate than Woodman in the management of his Wisconsin lands. In 1856 he arranged with William Weston to have 4200 acres entered for him at the Stevens Point office with military warrants which had cost him $1.06 an acre. Two years later he estimated that the land had cost nearly $2 an acre, figured as follows:

4200 acres at $1.06	$4,460.40
Agents' fees for entering tracts	300.00
Taxes, 1858–1867	3,269.37
Agents' fees for paying taxes, at 5 per cent	163.45
Redeeming land from tax sale	50.00
Total	$8,243.22

As money generally brought 10 per cent interest in the West at this time, Mason estimated that the total cost to him in 1868, including interest, would be at least $15,000. When he visited Wisconsin in the late sixties he found to his dismay that the selections had been poorly made. Weston, it seems, had not even inspected the land before entering it. It was impossible to approach within sixteen miles of it by horse and carriage, so distant was it from roads, and Mason was advised that better land could then be entered at the Stevens Point office than he had acquired in 1856. Disgusted with his ill-fortune, he contemplated abandoning part of the land.[33]

Charles W. Pairo, a Washington banker, bought 40,000 acres of land in five states and two territories, 13,000 acres being located in

---

[33] MSS: "Statement of Wisconsin Lands, Sept. 28, 1868" (Mason MSS, Iowa State Department of History and Archives, Des Moines, Iowa); MSS: "Life and Letters of Judge Charles Mason of Iowa," vol. viii (Cornell University).

Polk and Marathon Counties, Wisconsin. He became bankrupt in 1857 because he had overinvested in unproductive land, but his trustees continued to pay taxes on his Wisconsin property until 1869. At that time they sold 5,120 acres in Polk County to Caleb Cushing for $1.50 an acre.[34] Cushing was an inveterate speculator whose Wisconsin schemes uniformly went awry. His income from his law practice was sufficiently large, however, to enable him to take part in three successive efforts to develop a city at the site of St. Croix Falls, each one of which brought him nothing but additional debts.[35]

An equally unpromising venture that subsequently was made to pay well was that of Miles White, president of the Peoples Bank of Baltimore. He and his son Elias made frequent trips into the West in the fifties and sixties, attending the various land sales and arranging to loan funds at the usual frontier rates to pre-emptors and others wishing to buy land. During these two decades the Whites entered more than 150,000 acres in Iowa, Nebraska, Minnesota and Wisconsin, either for settlers or for themselves. Much of the land entered for squatters was forfeited to the Whites through the inability of the claimants to raise the funds necessary to complete their purchases. Many of these tracts were held for forty years before they were sold at the price demanded, although, in the meantime, rents were received from some of them. In Wisconsin the Whites entered or bought from others some 12,000 acres. Most of the entries were for settlers, and, although payments on them seem to have been fairly well met, the Whites received little return from their investment because they had a misunderstanding with their agent.[36] He claimed a partnership in the enterprise, while White insisted that he had acted solely as agent. White sought to press the claim against the agent in the courts, only

---

[34] William Nourse, Washington, April 31 [sic], 1869, to Caleb Cushing (Cushing MSS, Library of Congress).

[35] There is much correspondence in the Cushing papers concerning the establishment of the Great European American Emigration Land Company, which bought the Pairo lands and the Wisconsin State Agricultural College lands in Polk County, amounting to 54,000 acres. The effort to settle these lands with Swedes was not successful.

[36] The White land business can be reconstructed from the Woodman MSS and the papers in the possession of Miles White, Jr., of Baltimore. See especially George Woodman, New York, October 8, 1859, to Cyrus Woodman; Cyrus Woodman, Mineral Point, Wisconsin, April 6, 1861, to Alanson Eaton (Woodman MSS).

to find that local juries were not friendly to outside speculators, and he lost his case.[37] He did, however, succeed in recovering land to the amount of 9,260 acres which, with the exception of one or two pieces, was sold by 1907 for $99,474.[38] The Whites' ventures in Wisconsin thus proved profitable in the long run.

The firm of Easley & Willingham of Halifax Court House, Virginia, consisting of James Stone Easley and William W. Willingham, invested very heavily in western lands. In Iowa, Missouri, Minnesota, Kansas, and Nebraska the firm acquired nearly 335,000 acres, either for speculation or for squatters. In Wisconsin it entered 17,640 acres at the Menasha and Stevens Point offices.[39] The panic of 1857 obliged many of the settlers to relinquish their claims and the firm was forced to carry a large proportion of its land entries for many years and very soon it ran into difficulties. In 1859 a local agent in Wood County commented upon the high taxes being assessed upon the lands, the result of the construction of a "main thoroughfare" which gave settlers "a chance to get into that portion of the county." [40] In 1860 Easley and Willingham were doubtless gratified at the advice not to sell some of their Door County lands for $3 or even $5 an acre, so promising did the future seem.[41] Thereafter they could take little comfort in their dispatches from Wisconsin.

During the Civil War confiscation proceedings were brought against the lands of Easley & Willingham because they were both living in the Confederacy and as a result their titles became clouded. Furthermore, since it was impossible to transmit funds to Wisconsin, their

[37] Miles White, Baltimore, Maryland, December 16, 30, 1859, July 5, 1862, to Cyrus Woodman; Cyrus Woodman, Mineral Point, Wisconsin, September 25, 1860, to Alanson Eaton; A. Eaton, Stevens Point, Wisconsin, June 30, 1862, December 10, 1863, to Cyrus Woodman (Woodman MSS).

[38] Compiled from manuscript volume, "Land Record, Francis White" (Miles White MSS).

[39] James S. Easley attempted to make sure that only "good land" would be entered on the time-entry basis, but his agent, who was paid only $10 for each quarter-section claim, was not inclined to spend much time investigating the land. Had Easley worked through a local—instead of a Chicago—agent his efforts to secure "good land" might have been more successful.

[40] Lemuel Kromer, Grand Rapids, Wisconsin, December 30, 1859, to James S. Easley (Easley MSS).

[41] S. Harris, Sturgeon Bay, Wisconsin, May 20, 1860, to Easley & Willingham (*loc. cit.*).

taxes remained unpaid and tax titles were issued on most of their tracts. These tax titles were bought by residents who cut the timber and then abandoned the land.[42] When the war was over and Easley & Willingham could again look after their land, they found that the Wisconsin titles had become so involved and that it would be so expensive to clear them of conflicting claims that it seemed best to let the land go for a time in the hope that later something could be retrieved from it. In 1868 they were informed that other absentee owners in Door County were abandoning their lands, so heavy were the taxes and so difficult was it to prevent depredations.[43] The same year Easley was told that the best timber was rapidly disappearing from his land and that if he did not sell his title shortly there would be nothing of value left.[44] Thus warned, Easley, in November, 1868, offered to sell his Wisconsin property for $1.25 an acre, but he received no bids.[45] Finally, in 1870, Easley sold 1834 acres in Portage County for the low price of $400.[46] The Door County lands promised better, despite the fact that they were being pillaged, because they were wanted by settlers. Another factor which made for somewhat better prices was that in 1876, when their lands were being sold, the old question whether tax titles had any value was revived by a decision of a lower court which cast doubt upon such titles. Of the Door County lands 1860 acres were sold for $2528 and the remaining 5000 acres would, it was estimated, bring $4500.[47] Such prices, after a wait of fifteen or twenty years, indicate the hazards involved in Wisconsin land investments. It should be remembered, however, that the investments of Easley & Willingham, like those of other southerners who held land in the Door peninsula and in central Wisconsin, had been impaired by the confiscation proceedings begun against them and by the numerous tax titles issued on their lands.

---

[42] George W. Hungerford & Bros., Stevens Point, Wisconsin, December 12, 1865, to Easley & Willingham (*loc. cit.*).

[43] J. H. Rees & Co., Chicago, March 14, 1868, to Easley & Willingham (*loc. cit.*).

[44] Josiah Bond, Chicago, June 2, 1868, to James S. Easley (*loc. cit.*).

[45] James S. Easley, Halifax Court House, Virginia, November 27, 1868, to C. Guard, Fabers Mills, Virginia (*loc. cit.*).

[46] *Id.*, March 30, 1870, to Hungerford & Bros. (*loc. cit.*).

[47] Josiah Bond, Kenosha, Wisconsin, September 7, 1876, to James S. Easley (*loc. cit.*).

Mason, White, Easley & Willingham, the Boston & Western Land Company, and numerous other absentee speculators found that their investments in Wisconsin lands in the thirties and fifties either paid little in the way of net profits or left them with a positive loss. Professor Schafer has studied other investments in Wisconsin lands, notably the estate of Charles Augustus Murray of England and the purchases of Hubbard, Olcott, and Hall of New Hampshire, and has found the net returns on these speculations very meager. These studies led him to the conclusion that land speculation in Wisconsin was "a precarious business." [48]

The records thus far presented indicate that in the early period of Wisconsin's history absentee investors who bought lands sight unseen and who were forced to depend upon local agents more interested in immediate commissions than in getting the highest possible price, did not secure their anticipated profits. Others who could hold on for a time and who either had an able and conscientious agent, or whose investments were large enough to warrant their spending much time in Wisconsin, did profit, provided their selections had been wisely made. Values of farm and pine land continued to rise in Wisconsin and many fortunes were made by residents and absentee owners. Among the local residents who did well might be mentioned Cyrus Woodman, Cadwallader Washburn, and Henry C. Putnam; absentee owners whose success was outstanding are Abner Coburn, William A. Woodward, and the firm of Sage & McGraw. Coburn, a millionaire lumberman from Maine, bought land in the Eau Claire River Valley in 1854 for less than $30,000 which twenty-eight years later was sold for $600,000.[49] The Sage & McGraw transactions will be discussed later and the business of Woodward has received attention.

---

[48] *Wisconsin Domesday Book, Town Studies,* i, 10, and *The Wisconsin Lead Region, Wisconsin Domesday Book, General Studies,* 3 (1932), 153. Professor Schafer's studies are instructive but do not entirely warrant his conclusions, the reason being that he has neglected two items which would considerably change the balance sheet. Commissions for sales, which he estimates and deducts from gross sales, were generally paid by the purchaser and therefore would not be deducted from the purchase price. Furthermore, the item of rents, which in southern Wisconsin were coming to be important, is neglected.

[49] *Northwestern Lumberman,* October 14, 1882, p. 10. The acreage is not given, but it was probably less than 30,000.

Suffice it to say here that Woodward, more frank than other land speculators, freely admitted that he made a good profit on the 40,000 acres of land he entered for himself and others in Wisconsin and neighboring states. His account of the land deals in which he engaged is a valuable document; it not only reveals real profits but it also shows the reasons why he succeeded where Easley & Willingham, Mason, White, Pairo, and other non-residents failed.[50]

There were numerous hazards of which the innocent investor in western lands was ignorant and these hazards wrecked many a promising speculation. The cautious investor did not scatter his lands over too wide an area, unless he was entering them on a hit-or-miss basis, in which case scattered locations might work better than otherwise. It has already been pointed out that those speculators who invested their all in land and did not reserve sufficient funds to meet the taxes and other expenses over a long period of years, during which there would be little income from the land, were generally unsuccessful. Prairie land rose slowly in value but could not be pillaged; timbered land, on the other hand, was at the mercy of neighboring settlers who had long since learned that timber on vacant land—owned either by the government or by absentee holders—could be "hooked" or stolen without fear of punishment. Few prosecuting attorneys dared to take action against such plunderers; the local judge, dependent upon popular support for re-election, could not afford to challenge the prevailing custom; and rarely would a frontier jury convict timber thieves. Absentee-owned timber land was, then, difficult to protect, and even large land companies which employed timber agents to ferret out plunderers and prosecute them found the expenses heavy and the returns meager.

The West displayed much ingenuity in discriminating against and penalizing absentee owners. In Wisconsin it was a common practice for residents to organize new counties and towns, often unnecessarily, construct expensive school buildings and courthouses, lay out little-needed roads through the woods, build substantial bridges, vote heavy subsidies to proposed railroads, and in each case give the lucrative

[50] *Woodward vs. Cornell, passim.*

contracts to themselves and friends, knowing full well that the burden of such expenditures would rest upon non-residents. One observer, in explaining this tendency in Wisconsin pineries, said:

Very bad abuses are commencing . . . by exorbitant contracts for making roads, etc., a few settlers combining to vote large appropriations for roads, and obtaining contracts at high prices. The early settlers are tempted to obtain a compensation for the hardships of a wilderness life by road contracts in which nearly all the residents of the towns are interested.[51]

Another writer explains how taxes were made unbearable upon absentee-owned lands:

During the time when a large portion of the land belonged to speculators, the people adopted a shrewd device for building their school houses with slight cost to the inhabitants. They attached the sections thus owned, successively, to every district which wished to build a school house, promising the few scattered inhabitants that the taxes levied on them should be refunded by contributions out of their own pockets. They levied the highest possible taxes on speculators' lands, they supplied themselves, cheaply, with school buildings, astonishing the said speculators, who could not understand how they were taxed, for several successive years for the construction of those buildings, and yet have none within miles of their lands.[52]

One speculator in western lands escaped these discriminations by "a liberal course, always giving lots for schoolhouses, assisting in their erection, and encouraging opening and working roads, and occasionally sending a donation of $25 towards a new church." He added, "They give me credit for liberality, even if my conduct is governed by worldly wisdom."[53]

The problem of paying taxes was one that called for infinite patience on the part of absentee landowners. In some states taxes on wild lands could be paid at the capital, but in Wisconsin they had to be paid at each county seat. The local tax collector sent out no tax bills but expected landowners to appear at his office and pay their taxes promptly after they were assessed. It was practically impossible for owners to

---

[51] B. Brett, Stevens Point, Wisconsin, March 13, 1860, to Charles Mason (Mason MSS).
[52] Henry L. Boies, *History of De Kalb County, Illinois* (Chicago, 1868), p. 471.
[53] William A. Woodward, Vail's Gate, New York, March 28, 1865, to Ezra Cornell.

pay by mail and they either had to attend the local offices in person or employ an agent. The tax receipts had to be closely scrutinized to make sure that the proper entries were made, so careless were the tax clerks. If the taxes were not paid on time the lands would be advertised for sale and if an owner wished to protect his equity before sale he had to pay a penalty plus the cost of advertising. If he did not take prompt steps the lands would be sold and he would then have to buy the tax title from the new owner, who could charge him an exorbitant rate of interest and penalty for the use of his money during the time he had the title. Hundreds of easterners hopefully invested in western lands only to find that the cost of protecting their holdings against depredations, the high taxes, the difficulty of paying taxes and avoiding penalties, and the frequent clashes with agents over commissions, prices, and terms were so great that there was little or no profit in the enterprise.

In summary, it would appear that the Wisconsin pineries were a hazardous area in which to undertake a large-scale speculation. The prevalence of numerous absentee-owned estates had developed an anti-monopoly and anti-alien feeling which boded ill for large landholders living outside the state. Not only was unfriendly legislation threatened, but the counties and townships could be counted upon to be extravagant where the land was chiefly owned by outsiders, for the express purpose of raising the tax costs. Timber stealing was a major occupation in Wisconsin. Western agents who represented eastern capitalists were always dealing in lands on their own account and were likely to push their own interests even against those of nonresidents by whom they were employed. At a time when fire protection did not exist and forest fires annually raged unchecked it was no small risk to venture a large investment in the most inflammable of the forest lands. Furthermore, heavy winds swept through the Wisconsin pineries frequently and laid low many thousands of acres of standing timber. In the sixties no one thought that the area of white pine in the Lake States would be exhausted for many decades and few there were who would predict a rise in stumpage values. On the contrary it was to be expected that pine land would go begging during the inevitable deflation of the post-war years. There was, then, much to make Wisconsin pine lands unattractive in the sixties, and yet Ezra Cornell, under the strong urging of William A. Woodward and Henry C. Putnam, ventured to locate the bulk of the New York land scrip there and, to the surprise of many Wisconsin lumbermen and of some of the trustees of Cornell University, carried the business through to success.

CHAPTER FIVE

Cornell Acquires Wisconsin Pine Land

By 1865 the public domain in Wisconsin had been reduced to ten or eleven million acres, most of which was in the northern half of the state.[1] Although there was to be a considerable agricultural development within this area at a later time, the chief value of these lands was in their timber, especially their white pine. This tree, the monarch of the Wisconsin woods, was found in clumps, usually on sandy soils and surrounded by other soft woods or mixed soft and hard woods. The best stands of white pine in Wisconsin were on the Chippewa River, and a large part of this pine was still in public hands. It was to these pine lands on the Chippewa and its tributaries that Cornell's attention was drawn by Woodward and Putnam.

When the Chippewa lands were brought into the market in the fifties there was considerable competition between speculators, looking for choice locations of pine land, and the agents of the sawmills, who felt it necessary to buy select tracts to save them from the speculators. Thomas Randall, the first historian of the Chippewa, says that "vast quantities" of land warrants "were sent to agents in this valley, to be located on the choicest spots; some with instruction to secure pine lands, others wanted 'timber and prairie well watered,' and large tracts of the best land in the valley were thus absorbed, which greatly retarded actual settlement, and increased the hardships of that other class, whose object was to acquire a home and a competence by honest toil." The actual settlers and mill owners, adds Randall, "looked on with alarm and consternation at this absorption of the

---

[1] The Commissioner of the General Land Office, in his *Annual Report* for 1869, page 403, gave the amount of public land remaining unsold and unappropriated on June 30, 1869, as 8,694,316 acres. To this should be added more than 2,000,000 acres disposed of between 1865 and 1869.

pine timber, and made strenuous efforts to secure all their means would possibly afford. . . ."[2]

The struggle between the speculators and the mill men was over the pine land located close to the towns of Menomonie, Eau Claire, and Chippewa Falls, and there is no indication that there was a rush for land on the upper reaches of the Chippewa. The lumbermen obviously did not find it necessary to buy when the laws against timber stealing were not strictly enforced, and speculators were not attracted to areas where timber rights were not respected. As late as 1866 a Chippewa Falls dealer could write: "As yet but a little of the land has been located upon the new survey. Our mill owners with the exception of two or three own no land & they could get a supply of logs without buying land & have concluded it would always be so. . . ."[3]

The Chippewa pineries were open to sale and entry at the land office in the city of Eau Claire. This office was technically in the hands of Gilbert E. Porter, register, and H. Clay Williams, receiver. Porter was at the same time editor of the *Eau Claire Free Press*, a paper which reflected the attitude of the sawmill industry of Eau Claire, in which he was also engaged.[4] The salary of $500 which the register received was to him a mere bagatelle, and, even if business had been sufficient to bring his total income, including commissions, to the $3,000 which the law allowed, it would still have been a matter of small interest to him.[5] Williams continued to practice law while receiver and there is little indication that he paid any attention to the work of the land office.

In 1864 Henry C. Putnam became clerk of the land office at Eau Claire. Putnam was born in Madison, New York, in 1832. He became a railroad engineer and was thus employed in New York, Florida, South Carolina, and Tennessee. In 1855 he settled in Wisconsin, where he became connected with various railroads. Two years later he moved to Eau Claire, a part of which he laid out, and he remained

---

[2] Thomas E. Randall, *History of the Chippewa Valley* (Eau Claire, 1875), pp. 50, 52.
[3] W. J. Cornell, Chippewa Falls, Wisconsin, April 2, 1866, to Ezra Cornell.
[4] The *Eau Claire Free Press* is valuable for the story of the lumber industry of the Chippewa Valley. There is a sketch of Porter in *History of Northern Wisconsin* (A. T. Andreas, compiler), p. 312.
[5] Act of February 2, 1859, 11 *U. S. Stat.*, p. 378.

closely identified with the city and with many of its banking and lumbering enterprises until his death in 1912.

Putnam soon made himself familiar with "every section, corner and trout brook" of the Chippewa Valley.[6] He became an agent for eastern investors like Woodward who wanted to place their funds in time-entry loans. The loan business brought Putnam and his eastern principals profitable returns, but it soon became clear to him that the area suitable for settlement in the Chippewa Valley was limited and that it was not attracting settlers like parts of Iowa and Minnesota. Consequently the extensive pineries claimed his attention.

As a result of investigations which he made himself and through landlookers Putnam acquired records of numerous tracts of land on the Chippewa containing large amounts of valuable pine.[7] The landlookers were themselves an important class on the pine-land frontier. They were employed by capitalists, lumbermen, and agents to cruise timbered sections and to estimate the amount of pine timber of the size in commercial demand. They developed a high degree of skill in making their estimates and some of the ablest acquired a reputation for accuracy which assured them a steady demand for their services. Putnam knew most of the landlookers of the Chippewa and St. Croix Valleys and employed many of them to cruise tracts which the surveyors' notes showed to be heavily timbered. He accumulated records of the amount of pine on 50,000 to 100,000 acres of land and he offered to sell this information to capitalists or lumbermen who were looking for pine. In Wisconsin the usual practice of land agents who selected pine land for others was to ask for part of the tract as compensation, one-fourth of the land usually being demanded. The price for entering farming land ranged from $15 to $25 a quarter section. Some agents selected and entered land for $10 a quarter section, but, as Putnam pointed out, they did nothing further in the way of managing the land.[8] Putman made a number of large entries for absentee owners including John McGraw, Jeremiah W. Dwight and Charles D. Gil-

[6] W. A. Woodward, Eau Claire, Wisconsin, July 25, 1866, to Ezra Cornell.
[7] Putnam, Eau Claire, January 10, 1866, to Ezra Cornell.
[8] *Id.*, Eau Claire, January 24, 1866, to *id.*

more, for which he received from one-fourth to one-fifth of the land.⁹

Putnam was not only a successful land agent and town and railroad promoter; he was also a dextrous politician. Among the offices that he held were those of register of deeds, county surveyor, deputy United States assessor, town clerk, agent for the university, school, and swamp lands of the state of Wisconsin, and agent for the lands of the West Wisconsin and the Wisconsin Central Railroads.¹⁰ When he was made clerk of the land office Porter and Williams left their duties and powers as register and receiver completely to him.¹¹ These two offices were supposed to be in separate hands so that the records of one would provide the government with a check upon the records of the other, but in the Eau Claire office this intention was subverted and remained so during the entire time the Cornell lands were being entered. Regardless of who drew the salaries, Putnam ran the land office from the time of his becoming clerk until 1872 and no action could be taken without his approval. Neither Porter and Williams nor Bart-

⁹ *Id.*, Eau Claire, January 10, 1866, to *id.*

¹⁰ *Eau Claire Free Press*, December 30, 1860, October 9, November 13, 1862, July 2, 1863, October 29, 1868, December 15, 1870; W. A. Woodward, Eau Claire, July 25, 1866, to Ezra Cornell; and H. C. Putnam Sales Book.

¹¹ In a letter of January 14, 1875, to Barnes & Grimes, Putnam said: "I have been running the U. S. Land Office here from 64 to 72, & know most of the parties who want Land." In 1866 Putnam considered making an effort to secure the position of register or receiver, if either officer decided to resign. Porter, who drew the maximum income the law allowed, was willing to resign, provided he could be sure that Putnam would be appointed in his place. The latter attempted to secure promises of support for the office and Woodward and Cornell both used their political influence on his behalf. It was eventually decided that the best policy was to continue the *status quo* for fear that President Andrew Johnson might appoint someone unfriendly to Putnam and the Cornell interests. In 1869 there was fear that Porter and Williams would be replaced, and again Woodward, Putnam, and Cornell, as well as Cyrus Woodman, did their best to prevent any change. Putnam planned to visit Washington to interview Cadwallader Washburn and other members of the Wisconsin delegation in the hope of winning their support for the retention of the present officers, but Woodman counseled against it. He especially urged Putnam not to approach Washburn with "any offers that would seem like bribery or giving him improper advantages in relation to lands in the District. He will naturally want officers who are personally & politically friendly to him." (Cyrus Woodman, Cambridge, Massachusetts, February 19, 25, and other dates, 1869, to Putnam; W. A. Woodward, New York City, October 20, 1866, to Putnam; E. Cornell, Ithaca, October 24, 1866, to Woodward; H. C. Putnam, Eau Claire, October 17, 1866, to Woodward; *id.*, Eau Claire, October 30, 1866, to Ezra Cornell; Cornell, Albany, November 12, 1866, to Putnam; Woodward, Ithaca, February 16, 1869, to Putnam.)

lett and Stocking, who succeeded them, had any active share in the administration of the office.

The positions of register and receiver were extremely important and indeed no national officer, except the territorial governor, exercised as much power on the frontier. The land officers had charge of the surveyors' plats and of the entry books, recorded entries, received fees and the government land price, acted as a court when disputes arose over claims, and were instructed to enforce the laws against timber thieves. They could exercise considerable latitude in carrying out these duties, although there was always an appeal from their decisions to the authorities in Washington. Surveying was done by another branch of the General Land Office, but the surveyors' plats were made available to the land officers before the public had an opportunity to see them. Aided by this advance information, the land officers could—themselves or through others—easily enter those tracts which the notes indicated to be heavily wooded or prairie land suitable for farming. Furthermore, there was a spirit of coöperation between the land officers of the various districts in Wisconsin which gave them advantages not enjoyed by others. Putnam, for example, was on intimate terms with the land officers in Wausau, St. Croix, Bayfield, and Stevens Point, all of whom did special favors for him in expediting land entries and reserving tracts to an extent not warranted by law. Land officers had long been active speculators in western lands and many had risen to positions of affluence through their deals. The special advantage which they had in private land deals, the income from salary and fees, and the prestige which went with the appointments all made the land offices much sought after and highly prized.

It was Putnam's good fortune to come into control of the Eau Claire office just as land entries began to increase. No man in Wisconsin could better serve capitalists and lumbermen in securing choice pine land than he, not only because he was thoroughly familiar with the Chippewa Valley but also because he controlled the plats and the entry books in the Eau Claire office, and no one knew this better than William A. Woodward. When, therefore, Woodward first learned that Ezra Cornell contemplated entering the New York land scrip, it was natural that he should think of the advantageous position which Putnam then held and to dream of entering the scrip in the Chippewa Valley through him.

Putnam's first reaction when approached by Woodward was to think in terms of monopoly. The amount of scrip was sufficient, he believed, to enable Cornell to secure a monopoly of the best pine on the upper Chippewa, and he proposed to Woodward and Cornell that this be their goal.[12] It was Putnam who convinced Woodward and through him Cornell that a fortune could be made in pine land for the university. The vastness of the project troubled none of the men, nor did they have any doubts about their ability to make a success of the venture.

Putnam and Woodward were not the first to think of establishing a monopoly of pine or mineral land in Wisconsin. In 1836 a group of influential easterners made an effort to secure a monopoly of the lead-bearing land of southwestern Wisconsin, among them being Senator Henry H. Hubbard of New Hampshire, Daniel Webster of Massachusetts, Henry H. Sylvester of Washington, and A. E. Dougherty of Philadelphia.[13] In 1852 Abner Coburn, a wealthy lumberman of Maine, was said to be contemplating the acquisition of all the valuable pine on the Black River. Another group, consisting of Caleb Cushing, Robert Rantoul, and Daniel Webster tried, through their purchase of the property at the falls on the St. Croix, to control the surrounding timber land. Successive efforts to exploit the area failed, but that which came nearest to success was made in 1869, when Cushing, still optimistic, helped to organize the Great European American Emigration Land Company which was to buy up additional land and settle it with immigrants from northern Europe. The company bought 50,000 acres of Agricultural-College land in Polk County from the

[12] Putnam asserted in 1866 that 300,000 or 400,000 acres would include all the pine on the Chippewa (H. C. Putnam, Eau Claire, May 5, 11, 1866, to Ezra Cornell).

[13] H. Sylvester, Washington, January 6, 1837, to Moses Strong; copy, letter of Moses Strong, Cincinnati, Ohio, November 20, 1837 (Strong MSS). Webster and Hubbard tried to induce the government to permit them and their associates to enter 72,000 acres of mineral land, but neither Jackson nor Van Buren had any desire to aid such a monopolistic enterprise. Joseph Schafer has described this venture in "A Yankee Land Speculator in Wisconsin," *Wisconsin Magazine of History*, viii (June, 1925), pp. 377–392.

State of Wisconsin and 12,000 acres from other parties and began a large emigration promotion campaign in Europe, but, being poorly managed, soon failed.[14]

Most spectacular of all these schemes was that undertaken by Cyrus Woodman and Cadwallader Washburn to control or "monopolize" all the valuable pine on the upper Mississippi and described in the following quotation:

We have taken up the idea of monopolising all the pine timber lands in the valley of the Miss. & if we carry out our plans a mint of money will be the result. The only pine in all this vast valley is in Wisconsin & Minnesota, & as yet it is nearly all gov't land subject to entry any day. There are probably 200 saw-mills engaged in making pine lumber on the Wisconsin, Black, Chippewa, St. Croix, Rum & Wolf Rivers all of which greatly depend upon getting their timber from gov't land. We propose sweeping of this land at one fell swoop. We are about starting our explorers, who are thoroughly acquainted with the business of lumbering, and by fall I shall have all the data to show where every pine tract is in the Miss. Valley. We suppose that it will take $200,000 to monopolise it.[15]

A year later Washburn's partner announced that in conjunction with some Maine lumbermen—among them Dorilus Morrison—the firm had been "recently entering all the choice pine lands in Wisconsin and Minnesota. . . ." [16] On April 19, 1854, Cyrus Woodman said that the group had "monopolized a good portion of all the pine lands in the valley of the Mississippi above the mouth of the Ohio. . . ." [17]

[14] The *Polk County Press* (August 27, 1869) of Osceola Mills—probably under obligations to Cushing, Barron, and Reymert of the Emigration Land Company—commented upon the purchase of the State Agricultural College lands in the following manner: "This sagacious and liberal measure, by which any attempt of land speculators to corner the land market on the influx of immigrants, is effectually prevented, will ensure the rapid filling up of that district with a hard[y] and industrious population." In the Cushing MSS in the Library of Congress are many letters between Caleb Cushing, James D. Reymert, Isaac Freedland, Henning A. Taub, and H. D. Barron concerning the land speculation in Polk County.

[15] C. C. Washburn, Mineral Point, Wisconsin, April 24, 1853, to his brother (Washburn Letter Book, Washburn MSS, Wisconsin Historical Society). On May 7, 1853, Washburn and Woodman instructed George Messersmith, of Dodgeville, Wisconsin, to search for timbered lands which he is to classify according to quantity. Messersmith was urged "not to breath a word to a human being" concerning the object.

[16] Cyrus Woodman, Mineral Point, Wisconsin, January 26, 1854, to E. Wilder Farley (Woodman MSS).

[17] Woodman, Mineral Point, Wisconsin, April 19, 1854, to Francis O. Watts (*loc. cit.*).

Washburn and Woodman entered between 150,000 and 200,000 acres of land which, combined with that acquired by their associates, brought the total to a quarter of a million acres. This did not give the firm a monopoly of pine on the upper Mississippi, though it did enable it to dictate prices to a considerable degree within certain areas.

It was the prospect of securing a monopoly of the pine lands on the Chippewa that Woodward used to induce Cornell to make him his agent. Woodward well knew that his fortune would be made if he had charge of the scrip, and as soon as he learned of Cornell's plan to enter it he plied him with information concerning the Chippewa, the special advantages which he had in entering lands, and the profits which might be expected if Cornell would permit him to use the scrip to corner the Chippewa pine lands. As a matter of fact, all the information which Woodward possessed concerning Wisconsin pine-land values came from Putnam, and it was Putnam who was to make the entries, secure titles, pay taxes, make sales, and prevent depredations on the Cornell lands during the first decade of their existence. Cornell, as has been seen, sought information from others concerning the land business, but either his other correspondents were less certain of the amount and quality of land they could enter or else they could not persuade him of their qualifications to deal in land on a large scale. Woodward had entered a large amount of land in Wisconsin from which he and his associates were enjoying good dividends; he therefore had experience and success. His experience—plus the bait of monopoly that he continually held out—were sufficient to persuade Cornell that he was the man to be entrusted with the work. Having reached this point, Cornell made a major error that he might have avoided if he had been more familiar with the western land business: he neglected to make a contract clearly stating the terms under which Woodward was to conduct the business for him.

Cornell had numerous admirable traits and was a man of strong character, but he cannot be classed among the giants of modern business. The fact is that he got in on the ground floor of the rapidly expanding telegraph business and had sufficient confidence in it to retain his share until it brought him a fortune. But of capacity for business leadership in the way it was possessed by Commodore Vanderbilt, Peter Cooper, or Amos Lawrence, he seemed to have little. Nothing bears this out more than the haphazard manner in which he turned over the land business to Woodward.

At the risk of repetition it is necessary to point out that Woodward was a business man, first and last, and his share in the administration of the Cornell lands was part of his normal affairs from which he expected to make a large profit. True, he professed a keen interest in the proposal to establish a great university for the children of farmers and mechanics as well as for those of the more well-to-do class, but this appears to have been to insinuate himself into the good favor of Cornell. There is nothing which reveals any other motive than that of self-interest. Cornell was pleased with his interest in the university, which he accepted as sincere, and was impressed by his understanding of business methods and his knowledge of western land. Woodward's persuasive manner, fluency in conversation and writing, and understanding of land speculation were all in sharp contrast to Cornell's shy, reticent speech, his awkward writing, and his ignorance of land speculation. Cornell accepted Woodward slowly and with some hesitation, but, finding no one better, he came to place great confidence in him.

Woodward's slow progress in winning Cornell's favor can be traced in the correspondence between the two men during 1865 and 1866. Woodward persistently urged the advantages he had over others in locating land and sought to hasten the matter and bring Cornell to terms. Cornell, confused by the vastness of the project he had undertaken, took the bait slowly. He first agreed to turn over to Woodward a small amount of scrip as an experiment and, when he was informed that some of the best opportunities for locating land were rapidly slipping away, he hastily sent additional scrip. Woodward meantime stated the terms on which he proposed to locate and manage the lands, and on a number of occasions attempted to get Cornell to come to a definite agreement as to the compensation to be paid. Woodward proposed to make careful investigations of farm and pine lands in the Chippewa Valley, enter the lands and pay the entry fee of $4 a quarter section, set up a system of books, and superintend the administration of the lands, all for a price of 30 cents an acre or $48 a quarter section.[18] Although it was not at all clear what "superintending" the lands actually included, nor precisely how Woodward proposed to ensure the entry of first-class farm and pine lands, there could be no doubt as to the compensation he expected.[19] Cornell evaded a definite agreement and later stated that Woodward proposed to locate farm land for $15 and pine land for $25 a quarter section, but the documents do not sustain his contention.[20]

Neither was any understanding reached about the scrip, and as a result a sharp controversy developed. Woodward expected to sell part of the scrip to western settlers from whom he could get a much higher price than it brought in the East. The profits from this part of the business he expected to share with Cornell, and he assured him that they would be sufficient to carry the land investment until sales could be made.[21] Woodward contended that he had the right to sell part of the scrip and, when denied that right, he argued that he had been damaged, while Cornell maintained that Woodward never had any

[18] W. A. Woodward, Vail's Gate, Orange County, New York, May [n.d.], 1865, to Victor Rice, Secretary to the Board of Trustees of Cornell University (*Woodward vs. Cornell*, pp. 8–14). Also letters of Woodward to Cornell of October 4, December 7, 20, 1865, October 30, 1869 (Cornell MSS). Woodward billed Cornell for commissions at the rate above mentioned, but Cornell, according to his own testimony, neglected to study the accounts, and the commissions and fees were not settled for by 1871, when matters between the two reached the breaking point. Cornell demanded the return of certain books and documents which Woodward insisted on retaining in his own hands until the accounts were satisfied. Woodward was then dismissed as agent in charge of the lands and Henry C. Putnam, with whom Woodward had previously quarreled, was put in his place. Woodward brought suit to recover the full commission, and the testimony which has been published contains numerous letters between Woodward, Cornell, and Putnam bearing on the land business.

[19] Woodward's methods of examining lands are outlined in his testimony (*Woodward vs. Cornell*, pp. 39–40).

[20] The only justification for Cornell's stand is in an early statement of Woodward to the effect that he had formerly paid $15 and $25 respectively for the location of farming and pine lands (*Woodward vs. Cornell*, p. 8). In all subsequent communications Woodward stated his price for entering land to be 30 cents an acre. That Cornell knew he was not correct is indicated in a confidential letter to Putnam, October 25, 1869, in which he admits that Woodward's letters "sustain his position" concerning the fees. In his testimony given in the resulting suit Cornell insisted that the price agreed upon—or at least the price stated by Woodward—was $30 a quarter section (*id.*, pp. 797–810).

[21] W. A. Woodward, Vail's Gate, December 7, 1865, to Ezra Cornell.

right to use the scrip for any other purpose than that of entering land. Lacking a contract or definite agreement, Woodward assumed that Cornell accepted his terms when he continued to send him scrip and he did not permit Cornell's evasion of the issue to trouble him. It was in this vague and indecisive way that the scrip was gradually turned over to Woodward by Cornell. Woodward was never informed how much land it was intended to locate, but whenever he urged that additional scrip be forwarded to Putnam to take up locations already selected it was generally sent until 1867, by which time 511,069 acres had been located with 521,120 acres of scrip.[22] The university's need for funds and the growing reluctance of the trustees to add to the heavy burden of financing the land assumed by Cornell led to the decision to make no further entries and the remaining scrip was sold, as is related elsewhere.

Woodward's commission of 30 cents an acre or $48 a quarter section was high; W. J. Cornell had offered to enter land for a quarter share of the acreage entered, which would have been equivalent to 20 cents an acre, and other bids were made at even lower rates. Through Putnam, Woodward had unparalleled advantages in entering land, but even so his price was high. Woodward agreed to pay Putnam $6 and $7.50 a quarter for selecting and entering farm land and $10 a quarter for selecting pine land.[23] The entire burden and responsibility for selecting suitable land and the success or failure of Cornell's great speculation depended therefore almost completely on Putnam, not Woodward. The small compensation given Putnam was barely sufficient to pay the land hunters, leaving him little or nothing save a vague promise of future benefits to be derived from the management and sale of the land. Had Putnam been more generously treated he doubtless would have given more attention to selecting the land and would have secured more heavily timbered tracts. Some of the

[22] Many quarter sections containing less than 160 acres were entered, and sometimes 80- and 120-acre tracts bearing heavy stands of pine were acquired. Since a piece of scrip had to be used for each tract, the actual amount of land entered by Cornell was less than the total acreage of the scrip thus used.

[23] Putnam later stated that he could have entered the lands for one-third the amount charged by Woodward (H. C. Putnam, Eau Claire, March 15, 1870, to John McGraw).

financial difficulties and subsequent cancellations of sales in the seventies would thereby have been avoided.

In the summer of 1866 Woodward went to Eau Claire to aid Putnam in entering the land. He prepared a set of books in which details of entries, descriptions of land, and tax payments were recorded. He also gave Cornell some assistance in organizing an abortive company whose purpose it was to buy part of the Cornell land and cut off its timber.

Until 1868 or 1869 Woodward acted chiefly as an intermediary between Cornell and Putnam, by which time the two were in direct communication with each other. It was becoming increasingly apparent that Woodward's services were unnecessary, since all that he did could have been done at less expense by Putnam and a full-time salaried attorney to manage the books. Such an appointment was eventually made, but not until the land matters had got into a serious tangle which threatened for a time the entire enterprise.

Putnam began making land entries for Cornell with real enthusiasm. Here was his main chance to use to full advantage the dominant position he held in the Eau Claire land office and his special knowledge of pine-land locations. But Woodward's experience prejudiced him in favor of farm land, although he had talked to Ezra Cornell about securing a monopoly of the pine land, and he instructed Putnam to enter the Cornell scrip on land suitable for settlement.

During the post-war years Eau Claire and Chippewa Counties were growing rapidly as a result of an influx of immigrants. Some newcomers took up homestead claims to which they could get title after five years of residence, but meantime they could not borrow on their claim to finance improvements, nor could they sell their interest in the property if circumstances made their stay on it intolerable. Furthermore, the government required the entry fee of $10 to be paid at the time of entry. The five-year clause was designed to ensure permanent settlement and the fee system was to compensate the local officers. Immigrants hesitated to tie themselves to a piece of property for as long as five years, and others could not raise the entry fee.

Consequently, after the Homestead Law was put in operation, there were still many prospective settlers arriving penniless on the frontier who looked not to the government but to loan sharks or land agents to assist them in getting a piece of land. In 1865 the Secretary of the Interior estimated that from 40 to 50 per cent of homesteaders would decide to commute their claims into a pre-emption entry in order to secure an early title.[24] Woodward and Putnam were familiar with the "parties who desire to be able to transfer their interest & renew their travels toward the setting sun" and prior to 1865 they had aided many homesteaders in commuting their claims to pre-emption entries.[25] They now proposed to carry on the business on a large scale by loaning the Cornell scrip to the homesteaders at a usurious rate of interest. This business, Woodward argued, would bring in quick profits and would be a "soothing syrup for our anxiety while waiting" for the pine-land entries to become marketable.[26]

Numerous tracts in Clark, Taylor, Eau Claire, and Chippewa Counties were entered for homesteaders, who agreed to pay in a year from $1.25 to $1.37 an acre. Larger amounts of land considered suitable for farming were entered to be held as a speculation. Such lands were easily selected, their value was not destroyed by depredations, and settlers were certain to want them in a relatively short time. The amount of land suitable for settlement was limited, however, and when between 50,000 and 100,000 acres of such land, much of it bearing some pine, were located, Putnam had his way and the remainder of the lands selected were chosen for their pine. Putnam had more confidence in Chippewa pine land than in farm land in the lower part of the valley, and in 1866 and 1867, when he was told to go ahead and locate the Cornell scrip on timbered areas, he began operations in a large way.

Putnam employed a corps of land hunters to roam through the valley of the Chippewa and those of its main tributaries the Flambeau,

---

[24] "Extract from report of the Secretary of the Interior relative to the report of the Commissioner of the General Land Office," in *Report*, Commissioner of the General Land Office, 1865, pp. iii–iv.
[25] W. A. Woodward, Vail's Gate, New York, February 27, 1866, to Ezra Cornell.
[26] *Id.*, Vail's Gate, February 27, 1866, to *id.*

the Jump, the Thornapple, and the Red Cedar, looking for land bearing pine in commercial quantities. Among these hunters were W. J. Cornell, Edward Rutledge and James S. Becky, who were thoroughly familiar with the Chippewa pineries. They had spent years in selecting lands for themselves and for some of the largest operators in the valley. Putnam paid them $10 for each quarter section which they reported to have pine in commercial quantities and to be close to rivers suitable for floating logs to the mills, and he gave some of them expenses in addition. This sum was insufficient to make it worth their while to estimate the amount of board feet of pine on each quarter section. Their method was to find the major pine-bearing areas and walk the lines to ascertain the sections which contained them. Their descriptions were, therefore, somewhat general, and because they did not inspect the land more thoroughly they included in their recommendations some land on which the pine was scattered and thin, too small, of poor quality, or even absent altogether. This was unavoidable. On the other hand the selections included more of heavily timbered land on which pine predominated than of poor land, and eventually these tracts yielded several times the minimum of 4000 board feet of merchantable pine to the acre which Cornell and Putnam had established.

When Cornell first suggested to Woodward that he might locate the New York scrip in Wisconsin the latter urged the necessity of haste, for he knew that, although the upper Chippewa Valley was still virtually untouched, land speculators and dealers in pine would soon be attracted to the region. This was apparent by 1865 to anyone who had observed the rapid rise in lumber prices during the Civil War and the expansion of the lumber industry. In 1866 the rush for Chippewa pine began. Rapid sales at Stevens Point and Menasha in the fifties had exhausted the government supply of first-rate pine land in the northeastern section, and now lumbermen from other parts of Wisconsin and Michigan began to focus their attention on the Chippewa.

Among those looking for choice pine land at this time were Cadwallader Washburn and his partner Cyrus Woodman, whose earlier dream of securing a monopoly of pine on the upper Mississippi was as yet unsatisfied. Francis Palms, one of the richest pine-land dealers in America, whose holdings in Michigan and Wisconsin were ultimately to equal in amount those of Cornell, had timber cruisers searching for choice tracts on the Chippewa. Sawmill operators like Pound, Halbert & Co. of Chippewa Falls, Smith & Buffington, and Carson & Rand of Eau Claire were also taking more interest in land entries than formerly, perhaps realizing before other millmen of the Chippewa and the Mississippi that if they did not secure pine land now they would have to buy it later from speculators at enhanced prices. Land cruisers seemed to be all through the Chippewa pineries in 1866 and 1867, but those of Putnam roamed farther afield. Francis Palms located land on the Jump and the lower Flambeau; Pound, Halbert & Co. selected land on the Thornapple and on the Flambeau, and Smith & Buffington likewise made entries in the lower portion of the valley. By ranging farther afield in the present counties of Ashland, Price, Rusk, and Sawyer, in areas then regarded as remote, Putnam's hunters secured the first and presumably the choicest selections.

Putnam had no intention of making all of his entries far up the Chippewa. The more distant pine lands, although adjacent to floatable streams, were not as attractive to lumbermen as land of equal or even poorer quality closer to roads and to farming and village communities. Remote tracts would not find a market for perhaps a generation, and Putnam knew that part of the land which he was entering must be salable at an early date or the land business would not carry itself. The land hunters of Palms and Woodman and of some of the mill owners were cruising the pineries close to Eau Claire and Chippewa Falls, and they threatened to forestall him in entering well timbered tracts. Many selections had been made by his landlookers, but the Cornell scrip was not transmitted with sufficient dispatch to make possible the entry of the lands before other agents learned of them. However, Putnam had a trump card which he brought into play and by means of it secured practically all the tracts his hunters recommended.

Putnam's scheme was to prevent others from securing land which he wanted but could not yet enter for lack of scrip or on which he was awaiting a report, by simply pointing to the books which he had written up to show that applications had already been made for the land. Of course, if anyone wished to make trouble for what was patently a breach of the Federal land laws he might do so, but there were few who dared challenge the register and receiver of the land office or, in this case, the person to whom they had delegated their responsibilities. Putnam could make it extremely unpleasant for those who opposed him, and it was generally found advisable to accept the situation and enter other lands. By this means Putnam succeeded in withholding lands from entry until he had received the reports of his timber cruisers or until he had the scrip. If the reports were not favorable the tracts would be reopened to entry; otherwise they would be entered in the name of Ezra Cornell. The latter may not have learned precisely how he was enabled to get the valuable pine lands of the Chippewa, but Woodward had no doubts about it.[27]

Meantime Putnam concealed the fact that he was making large selections for Cornell, fearing that the news would produce a scramble for pine which would make difficult the attainment of the monopoly for which he and Woodward were working. He was also aware that the Chippewa millmen would resent the intrusion of Ezra Cornell and his university into the pine-land business and would consider him as poaching on their preserves.[28]

The letters of Putnam and Woodward of 1866 and 1867 constantly stressed the reasons for speedy transmission of the scrip, but delay was caused by the difficulty of getting the Comptroller of the State to turn it over to Cornell as wanted. Furthermore, it was becoming apparent to Andrew D. White and other trustees of the university that the land investment would not return profits for some years. In the meantime there was the greatest need for money and the only solution seemed to be to cease making additional land entries and to sell the remaining scrip at the current market price.

From the outset Woodward had assured Cornell that the returns

---

[27] Woodward to Cornell, August 2, 1865, January 24, February 20, 24, July 7, 1866; H. C. Putnam, Eau Claire, May 5, 1866, to Cornell; *id.,* January 13, February 9, 1866, to Woodward; Cornell, Ithaca, January 26, 1866, to Woodward.

[28] Woodward, Vail's Gate, April 12, 1867, to Cornell.

from early sales, interest upon contracts and time entries, and profits to be derived from dealing in the scrip would be sufficient to carry the entire land venture until sales could be made in volume. But taxes quickly became a heavy drain and, together with the charges made by Woodward, they assumed proportions which were alarming to Cornell. It is true that Woodward had been disappointed in not being permitted to sell a portion of the land scrip, and to this alleged change in plan he blamed his heavy drafts on Cornell, but this was merely an excuse to hide the fact that the early sales at high prices which he had promised were not being made. The land business could not, at the outset, carry itself.

Cornell had dreamed of entering in the West the entire amount of New York scrip remaining unsold, which was more than 900,000 acres, but the continued urging of White and the trustees, the pressing needs of the university, and the failure of the land investment to carry itself, brought him to the realization that he had attempted too heavy a task. Reluctantly he concluded that he could make no further land entries.

By 1867 Ezra Cornell had acquired 499,126 acres of pine and farming land in Wisconsin. He had also made small ventures in Minnesota and Kansas amounting to 7968 and 3974 acres respectively. This made Ezra Cornell and through him Cornell University the largest owner of pine land in the Northwest, aside from one or two railroads and the governments of Wisconsin and the United States. His chief concern now was whether or not the Chippewa lumbermen would have to come to him for land before the tax burden threatened to swallow up the enterprise.

CHAPTER SIX

The Pine-Land Ring

FROM the time when he came into control of the Eau Claire land office, Henry C. Putnam had been planning to secure a monopoly of the valuable pine land on the Chippewa River. Lacking capital with which to buy a large volume of land, he was forced to employ a variety of means to exploit more fully his extensive information and his special position in the Eau Claire land office. When the Cornell land business was presented to him, through the agency of W. A. Woodward, he believed that Cornell could practically corner the good pine land on the Chippewa, and he expected to make his profit from service charges and commissions on sales. This expectation was never fully realized. Woodward allowed Putnam only a small sum for entering the land, and Ezra Cornell, on Woodward's advice, promptly set such high prices on the land that he could not make sales. Furthermore, Cornell did not locate the 900,000 acres which he had originally planned to acquire, and the Chippewa pineries proved to be larger than Putnam had earlier estimated. In consequence he sought other means of establishing the monopoly of which he dreamed. He now planned to make large entries of pine land for others who would be friendly to and willing to work with him and Cornell University. Woodward could aid in this matter because he had access to eastern capitalists whom he could induce to invest in Chippewa land. Putnam expected, through Woodward's assistance, to make himself the agent and manager of a combination of pine-land owners who, working together, could dictate the price of pine land to the mill owners for years to come. Putnam would profit from the increased value of the pine land he already owned and from the land entries made for others, a percentage of which he would secure as compensation.

Woodward fully realized the advantageous position Putnam held at Eau Claire. By utilizing that position he hoped to make for himself large profits. He assured Putnam that he would treat him fairly, but the latter soon realized that Woodward intended to have the lion's share of the returns from their partnership. Because he was playing an intermediary and by no means necessary role between eastern capitalists and the western land agent, Woodward feared that he might be by-passed and his services dispensed with. He therefore tried to prevent Cornell and Putnam from having any direct correspondence with each other, and he watched with much suspicion the activities of Henry W. Sage and John McGraw, who were, he feared, attempting to undermine his influence with Cornell. These two lumbermen had told Cornell that 25,000 acres of scrip might well be located in Michigan, and Woodward, fearful lest he lose his share in the business, warned Cornell that Sage had probably located all the best land on the Saginaw, that taxes were higher there, and that there was a greater prejudice against easterners in Michigan than in Wisconsin. Woodward was also afraid that Sage and McGraw would anticipate him and Putnam in their plans to secure a monopoly of the pine on the Chippewa.[1]

Later events soothed Woodward's fears, and in 1868 he turned to John McGraw and his partner, Jeremiah W. Dwight, for aid in acquiring the monopoly which he and Putnam were planning. McGraw had already made large investments in Michigan pine lands in association with Sage, and now, like so many other Michigan operators, was transferring his interest farther west, where he might anticipate his future needs. Both McGraw and Dwight had enough money to enable them to speculate in lands in a large way. Woodward made them the same glib promises that he had made Cornell and stressed his connection with Putnam and the opportunity it gave him of monopolizing the remaining pine land on the Chippewa. This was the chief bait and

[1] E. Cornell, Ithaca, November 1, 1865, to W. A. Woodward; Woodward, Vail's Gate, November 4, 1865, March 27, 1866, to Ezra Cornell. In 1866 both Cornell and Woodward suspected, from rumors which they heard, that Sage and McGraw had agents on the Chippewa looking for land. Woodward hoped to "expose these men who have done so much to thwart our legitimate operations" (Woodward, Ithaca, September 23, October 9, 1866, to Cornell).

again it worked. McGraw & Dwight agreed to enter through Woodward and Putnam all the "good merchantable pine land" on the Chippewa up to 120,000 acres or even more if it were available, "no matter who else applies for them." [2] Putnam was not to enter any lands for others and was expected to do everything possible to assure McGraw & Dwight the best remaining land bearing 4000 feet or more of pine to the acre. Woodward was to receive as compensation one-fifth interest in the land. Of this amount one-fifteenth was to go to Putnam.[3]

Putnam proceeded to enter some 23,000 acres of land for McGraw & Dwight, but by that time complications had set in. Dwight had learned through private reports that the lands did not bear the required amount of pine. Friction developed between Woodward and the others, and Putnam became restive when he learned how small his compensation was compared with that of Woodward. The blame for the poor entries was put on Woodward, perhaps rightly, as the small return he permitted Putnam was insufficient to warrant paying land hunters for careful inspection. McGraw & Dwight had meantime drawn closer to Putnam, whose qualities they deeply respected, and eventually they decided to drop Woodward and to work directly through Putnam, a decision which Ezra Cornell was subsequently to make.[4] Putnam pushed the entries rapidly thereafter, and a total of 29,500 acres of Federal land and 23,149 acres of state land was acquired for McGraw & Dwight in the Eau Claire district. That the entries were generally acceptable is shown by the fact that within two years 27,886 acres were sold at $3.89 an acre to A. P. Brewer of East Saginaw, Michigan. This was an appreciation of more than 200 per cent.[5] McGraw & Dwight also entered 5100 acres at Stevens Point and Henry W. Sage and McGraw at the same time entered 44,330 acres at Eau Claire and Bayfield. Altogether this group, all closely

[2] W. A. Woodward, Vail's Gate, December 8, 10, 1868, to H. C. Putnam. The contract between Woodward and McGraw & Dwight is in *Woodward vs. Cornell*, pp. 1274–1276.

[3] Woodward, December 8, 22, 1868, to Putnam.

[4] As in the case of the Woodward-Cornell relations, a suit was brought to determine the rights of Woodward under the contract with McGraw & Dwight (*Woodward vs. Cornell*, pp. 1244–1245).

[5] *Clark County Republican*, March 28, 1874. See also testimony of McGraw, Dwight, and Brewer in *Woodward vs. Cornell*, pp. 1221 ff.

associated with Ezra Cornell, entered 101,079 acres of Federal and state lands in Wisconsin. With purchases subsequently made from Cornell, the group became one of the largest holders of pine, not only in Wisconsin but in the United States.

Putnam was too canny a dealer to work only through Woodward and the group of Ithaca, New York, lumbermen. He was ever restive under the flow of complaints that Woodward directed at him because of his alleged failure to keep his accounts in the careful way the latter required, and he could not but feel that Woodward was getting far more advantage out of the mutual association while contributing little to it. Furthermore, Woodward, after exploiting to the fullest degree Putnam's peculiar position in the land office, intended to replace him as his western agent by his son, Francis, who had settled in Eau Claire in 1869. Putnam and Cornell saw through Woodward's scheme, and when the break came in 1870 and 1871 Cornell sided with Putnam, who was then put in full charge of the Wisconsin lands. But by that time Putnam had secured additional capital for his land deals.

Cyrus Woodman and his partner Cadwallader Washburn had not forgotten their earlier plans to acquire a monopoly of the pine on the upper Mississippi. Despite their large purchases they soon found a real monopoly of pine to be very hard to acquire. While they were scattering their entries on the Wisconsin, Black, St. Croix, and Chippewa Rivers they found to their dismay that Francis Palms, Ezra Cornell, Sage, and McGraw & Dwight had come into the Chippewa area and snatched from under their noses a vast amount of pine. Woodman wrote to his associate, "We were smart to let Cornell & Michigan men come in and gobble up such an enormous quantity of valuable pine." [6] Woodman had long been associated with Putnam in land deals, and in 1868 and 1869 the two laid plans to secure between 25,000 and 50,000 acres of the remaining pine land on the Chippewa.[7]

Early in 1869 the government ordered a public sale of 247,680 acres of land on the Chippewa which had previously been withdrawn

---

[6] Cyrus Woodman, Plattsmouth, Nebraska, August 22, 1869, to C. C. Washburn, La Crosse, Wisconsin (Woodman MSS).

[7] Cyrus Woodman, Cambridge, Massachusetts, February 25, 1859, and numerous other dates, to H. C. Putnam.

from entry for railroad purposes.[8] By this time most of the desirable pine was in private hands, and mill owners now recognized their mistake in not anticipating future needs. There still remained an abundance of pine which, at existing rates of cutting, would last perhaps two generations, but it was held by Cornell, Palms, Sage, McGraw & Dwight, and other eastern capitalists. Hence great excitement prevailed when it became known that one of the last tracts of Chippewa pine in public hands which was considered merchantable was to be sold.[9] On the day of the sale there were in attendance at Eau Claire not only the lumbermen of the Chippewa and the Red Cedar—Thorp, Chapman & Co. and Knapp, Stout & Co.—but also many lumbermen and pine-land owners of other sections. The presence of such persons of means as Philetus Sawyer of Oshkosh, Henry Hewitt of Ripon, Washburn & Woodman, Jeremiah W. Dwight, John McGraw, Francis Palms, William A. Rust of Saginaw, Michigan, John F. Rust of Philadelphia, H. W. Early of Williamsport, Pennsylvania, and William A. Woodward assured an exciting sale.[10] So crowded was the town that both taverns were full and accommodations had to be engaged in private homes.[11]

It was a rare occasion when such a group of successful loggers and pine-land dealers came together at a public auction, and since only a relatively small amount of land was available it was a certainty that competition would drive up the bids. Furthermore, Thorp, Chapman & Co. and Knapp, Stout & Co. had no intention of permitting outsiders to monopolize the land. When the sale began prices were raised to two, three, four, and even six dollars an acre, and the highest

[8] Manuscript volume, "Record of Proclamations for Public Land Sales, etc., 1857–1875," General Land Office, Department of the Interior.

[9] Cyrus Woodman, Eau Claire, May 21, 1869, to George Woodman (Woodman MSS); *Eau Claire Free Press*, June 3, 1869. There was valuable pine on the Indian reservations in Wisconsin which was subsequently to become the subject of much controversy.

[10] Both Woodward and Putnam, while representing Ezra Cornell, continued to deal in lands for themselves as well as for other persons. In 1869 Woodward instructed Putnam to enter 3040 acres for him (Woodward, Ithaca, January 5, 1869, to Henry C. Putnam). Woodward attended the sale at Eau Claire in May, apparently to watch over his own interests and those of McGraw & Dwight, but debited the cost of the trip to Cornell (*Woodward vs. Cornell*, p. 162).

[11] Cyrus Woodman, Eau Claire, May 21, 1869, to George Woodman, and May 23, 1869, to his wife (Woodman MSS).

bidder got his tracts. The well laid plans of Woodward, McGraw, and Dwight to work through Putnam and thereby control entries did not succeed at the outset. But cooler tempers soon prevailed and a "ring" was formed to prevent competitive bidding. At the suggestion of Putnam the insiders agreed to divide the land among them and end the expensive competition. Henceforth the sale proceeded smoothly. When it was completed, Knapp, Stout & Co. and Thorp, Chapman & Co. had each acquired 14,000 acres; William A. Rust, 13,000; George Burnham, 9000; Philetus Sawyer, 5600, and others smaller amounts. Woodman, despite the aid rendered by Putnam, secured but a small tract, and he doubted whether the entire business had been worth his time.[12]

Putnam did not cease his efforts to secure a monopoly of pine on the Chippewa with this sale. Convinced that lumbermen and landlookers had misjudged numerous tracts of land which had pine and hemlock in merchantable quantities, he sought to induce others to join with him in buying these neglected sections. With William Griffin of Troy, New York, he entered 12,500 acres on the Red Cedar which in less than fifteen years was sold for $200,000.[13] He also agreed to enter 75,000 acres for General Charles D. Gilmore of Washington, D. C., for a one-fourth share in the land.[14] With other parties too Putnam arranged to enter land, and by 1872 he was either agent for or part owner of much of the best pine land on the Chippewa.

Putnam's selections of land for General Gilmore took practically the last of the pine land open to public entry in the Eau Claire district. There was in 1873 still another chance for the "ring" to function when a small lot of land, previously withheld from market for the selection of railroad land, was offered. Again great excitement prevailed. Loggers, millmen, and pine-land dealers flocked to the sale,

---

[12] "Going to Wisconsin didn't pay. Too much competition" (Cyrus Woodman, Eau Claire, May 28, 1869, to C. C. Washburn), *id.*, Cambridge, Massachusetts, June 7, 1869, to George Woodman; H. C. Putnam, Eau Claire, undated but in August, 1869, to Cyrus Woodman (Woodman MSS); W. A. Woodward, Eau Claire, May 28, 1869, to Ezra Cornell.

[13] *Chippewa Herald*, January 19, 1883, quoting the *Northwestern Lumberman*.

[14] In 1877 Putnam held the Gilmore land for sale at $2 an acre (H. C. Putnam, May 19, 1877, to J. W. Williams).

organized a "ring" and attempted to prevent competition.[15] The *Chippewa Herald* reported that the ring got its signals mixed and that in the rush to buy, participated in by at least a hundred persons, bids were forced up as high as $19.75 an acre.[16] Putnam, who was attempting to get a share of the land for himself and Congressman Jeremiah M. Rusk, said that the advance arrangements were broken up and the buyers got no aid from the land officers, who were powerless, so strong was the demand for the pine. A night of rest enabled the bidders to realize their error, and on the following day the tracts which brought such high prices were forfeited and offered again, this time bringing about $3. The combination had been re-established and throughout the remainder of the sale it functioned smoothly.[17]

No other man in the Chippewa Valley had as many influential connections or as strong a hold on its resources as Putnam. His familiarity with the pine lands and his position in the land office brought to his door the larger operators, who asked for favors, sought assistance, and followed his leadership in plans for securing river improvements, railroad connections, reductions in taxes, and control of local governments. In the late sixties and early seventies Putnam was emerging as one of the principal leaders of the Chippewa pine-land and lumbering industry, and his advice and assistance were much sought.

Success and fortune invite jealousy, and Putnam's lot was not an easy one. It is true he does not seem to have incurred the animosity of the Chippewa lumbermen, despite the fact that it was his influence that had made possible the large entries of Cornell in the valley. Although Ezra Cornell and subsequently Cornell University were criticized by numerous individuals and newspapers for their land acquisition and tax policies, Putnam, while defending his employer, managed to gain prestige among his Wisconsin associates. But Putnam's hold over the land office was not to last. Through that opportunity and his shrewd knowledge of pine he had accumulated a small fortune. He had, however, broken with Woodward, and for good

---

[15] Among those present were G. B. Burrows of Madison, J. S. Young of Clinton, Iowa, C. D. Gilmore, and H. C. Putnam (*Eau Claire Free Press*, August 18, 1873).
[16] *Chippewa Herald*, August 29, 1873. Peter Truax bid this price for a small tract.
[17] *Id.*, August 19, 20, 22, 25, 1873.

reason. In retaliation, Woodward, as has been seen, sent his son Francis to Eau Claire to replace Putnam as Cornell's agent. A sharp clash between the two resulted in an embarrassing situation for all concerned, including Ezra Cornell.

Woodward's insistence upon the full payment of his charges for entering the university's land brought about a gradual break between him and Ezra Cornell and led Cornell to rely upon Putnam for assistance in managing the western lands. Cornell could not afford to break openly with Woodward, however, until he had secured the certificates of entries or patents which Woodward had retained. Eventually the question of jurisdiction in Wisconsin had to be settled, for both Putnam and Francis Woodward were attempting to pay taxes, manage sales, and keep the books. The upshot was an announcement in September, 1871, that Putnam had superseded Woodward as agent for the Cornell lands.[18] This was the final break, and although it seemed a victory for Putnam it was to have an unpleasant aftermath.

Francis Woodward did not lose the opportunity of managing the Cornell lands without striking back at his successful rival. He had another grievance—the hold which Putnam had on the Eau Claire land office. That made it unpleasant, if not impossible, for Woodward to have business dealings there. When Woodward sought to enter a tract of land marked "E" on the plats he was informed that it had been entered. Subsequently he learned that the entry was made not before but two hours after he had presented his application. In a letter of complaint to the General Land Office, Woodward charged that this practice of withholding lands from those applying until insiders could enter them was common and he demanded an investigation.[19]

This was not the first accusation brought against the Eau Claire land officers. Similar complaints had been made about Porter and Williams in 1869. Fearful of losing his hold over the office if they should be removed, Putnam had tried to defend them, and when told

[18] *Chippewa Herald*, September 30, 1871.
[19] Copy, letter of Francis Woodward, Eau Claire, July 30, 1871, to Willis Drummond.

that they were to be removed he had sought to secure the office of register for himself.[20] He failed in this respect but was successful in having two men appointed to the offices of register and receiver who permitted him to retain charge of the land office as their predecessors had done.[21] The Grant administration, having made the new appointments, was forced to make at least a perfunctory investigation of Woodward's charges, which were well supported by evidence.[22]

A month after receiving Woodward's complaint, Willis Drummond, Commissioner of the General Land Office, ordered the register and receiver to make answer to it. A delay of more than two months followed, during which no reply was made, probably because the officers hoped the matter would blow over. On November 9, 1871, Drummond peremptorily demanded a reply and dispatched a special agent to Eau Claire to investigate the situation and to close the office. It soon became apparent there could be no whitewashing of the officers, as even more serious charges followed.[23]

The *La Crosse Republican and Leader* summed up the accusations —in an unfriendly spirit, it is true—in the following words:

> The operations of a powerful Pine Land Ring, that has, for several years past, exercised a fearful and terrible monopoly of the most valuable pine lands on the Chippewa and its tributaries, has caused considerable consternation and surprise. . . . The Chippewa Pine Land Ring has been a formidable and dangerous monopoly. It has controlled the appointments in that office, in such a manner as to keep its clutches upon the great prize; and already over a million of acres of the best pine lands of the Chippewa country have been secured by half a score of monopolists, upon terms that debarred the people from a fair and equal participation in the benefits of a system that was designed to promote the general welfare.

[20] Porter and Williams were threatened with removal when Putnam and Woodman were engaged in entering land for McGraw & Dwight. Fearing that any change would damage their chances for securing the desired tracts, Woodward told Putnam to "enter land as fast as you can. . . . I shall work to keep Porter & Clay [Williams] in land office."

[21] H. M. Stocking and E. M. Bartlett, receiver and register respectively, assumed office in May, 1869.

[22] The *Chippewa Herald* (January 27, 1872), a Republican organ, said there had been innumerable complaints made by injured persons against the management of the land office but that Woodward's was the first in writing.

[23] *Dunn County News*, January 13, 1872.

In more detail, the *Leader* went on to say that McGraw & Dwight, prominent beneficiaries of the ring, had acquired 250,000 acres of pine lands through "such favored terms of intimacy with the Land Office that few outsiders could enter any valuable tracts of land without being compelled to undergo the ordeal and inspection of the select Ring." The *Leader* accused Putnam not only of withholding land from legitimate entry but also of violating the spirit if not the letter of the law by combining in his own person the functions of register and receiver. As a result, Putnam had become, "in common with his favored associates, a very wealthy and extensive owner and is a representative of enormous tracts of the best pine lands on the Chippewa." Putnam was also accused of accepting cash for entries but actually using warrants, and then pocketing the difference between the small cost of the warrants and the cash paid at the rate of $1.25 an acre. Another complaint concerned the withholding of two townships from sale while bogus pre-emptors made claims to the land.[24]

Alarmed at the course of events, Putnam wrote a frantic letter to Ezra Cornell in which he said: "The Charges are all as false as Hell & I can prove it in time." He urged Cornell to see McGraw and Dwight and to have them write Commissioner Drummond and "tell him that you know me." [25]

Cornell University, while frequently under attack in Wisconsin on account of the large amount of pine land which had been entered for speculation in its name, escaped notice in this flareup, although the university and Sage, McGraw, and Dwight were the chief beneficiaries of the irregularities. Woodward knew well what advantages Putnam took while in charge of the land office and he had full knowledge that the lands entered for Cornell University were withheld from entry by others until the scrip could be forwarded to Eau Claire. Woodward had frequently told Ezra Cornell of this special advantage which he and Putnam enjoyed in the Eau Claire office and in other

[24] *La Crosse Republican and Leader*, October 4, 1871.
[25] H. C. Putnam, Eau Claire, January 6, 1872, to Ezra Cornell. Putnam gave some details concerning the accusation against the land officers in a letter of March, 1879 (in the *Eau Claire Free Press*, March 12, 1879).

offices through friendly registers and receivers, but Cornell, never familiar with the business, probably had no real understanding of its character. He cannot be held responsible, since he had given full charge of the land entries to Woodward.

It should be pointed out that what Putnam had done in the Eau Claire office was not at all uncommon in the nineteenth century. "Rings" developed at most of the pinery land offices, and participating in them were such men as Cyrus Woodman, Cadwallader Washburn, Philetus Sawyer, Thomas B. Walker, and numerous other lumbermen well known at the time.[26] The temptation was great, the laws were poorly drawn, supervision by the General Land Office was lax, and at a time when timber stealing from state and Federal land was almost universally practiced public opinion condoned such deviations from the law.

Wisconsin opinion promptly sided with Putnam against the Government. It was pointed out that the original complaints had been brought by Francis Woodward, who had a personal grudge against Putnam. Although a good deal of evidence was offered in support of the accusations, much of it came from aggrieved persons. Many regarded the charges as merely part of a conflict between two groups sparring for control of the pine lands. Pinery newspapers, including the *Eau Claire Free Press,* the *Chippewa Herald,* and the *Dunn County News,* as well as the *Prairie du Chien Union,* sprang to the defence of the land officers and called the attack a "lot of bosh." [27] Public meetings were held to denounce the accusers, and resolutions defending and praising the conduct of the land officers were drawn up and signed by many of the prominent lumbermen of the section,

---

[26] Isaac Stephenson pictures a similar relationship between the land officers in the districts of Green Bay and Menasha, Wisconsin, and of Sault Ste. Marie, Michigan and the lumbermen, who took advantage of their cupidity. Judging by Stephenson's success as a land operator and by certain indiscretions which he permitted to creep into his memoirs, it may be conjectured that he was one who profited from this state of affairs. See his *Recollections of a Long Life* (Chicago, 1915), p. 120.

[27] *Dunn County News,* January 13, 1872; *Chippewa Herald,* January 27, 1872; *Prairie du Chien Union* in *Dunn County News,* January 27, 1872; *Eau Claire Free Press,* March 12, 1872; *Clark County Republican,* January 18, 1872; *Milwaukee News* in *Wisconsin River Pilot,* January 27, 1872.

among them being Captain William Wilson and John H. Knapp of Knapp, Stout & Co.[28]

When all the fireworks were over and the investigation completed the accused officers were found guilty of neglect but were not held responsible for the irregularities. They were merely censured. Since Putnam was not a responsible officer he could not be punished. The Commissioner saw fit to give the officers a "further trial," but did insist that Putnam should be dismissed as clerk.[29] Thus ended temporarily the long period of control which he had exercised in the Eau Claire office.

Unlike so many other successful Wisconsin lumbermen, Putnam apparently had no desire to enter political life. He had, however, come to have a good deal of political influence in Madison and in Washington. The accusations against him did him little harm, and when an attempt was made to remove the land office from Eau Claire to some point nearer the center of the district he was able to prevent the move, it was said, through his close friendship with the private secretary of President Hayes.[30] At the same time he succeeded in having his partner in the Chippewa Valley Bank, Vincent W. Bayless, appointed receiver of the Eau Claire land office, thereby restoring his influence, if indeed it had ever diminished.[31] From 1878 to 1885 Bayless held this office, at the end of which time the amount of pine land in the district was relatively small and of little consequence.

Meantime a constant shuffling of ownership of pine land on the Chippewa had taken place, large tracts passing from the weak hands of speculators to those of influential lumbermen who sought to assure themselves a plentiful supply of timber. At Chippewa Falls and Eau Claire on the Chippewa, at Menomonie on the Red Cedar, and at La Crosse, Winona, Dubuque, Clinton, Rock Island, Burlington, Mus-

---

[28] *Clark County Republican*, January 18, 1872; *Dunn County News*, January 20, 1872.

[29] Willis Drummond, Commissioner of the General Land Office, Washington, D. C., March 28, 1872, to Register and Receiver, Eau Claire, in *Dunn County News*, May 4, 1872.

[30] *Chippewa Herald*, February 15, 1878.

[31] *Chippewa Herald*, April 12, 1878; *Chippewa Times*, April 17, 1878; *Phillips Times*, April 22, 1882; *Barron County Shield*, August 28, 1885.

catine, Davenport, and St. Louis on the Mississippi were great mills which needed annually the cut of thousands of acres of pine. There gradually emerged from this group of mill owners a series of combinations, all revolving around Frederick Weyerhaeuser, whose mill was at Rock Island. These combinations, organized as the Mississippi River Logging Company and the Chippewa Logging Company, began to purchase great tracts of land on the Chippewa and its tributaries. Putnam sold a number of large tracts to this group and was well aware of its future needs. In 1875 he sought a partner with whom he might unite in one last great effort to "corner" the Chippewa pineries. With $50,000 or $100,000, he maintained, he could acquire all the good bargains in pine still to be had and could then force the combination to accept his terms for pine land. It is doubtful if the "corner" was established, but Putnam did control so large an amount of pine that the Mississippi River Logging Company and its constituent members had to offer him fancy prices for the tracts which they desired.

After 1880, when lumber prices increased appreciably, pine land which had been spurned by timber cruisers, loggers, and lumbermen came to attract attention and there was a scramble to secure it. Referring to the rush of land buyers at Eau Claire in 1887, the *Chippewa Herald* said sarcastically:

H. C. Putnam, W. A. Rust, J. G. Thorp, Thos. McDermott, Eugene Shaw, O. H. Ingram, George Buffington, Thos. Carmichael, George W. Mason, Peter Truax, John S. Owen, Dan Donnellan, H. P. Ellsmore, R. F. Wilson, Wm. Carson and other actual settlers are crowding the land office for the purpose of securing homes for themselves and families on the public domain.[32]

These lumbermen, the biggest on the Chippewa except for the downriver men, were making a last effort to buy the remaining timber land of the government before the restrictions on land purchases long advocated by land reformers were adopted.

Despite the efforts of Putnam, Woodward, Woodman & Washburn, and others, no individual or group had secured a monopoly of pine on the Chippewa, although the pine lands had been acquired by a rela-

[32] *Chippewa Herald*, September 23, 1887.

tively few dealers, loggers, and millmen. Putnam, the central figure in these efforts, was not through, however, and his subsequent efforts were devoted to concentrating still further the ownership of pine lands. He became closely associated with Frederick Weyerhaeuser and his partners in the Mississippi River Logging Company, who were to come near to realizing the earlier dreams of a Chippewa pine monopoly.

CHAPTER SEVEN

The Chippewa Lumber Industry

THE lumber industry of the Lake States—certainly as spectacular and as picturesque as other frontier developments—still awaits a narrator. Its rise was swift, its heydey short, its effects devastating, and its decline precipitate. From it were derived numerous family fortunes, the present owners of which live elsewhere and take no interest in the counties that were the source of their wealth. A few lumbermen gave libraries, parks, and colleges to the pine-land communities in which they made their money, but for the most part the wealth made in lumbering was not put back into the area from which it had been drawn. Other lumbermen, aspiring to political office, became congressmen, governors, cabinet members, and ministers to foreign countries, and almost every one of them regarded his public office not as a public trust but as a well deserved reward for his "contribution" to the development of the pine-land country. These self-made men, real individualists, were contemptuous of the rights of labor and they paid little heed to Federal and state laws which forbade certain practices in which they were engaged. Their struggle for wealth changed the rich pineries, the product of centuries of growth, into a shambles within a generation. Men of the twentieth century are attempting to undo some of the worst blunders of their predecessors by undertaking reforestation and social reorganization in these cut-over counties. With all its picturesqueness, its speed of destruction, its domination of politics, and its flamboyant display, the lumber industry has not yet attracted the historian as has the cattle industry, the mining rushes, the flood of immigration, or the expansion of the railroads.[1]

[1] The best brief account of the Wisconsin lumber industry is in Frederick Merk, *Economic History of Wisconsin During the Civil War Decade* (Madison, 1916). See

The lumber industry of Wisconsin was a child of the eastern lumbering frontier. From Maine, New York, and Pennsylvania, speculators came to buy Wisconsin timber land, loggers and woodsmen to get out the logs, and sawyers to operate the mills. They provided the leadership and they reaped the rewards, but not alone. For every Morrison, Higgins, Washburn, Sage, and McGraw from the eastern industry there was a Weyerhaeuser, a Denkmann, a Knapp, or a Stout who had made his start in the West.

As time goes, the lumber industry of Wisconsin had a swift development and an equally swift decline. First came the pioneer lumbermen who established their small mills where water power could easily be utilized. They did not own the land on which they cut, since there was no need to buy land when timber could be cut on the public domain for nothing. When a meddlesome commissioner of the General Land Office appointed a number of timber agents to prevent cutting on the public lands the lumbermen united in a common protest to their Washington representatives which promptly led to the dismissal of the commissioner and the special agents whom he had appointed. Henceforth, timber stealing from the public lands could be carried on with impunity, and the basis of many a Wisconsin fortune was laid by cheating Uncle Sam.[2]

The early mill towns of Wisconsin were on the shore of Lake Michigan or on the Mississippi River, but it was not long before lumbermen began to move up the Wisconsin, the Black, the Chippewa, the St. Croix, the Wolf, and Red Cedar, and to establish their mills at the site of waterfalls. Wausau, Mosinee, Stevens Point, Merrill, Oshkosh, Black River Falls, Menomonie, Eau Claire, and Chippewa Falls are some of the lumbering towns which flourished during the latter half of the nineteenth century.

As the industry progressed it required ever increasing amounts of capital. A constant stream of inventions for sawing lumber was cat-

---

also George W. Hotchkiss, *History of the Lumber and Forest Industry of the Northwest* (Chicago, 1898).

[2] The dismissal of John W. Wilson, forthright Commissioner of the General Land Office, in 1855, deserves study. There is much correspondence in the National Archives on the matter.

alogued in the journals of the lumber trade, and only those mills with the most modern machinery could survive the keen competition. Furthermore, as the pineries along the lower parts of the rivers approached exhaustion, the operators began to buy timber on the headwaters to assure themselves of an adequate supply of pine to keep their plants operating for years to come. Destruction of the forests made for rapid runoff of the spring floods. Each successive year floods were greater and consequently many streams were unable to float logs except during the freshet season. To extend the log-running season, lumbermen built "flash" dams on the driving streams to store up water which could be released when logs were ready for driving. Large amounts of capital were necessary to keep up with modern improvements, provide for large scale production, buy land in sufficient quantities to ensure an adequate supply of timber for the future, and construct flood dams at strategic spots on the rivers. The growing capital requirements of the industry brought about the gradual elimination of small mill operators and the establishment of great combinations. The Stephensons, Luddington, and Van Schaick in the Green Bay area, the Union Lumber Company of Chippewa Falls—later the Chippewa Falls Lumber and Boom Company—the Eau Claire Lumber Company at the junction of the Eau Claire and Chippewa Rivers, and Knapp, Stout & Co. of Menomonie were the largest of these combinations.

Isaac Stephenson—rare among lumbermen for a book of reminiscences—has described the beginnings of lumbering in the Green Bay area, which included the Menominee, the Peshtigo, and the Escanaba pineries. Small mills were quickly displaced by larger plants, great combinations were established, and soon a few firms had come to dominate the area. One may regret that Stephenson's political ambitions, which ultimately carried him to the Congress of the United States, where he had as colleagues such outstanding lumbermen-statesmen as Philetus Sawyer and William T. Price, are permitted so much space in his narrative, while the factors which explain his success in business are described in brief and very general terms.[3]

[3] Isaac Stephenson, *Recollections of a Long Life, 1829–1915* (Chicago, 1915).

The total land entries of Stephenson and those associated with him in Wisconsin and Michigan amounted to 300,000 acres. With a fortune made in the lumbering business, Stephenson extended his operations in the eighties to the South, where he acquired with others vast tracts of land and opened up new mills to exploit the longleaf pine of that section.[4]

The Union Lumber Company of Chippewa Falls was the outgrowth of a small sawmill erected in 1839 at the great falls of the Chippewa. Here, in the midst of the largest stand of white pine in the state, and with abundant water power at hand, was a unique site for a sawmill. In 1846 Hiram S. Allen acquired control of the small enterprise, enlarged it to include a modern sawmill, a planing mill, a shingle mill, a series of dams and booms, a grist mill, a blacksmith shop, and a general store. Allen established regular steamboat service on the Chippewa, bought quantities of pine lands to ensure a supply of logs for his mills, and was for a time the most influential man on the river. A flood on the Chippewa washed away many of his improvements and a large cut of logs. Allen did not recover from this disaster, and his mill passed into the hands of a group of lumbermen headed by Thaddeus H. Pound.[5] By 1870 the Union Lumber Company, as the group was now called, was capitalized at $1,000,000 and was rated as one of the largest mills in the world. For the next ten years this company had difficulty in keeping its head above water. For one thing it was troubled by the rising price of stumpage, of which it had an insufficient amount to meet its future needs. Although its operations were on as large a scale as those of Isaac Stephenson and his associates, the Union Lumber Company had not bought pine land in the same proportion. The total purchases of Allen and Pound and his partners probably did not amount to more than 50,000 acres before 1870. The Union Lumber Company may have been in W. J. Cornell's mind in 1866, when he said that the mill owners of the

---

[4] The *Lumber Trade Journal* (New Orleans), March 1, 1899, p. 24, reported that Stephenson and his associates owned 300,000 acres of longleaf-pine land in the South, of which 82,000 acres were in Louisiana. His Menominee (Michigan) mill, it was said, was to be moved to Alexandria, Louisiana.

[5] *History of Northern Wisconsin* (Chicago, 1881), pp. 193–197, 204.

Chippewa had not entered sufficient pine land to provide for their future needs because they expected to be able to continue to buy stumpage from the government as they needed it. In 1881 the company was sold to the Weyerhaeuser group.

Knapp Stout & Co. Company,[6] whose operations were centered on the Red Cedar, a tributary of the Chippewa, had a more successful development than the Union Lumber Company. The firm, consisting of Captain William Wilson, Andrew Taintor, John H. Douglas, John H. Knapp, and Henry L. Stout, bought control of the small mills on the Red Cedar in the vicinity of the present Menomonie in 1846. Conservative financial management permitted the firm to expand without increasing its debts. Profits were reinvested in pine lands and used to acquire competing mills at Waubeek and Downsville. Cadwallader Washburn had established at Waubeek a sawmill which was described by Thomas Randall as "rather sickly." [7] Knapp-Stout were ambitious to control the Red Cedar and the lower Chippewa, and in 1863 they purchased the Washburn mill, boarding-house, stable, blacksmith shop, and boom, together with 10,893 acres of pine land.[8] Practical control of the Red Cedar was obtained by Knapp-Stout in 1881, when they purchased the Jewett property, including the Cedar Falls Manufacturing Company and the Red Cedar Improvement & Log Driving Company, for which, together with pine lands, they paid $312,500.[9]

Unlike the Union Lumber Company, which went through numerous reorganizations, Knapp-Stout had continuity of management for a full generation, during which time they grew into a well integrated company. True, their members came to realize that the 135,000 acres

[6] Incorporated under that name, but hereafter in this study shortened to Knapp-Stout.

[7] Thomas E. Randall, *History of the Chippewa Valley* (Eau Claire, 1875), p. 62.

[8] Knapp-Stout agreed to buy 6,000,000 feet of good merchantable pine to be delivered at the mouth of the Chippewa and pay for it in quarterly installments during 1864, 1865, 1866, and 1867 (Barron County Deed Records, A, p. 68, conveyance of December 4, 1863). A second conveyance of July 30, 1867, transferred all of the property to Knapp-Stout by warranty deed for $60,000 (Barron County Deed Records, A, p. 638).

[9] The purchase was made of John J. Haley of Newton, Massachusetts, and Franklin W. Pitcher of Cedar Falls, Wisconsin (Barron County Deed Records, E, p. 274); *Chippewa Herald*, March 24, December 15, 1882.

which they had bought from the Federal Government were not sufficient stumpage for their needs, and in the seventies and eighties it became necessary for them to buy stumpage at high prices. But the company had the funds and credit with which to do so, not having overcapitalized or withdrawn capital from the enterprise in any large amount. Furthermore, Knapp-Stout's practical control of the Red Cedar virtually forced owners of pine land on that river to sell to them because the cost of separating their logs from the Knapp-Stout drive was too heavy.[10] Consequently, pine on the Red Cedar brought lower prices, generally estimated at between 50 and 75 cents a thousand board feet less, than pine on other branches of the Chippewa.[11] Between 1870 and 1881 Knapp-Stout developed a veritable little empire on the Red Cedar. Their great mills at Menomonie, Dunnville, Downsville, Chetek, and Rice Lake turned out between 100 and 150 million board feet of lumber a year.[12] They operated large farms to provide hay and grain for their horses and oxen, and vegetables for their many employees. In 1877 it was reported that they had 30,000 acres in crops, pasture, and mowing to provide for their 1200 employees and large number of draft animals. Five years later the number of their employees reached nearly 2500.[13]

Knapp-Stout was a highly successful enterprise. In the eighties it was said to be worth between six and seven million dollars. It doubtless made a profit from its milling operations, but the chief reason for its success was that its executives were shrewd judges of timber and knew when to buy. The company's original purchases from the government were greatly augmented by the addition of tracts bought from Cornell University, the West Wisconsin Railroad, and other owners of timberland. In this way Knapp-Stout was enabled to hold its own in competition with an even greater combination which was gradually forming on the Mississippi and its tributaries.

[10] H. C. Putnam, Eau Claire, June 3, 1875, to J. W. Williams.
[11] This difference in the price of pine on the Red Cedar and the Chippewa is brought out clearly in *McGraw-Fiske Testimony*, pp. 1843–1854, 1925, and elsewhere.
[12] *Chippewa Herald*, March 4, 24, 1882.
[13] *Eau Claire Free Press*, October 27, 1870; *Barron County Chronotype*, March 3, 1875, March 22, 1877; *History of Northern Wisconsin*, p. 281.

The greatest lumbering town on the Chippewa was Eau Claire, situated at the confluence of the Eau Claire and Chippewa Rivers. This site was destined to become an important sawmill town because of the abundant water power available there, the ease with which booming and sorting devices could be constructed, and the proximity of the pineries. The numerous small mills established at Eau Claire were later displaced or else combined in large corporations. Greatest of the companies operating at this point was the Eau Claire Lumber Company, whose founder was "Jim" Thorp. As additional capital was necessary to finance expansion of his plant Thorp and his associates took in William A. Rust, whose family fortune had been made in lumbering on the Saginaw River in Michigan, and Richard Schulenberg, who had a large mill and yard at St. Louis.[14] Thorp, Rust, and the Eau Claire Lumber Company entered a total of 112,000 acres in Wisconsin. In 1883 the capacity of their mill at Eau Claire was 100,000,000 board feet a season, which made it rank with the mill at Chippewa Falls and the Knapp-Stout mills at Menomonie. Smaller mills were operated by the company at Meridean and Sterling. In 1887 the Eau Claire Lumber Company was sold to the Chippewa Logging Company.[15]

Two other large lumber mills at Eau Claire were the Northwestern and the Empire, the respective capacities of which were 48,000,000 and 45,000,000 feet. The Empire Lumber Company came to be closely associated with the Weyerhaeuser combine in the eighties.[16]

While lumbering towns were developing in northern Wisconsin along the drivable streams, other milling communities were springing up along the Mississippi which were to come into sharp competition with the interior towns. Among these down-river towns were Winona and Wabasha in Minnesota, Prairie du Chien and La Crosse in Wis-

[14] *Eau Claire Free Press*, August 17, 1875.
[15] Letterhead of Eau Claire Lumber Company, William A. Rust, President, to H. W. Sage, January 31, 1881; advertisement in *Northwestern Lumberman*, January 8, 1881, p. 15; Taylor County Deed Records, 18, p. 244; *McGraw-Fiske Testimony*, pp. 425, 483.
[16] William Carson, president of the Valley Lumber Company, in a letter of February 12, 1885, to the Cornell agent at Eau Claire, said that his company owned between 150 and 200 million feet of pine stumpage, had a $240,000 interest in the Chippewa Logging Company, held real estate in Eau Claire valued at $150,000, and owned $6,000 worth of oxen and $20,000 worth of horses and harnesses.

consin, Dubuque, Clinton, Davenport, Muscatine, and Burlington in Iowa, Rock Island and Quincy in Illinois, and St. Louis and Hannibal in Missouri. These communities were situated in the heart of a rapidly growing area which provided a ready market for their lumber. Their proximity to urban markets and their ready access to the numerous railroads being constructed in the upper Mississippi Valley gave them an advantage over the more remote mills at Chippewa Falls, Eau Claire, or Menomonie. Many of the northern millmen were primarily dealers in pine lands and only secondarily lumbermen, but the owners of mills on the Mississippi were mainly concerned with their mill operations and had little to do with speculation in land.

The Mississippi millmen arranged with logging contractors for necessary supplies of logs. These contractors might be themselves owners of pine land or they might arrange to buy a tract from some speculator like Francis Palms of Detroit, D. L. Peck of Williamsport, Pennsylvania, H. C. Putnam of Eau Claire, or Cornell University on condition that the land should be paid for as the pine on it was cut. Numerous loggers like W. J. Cornell and Malcom José made such contracts for a "logging chance." At first it was their responsibility to cut the logs, drive them in the spring to the southern mill city, and deliver them to the purchaser. These small loggers were an important link in the lumbering business, but part of their work was gradually taken over by others. At Eau Claire and Chippewa Falls great dams and booms were being constructed which made it difficult to run the logs past these points. It was also difficult to separate the logs of one contractor from those of another because they became so hopelessly intermingled in the drive. The millmen of Eau Claire and Chippewa Falls were hostile to the millmen of the Mississippi, feeling that the logs of the Chippewa country might better be sawed at home instead of at some distant point, and they refused to permit logs to go through their booms.[17]

The open hostility of the Chippewa millmen to the down-river interests called for joint action to combat it. But there were other

[17] This hostility is well displayed in Thomas Randall, *op. cit.*, pp. 141 *passim*.

problems which were making even more difficult the continued operation of the mills on the Mississippi. The Eau Claire and Chippewa Falls operators had purchased quantities of pine land for present and prospective needs, but the Mississippi millmen had not done so. In the seventies, when stumpage prices were rising, the latter realized their error. Only those of them with ample credit could finance the purchase of a tract of pine land sufficient to meet their needs for some time to come. Furthermore, the Chippewa was a most undependable stream and it frequently happened that there was insufficient water during the driving season to float the logs to the Mississippi. Improvements on the Chippewa, such as the construction of dams and small reservoirs, were needed and only group action could make this possible. The necessity for joint drives was equally apparent. These factors brought the Mississippi lumbermen into a series of combinations which ultimately led to great changes in the Chippewa lumber industry.

The leader in the movement to bring together the millmen of the Mississippi for their mutual advantage was Frederick Weyerhaeuser, of Rock Island, Illinois. Many lesser persons appear frequently on the pages of American history, but Weyerhaeuser, perhaps because he was never a publicity seeker, has rarely been given even a footnote.[18] Yet he was as dynamic a figure in the lumber business as was Rockefeller in oil, "Jim" Hill or Edward H. Harriman in railroads, or Andrew Carnegie in steel. In the journals of the lumber trade his name appears constantly from 1870 onward; the local newspapers of the pinery section of Wisconsin gave him frequent notices; he made numerous trips to Washington to appear before committees to influence legislation. Withal, he has been disregarded by students of economic history. Weyerhaeuser's contemporaries on the Mississippi,

[18] Henry Hall, *America's Successful Men of Affairs* (2 vols., New York, 1895–1896), does not include a sketch of Weyerhaeuser. This was a commercial enterprise and Weyerhaeuser may not have been willing to purchase space in it. There is less justification for the omission from the *Dictionary of American Biography*, which found space for the Siamese Twins, Amelia Bloomer, and Lydia Pinkham, but none for Weyerhaeuser. There is interesting information on the Weyerhaeuser business today in "Bunyan in Broadcloth: The House of Weyerhaeuser," *Fortune*, ix (April, 1934), pp. 62 ff.

whether loggers, contractors, log drivers, sawmill operatives, or men engaged in wholesaling and retailing lumber, would find difficulty in understanding this neglect.

In 1870 the millmen of the Mississippi, whose principal source of timber was the Chippewa, organized the Mississippi River Logging Company, a pool with a capital stock of one million dollars divided into forty-three shares. The purpose of the company was to purchase for the pool land and logs on the Chippewa and its tributaries, and to drive the annual cut of logs to Beef Slough at the mouth of the river, form it into rafts, and float it down to the various mills on the Mississippi. Each member was to be permitted to take out of the pool approximately 6,000,000 feet of lumber for each share of stock that he held, but the amount of that dividend varied somewhat from year to year. Expenses of the pool were collected by assessments on the stock, the assessment for 1885 being $82,000 a share.[19] In the eighties, when the Mississippi River Logging Company and its affiliated companies had come to dominate the Chippewa lumber industry, shares of its stock were valued at $50,000 to $70,000 each. Firms like C. J. Lamb & Co. and W. J. Young & Co. of Clinton, Iowa, which needed many times 6,000,000 feet of logs annually for their mills, had to invest as much as $300,000 in this stock.[20] In time the Mississippi River Logging Company became a holding company as well as a log-driving company as a result of numerous purchases of pine lands and sawmills. From the start Weyerhaeuser was the leading figure in the company and after 1873 he was its president for many years.

At the mouth of the Chippewa River there was a series of sloughs which, if boomed, could be used for the storage of logs. Under the leadership of Francis Palms of Detroit, a dealer in land and logs, of

---

[19] *McGraw-Fiske Testimony*, p. 1127.

[20] The two companies at Clinton held six shares each. The *Northwestern Lumberman*, June 7, 1884, pp. 3–6, said that a share was then worth $100,000. On April 19, 1884, p. 3, the *Northwestern Lumberman*, generally a reliable trade journal, said that a number of years previously Weyerhaeuser had collected from the millmen on the Mississippi $1000 each for the improvement of the Chippewa. Out of this informal beginning the Mississippi River Logging Company is said to have developed. Shares were subsequently issued to those who had paid the $1000, and the business was thereafter conducted on an assessment basis. See also *McGraw-Fiske Testimony*, pp. 1095, 1120, 1124, 1143.

Moses M. Davis of Appleton, and of others, an effort was made to secure a charter and the right to construct a boom and other improvements at Beef Slough. The plan was opposed by the Eau Claire and Chippewa Falls millmen, who were attempting to prevent logs cut on the Chippewa from being driven to the mills on the Mississippi. Appeal to the Wisconsin legislature produced a long struggle which was carried on at the same time as the conflict between Eau Claire and Chippewa Falls over the Dells bill.[21] Finally the Chippewa Falls people, embittered by the Dells controversy, came to the support of the Beef Slough proposal. As a result the coveted right was secured and the improvements were promptly begun.[22] An elaborate series of devices was constructed at Beef Slough to store the logs and enable them to be separated and made into rafts for floating down the Mississippi to the mill towns. In 1872 the Beef Slough Manufacturing, Booming, Log-driving & Transportation Company was sold to Frederick Weyerhaeuser and associates, who enlarged the improvements and made Beef Slough a center of operations for separating and rafting all the logs driven down the Chippewa for the mills on the Mississippi.[23]

A major difficulty with which the Chippewa loggers had to contend was the variation in rainfall and runoff. In some years great floods would occur which took out all the small dams and numerous booms and sent enormous quantities of logs on to the Mississippi, where they were lost to their owners. In other years the rainfall was so scanty and the river so low that the drive was hung up on the river banks. If dams were constructed on the headwaters of the stream, water could be stored for use in dry seasons. Small improvements could be constructed by individual loggers, but dams which would hold back enough water for a main drive could be built only by the government or by united action on the part of the lumbermen. Wis-

[21] The Eau Claire millmen were anxious to construct a dam and booming works at the Dells, but were opposed by Chippewa Falls interests on the ground that any such works would obstruct the navigation of the Chippewa River.
[22] *Chippewa Herald*, December 9, 1871.
[23] The Beef Slough Company in 1884 owned 50 miles of shore rights on both sides of the Mississippi at the Slough and 20 miles along the Chippewa. Nearly 500 men were employed in rafting time (*Northwestern Lumberman*, June 7, 1884, pp. 3–6).

consin sought Federal assistance to improve the major log-driving streams, but, although much money was being wasted on unnecessary or useless river and harbor improvements elsewhere, the state's request was denied. This threw the matter back on the lumbermen who, under the leadership of Weyerhaeuser, organized in 1876 the Chippewa River Improvement and Log-driving Company to make the necessary improvements. This company invested half a million dollars in constructing dams and removing obstructions in the river.[24]

The superstructure of the Weyerhaeuser combinations in Wisconsin was the Chippewa Logging Company, which was designed to act as a pool in somewhat the same way as the Mississippi River Logging Company. The Chippewa Logging Company bought pine land for its members, purchased from them the logs they cut, engaged in logging operations through contractors, and drove the logs to Chippewa Falls and Eau Claire, where they were used in the mills of the Chippewa Lumber & Boom Company, the Eau Claire Lumber Company, and the Empire Lumber Company. The remainder of the log drive was supervised in its descent to Beef Slough by the Mississippi River Logging Company.[25] The membership of and stock ownership in the various Weyerhaeuser companies were not always the same, but in all of them Weyerhaeuser's influence was supreme. Both the Mississippi River Logging Company and the Chippewa Logging Company, as well as Weyerhaeuser & Denkmann and other members of the pool, bought great quantities of pine land on the Chippewa. There seemed to be a certain overlapping of activities, more apparent than real, it may be presumed.

Order was now brought out of the previously chaotic log driving on the Chippewa. This achievement was accomplished through the new alliance between the Chippewa Falls lumbermen and the Weyerhaeuser associates,[26] which is reflected in the growing subservience of the Chippewa Falls newspapers toward Frederick Weyerhaeuser. The next major step undertaken by Weyerhaeuser in establishing

---

[24] *Northwestern Lumberman,* June 7, 1884, pp. 3–6.
[25] *Eau Claire News* in *Phillips Times,* April 8, 1882; *Northwestern Lumberman,* June 7, 1883.
[26] *Chippewa Herald,* June 3, 1871.

control on the Chippewa was the purchase in 1881 of the great mill at Chippewa Falls. This mill, formerly the property of the Union Lumber Company, had been sold in 1879 to a group of easterners, chief of whom was D. M. Peck of Williamsport, Pennsylvania, for $1,000,000. Weyerhaeuser bought the Chippewa Lumber & Boom Company, as it was now called, with its 100,000 acres of pine land, half of which was uncut and the other half only partially cut, for $1,275,000.[27]

In rapid succession Weyerhaeuser and associates acquired the Meridean mill formerly owned by the Eau Claire Lumber Company;[28] organized the Shell Lake Lumber Company with a capitalization of $500,000 to operate in the vicinity of Shell Lake, Washburn County, and the North Wisconsin Lumber Company with a capitalization of $450,000 to operate in Sawyer and Washburn Counties; and secured an interest in the Atwood Lumber Company, the Rutledge mill on the Kettle River, and the C. N. Nelson Lumber Company of Cloquet, Minnesota.[29] In 1887 the Mississippi River Logging Company bought control of the Eau Claire Lumber Company, which employed 1800 men and sawed from 75 to 90 million feet of lumber a year. The price paid was $1,500,000.[30]

There now remained but one independent company of importance in the entire Chippewa Valley, namely, Knapp-Stout. Control of this interest would give Weyerhaeuser and associates a "gigantic corner" on the lumber industry of the upper Mississippi Valley.[31] Negotiations for the purchase were begun in 1887 and it was soon reported that a sale had been arranged for the record price of $7,500,000.[32]

[27] *Chippewa Herald,* April 8, 1881.
[28] *Northwestern Lumberman,* May 12, 1888.
[29] *Northwestern Lumberman,* May 14, 1887; George W. Hotchkiss, *History of the Lumber and Forest Industry of the Northwest* (Chicago, 1898), p. 583; William H. C. Folsom, "History of Lumbering in the St. Croix Valley, with Biographical Sketches," Minnesota Historical Society, *Collections,* ix (1901), pp. 309–310.
[30] *Northwestern Lumberman,* September 24, 1887, p. 9; October 1, 1887, p. 2. In 1857 the boom, sawmill, buildings at Eau Claire, ard 15,710 acres of pine land belonging to Carson, Eaton & Co. were sold for $125,000 to Chapman, Thorp & Co., the firm which afterward became the Eau Claire Lumber Company (Eau Claire County Deed Records, A, p. 355).
[31] *Northwestern Lumberman,* October 1, 1887, p. 10.
[32] *Id.,* p. 21; *Taylor County Star and News,* October 1, 1887.

The deal struck a snag, however, and was called off. Weyerhaeuser was doubtless disappointed at his failure, but he did succeed that same year in buying from Knapp-Stout 2497 acres of choice pine land for the almost record price of $38 an acre.[33]

Meantime, the various Weyerhaeuser companies had been picking up quantities of pine stumpage throughout the Chippewa Valley from all the larger holders like Francis Palms, Henry W. Sage, McGraw & Dwight, Henry C. Putnam, and Cornell University. In 1887 they acquired 680,000,000 feet of stumpage in a single transaction with the Eau Claire Lumber Company. They now held more pine land in Wisconsin than any other group. They also controlled more sawmill capacity.

The headquarters of the Weyerhaeuser companies were at Chippewa Falls, which was visited frequently by Frederick Weyerhaeuser in the eighties and nineties. The Lumberman's National Bank of Chippewa Falls was virtually a Weyerhaeuser affiliate. Its board of directors included Weyerhaeuser himself and such well known men as Edward Rutledge, William and Thomas Irvine, and A. B. McDonnell. Weyerhaeuser was also a director of the First National Bank of Chippewa Falls.[34] Meantime, the *Chippewa Herald* had come under the control of the pool and thereafter was regarded as its spokesman.

The formation of the pool or combination on the Chippewa River brought order to a turbulent industry, made possible numerous expensive improvements on the river, and facilitated the annual log drives. It may also have had some effect in reducing the competition for pine lands held by non-members. The members followed the practice of logging on their own lands when lumber prices were high and of buying logs from outsiders when the market was low. In 1881 the Chippewa Logging Company and the Mississippi River Logging Company offered such low prices for logs that H. C. Putnam, now

---

[33] Price County Deed Records, 8, p. 384; copy, F. Weyerhaeuser, Clinton, Iowa, October 7, 1887, to W. J. Young. Douglas Boardman, representing the estate of John McGraw, which had a large share in the W. J. Young Lumber Company, breathed a sigh of relief when the deal for Knapp-Stout failed (E. L. Williams, Ithaca, New York, October 18, 1887, to W. J. Young).

[34] *Chippewa Herald*, May 4, 1883; *Chippewa Current*, January 12, 1895.

one of the large owners of pine in northwestern Wisconsin, suggested that the independent pine-land owners should organize their own pool to combat the strangle hold of the Weyerhaeuser group.[35] Competition was not ended, however, for Knapp-Stout were still in control of the Red Cedar, and smaller lumbering companies were still operating at Eau Claire. By the eighties, moreover, white pine in commercial stands was becoming scarce, and a fear that it would soon be exhausted was sending stumpage prices up rapidly.

During the years after the Civil War the western prairies were becoming populated at a rate unparalleled in American history. The thousands of new settlers created an enormous demand for lumber. The principal gainers were those lumbermen who had capital resources large enough to expand their mills and storage yards and to increase their acreage of pine lands. It was in the eighties that the sawmills of Knapp-Stout, the Chippewa Lumber & Boom Company, the Eau Claire Lumber Company, W. J. Young & Co., and S. J. Lamb & Sons were enlarged and modernized.

When W. J. Young needed additional funds to finance expansion he went for assistance to John McGraw, whose plant at Bay City was considered, locally at least, one of the wonders of the world. McGraw bought a share in W. J. Young & Company which made it possible for them to enlarge their plant so that it could produce between 60 and 80 million feet of lumber a season. The equipment of this plant amazed a correspondent of the *Northwestern Lumberman,* who called it one of the largest lumber establishments in the world. It included two steam gang sawmills, planing, flooring, lath, and shingle mills, and three towboats. The company owned 60,000 acres of pine land and held stock in the Mississippi River Logging Company, the Beef Slough Company, and the Chippewa Lumber & Boom Company. In addition to the output of its sawmills it could manufacture in a season between 30 and 50 million feet of shingles and from 7 to 10 million feet of laths. In 1886 McGraw's half interest in W. J. Young & Co. —acquired in 1876 for $270,000—was sold for $700,000.[36]

---

[35] H. C. Putnam, Eau Claire, October 7, 1881, to Cornell University.
[36] *McGraw-Fiske Testimony,* p. 1993.

The *Northwestern Lumberman* of April, 1882, reported as follows the amount of lumber sawed during the year 1881 by some of the large mills on the Mississippi and its tributaries. The quantities are in board feet:

Knapp, Stout & Co., Menomonie, Wisconsin	90,000,000
Eau Claire Lumber Company, Eau Claire, Wisconsin	89,431,000
W. J. Young Lumber Company, Clinton, Iowa	62,000,000
C. Lamb & Sons, Clinton, Iowa	61,237,250
Weyerhaeuser & Denkmann, Rock Island, Illinois	37,212,400
Chippewa Lumber & Boom Company, Chippewa Falls	56,450,000

Even today such mills as these would seem large, except in comparison with the enormous plants of the Pacific Northwest. All but the first of the firms named above were subsequently associated with the Weyerhaeuser interests.

The growth of the Wisconsin lumber industry is best shown in a record of the annual cut of stumpage.[37] The amounts are given in *millions* of board feet:

1873: 1,240	*1879:* 1,470	*1885:* 2,710	*1892:* 4,010
1874: 1,200	*1880:* 1,920	*1887:* 2,890	*1893:* 3,490
1875: 1,250	*1881:* 2,190	*1888:* 3,210	*1894:* 3,100
1876: 1,340	*1882:* 2,580	*1889:* 3,270	*1895:* 2,800
1877: 1,000	*1883:* 2,750	*1890:* 3,660	*1896:* 2,080
1878: 980	*1884:* 2,950	*1891:* 3,010	*1897:* 2,430

Expansion of the lumber market and rising prices of white-pine boards produced a keen demand for pine lands which sent their values skyrocketing in the eighties. The Mississippi River Logging Company and its individual members and their competitors Knapp-Stout and independent loggers began scouring the woods for unentered government lands, a determined onslaught was made upon the pine on the Indian reservations,[38] and dealers in pine lands found their holdings in great demand. Cornell University was to profit largely from these favorable circumstances.

[37] Filibert Roth, *On the Forestry Conditions of Northern Wisconsin*, Wisconsin Geological and Natural History Survey, *Bulletin* No. 1, Economic Series No. 1 (Madison, 1898), p. 38.

[38] An important and complex problem awaiting the historian's attention is that of the policy of the Office of Indian Affairs toward the rich stands of pine on the reservations.

CHAPTER EIGHT

Tax Warfare

THE future of Cornell University became closely linked with that of Wisconsin as a result of the entry by Ezra Cornell of a half million acres of land in that state. Upon the success or failure of the pine-land business and the agricultural development of northern Wisconsin the university's future depended. The movement of population into Wisconsin, the extension of the railroad net, the rising demand for lumber in the Middle West, and the increase in stumpage values were changes followed with keen interest by its officials. Unlike other pine-land owners, Cornell was to do little to further the growth of the state. It simply waited for the expected scarcity of timber which would assure high prices for its lands.

It was not safe for Cornell's officials to be entirely passive in their attitude toward developments in Wisconsin, but, generally speaking, their interest was shown in a negative way. When high taxes were threatened by extravagant expenditures for roads, schools, and railroads, or by the extension of local government to practically unsettled areas, or by discriminatory and unfair assessments, the university's officials acted promptly to protect its rights. Cornell's interests were identical with those of other large holders of pine land, and frequently they all worked together to secure favorable legislation or lower assessments, but in many cases the other pine-land holders were also developers who were cutting timber, erecting mills, building dams, fostering industrial towns, and financing railroads. This difference in policy explains why the pinery newspapers frequently evinced a hostile attitude toward Cornell but rarely criticized other large holders of pine land.

Next to their desire to sell land as quickly as possible at good prices, the greatest concern of the Cornell officials was the burden of taxation on the property they were administering. Ezra Cornell, who had undertaken to finance the land business, found that he would be unable to do so for long unless the costs of administration and the taxes could be squeezed out of sales. It seemed essential, then, either to sacrifice a part of the land for what it might bring or to secure exemption from taxation. Since Cornell was not willing to sell land prematurely, he tried to induce first the Federal Government and then the State of Wisconsin to grant exemption. He urged his New York friends to introduce a bill in Congress to have

> all lands, located by colleges or educational institutions, or by individuals for the benefit thereof, on scrip donated to the several states and territories . . . and sold to said colleges . . . or to individuals for the benefit of said institutions by said states . . . declared to be exempt from taxation by . . . state or municipal authorities while thus held in the interest of education.

Copies of a proposed bill were submitted to Senator Edwin D. Morgan and Representative Giles W. Hotchkiss of his own state and to John M. Edmunds, Commissioner of the General Land Office, but nothing was accomplished.[1] Congress had no power to exempt land from state taxation, and furthermore a bill of this kind would have called attention to the fact that Cornell was violating the spirit, if not the letter, of the Agricultural-College Act, which forbade states entering land in other states.

A more determined effort was made to secure exemption through the Wisconsin legislature. Before any land entries were made, William A. Woodward proposed that steps be taken at Madison to secure tax exemption for five or ten years for land which might be located for Cornell University. He thought that the people would be happy to grant this exemption for the advancement of education, but, realizing that such idealistic considerations would not appeal to all interests, he added a more practical one. Granted exemption, said Woodward, Cornell University would locate a large amount of scrip

---

[1] Letters of Ezra Cornell, Albany, January 22, 1866, to W. A. Woodward, and February 12, 1866, to J. M. Edmunds and G. W. Hotchkiss.

in northern Wisconsin, heretofore neglected by settlers, and would make great exertions to people its lands with emigrants from the East and from abroad.[2] Ezra Cornell took up the latter argument and said that if exemption were granted, Wisconsin would secure for itself one of the best emigration agencies yet organized, since all the friends of the university would join together in directing emigration to the state.[3] For the next year or two Woodward and Cornell discussed at length plans to attract population to Wisconsin, but no organized emigration activity was undertaken. Woodward also called the attention of his Wisconsin correspondents to Cornell's plan to invest a relatively large sum of money in developing Brunette Falls, but that scheme fell through. Putnam, who had a good deal of political influence in Wisconsin, urged exemption upon his numerous friends in Eau Claire and Madison and suggested that Cornell and Henry W. Sage write to the governor and to other officials requesting tax exemption for the university.

A bill to grant tax exemption was introduced in the session of 1866. Henry D. Barron, of Falls St. Croix, speaker of the assembly, pushed it through that branch of the legislature, but it was defeated in the senate.[4] In preparation for the move to secure exemption from the next legislature, both Woodward and Cornell journeyed to Wisconsin to interview prominent leaders, and a strong supporting bloc was established. Speculators who were influential in the legislature were induced to favor the measure on the ground that the university would bring in purchasers for their land.[5] Such prominent lumbermen as Jim Thorp of Eau Claire, Thaddeus Pound of Chippewa Falls, Captain William Wilson and John H. Knapp of Knapp-Stout of Menomonie, and others were won over by promises that Cornell partisans would aid their designs for special legislation.[6] Pound was assured that Cornell would support boom legislation beneficial to Chippewa

---

[2] W. A. Woodward, Vail's Gate, January 27, 1866, to Cornell.
[3] E. Cornell, Albany, March 31, 1866, to H. C. Putnam.
[4] H. D. Barron, Falls of St. Croix, May 15, 1866, to Cornell; W. A. Woodward, Vail's Gate, May 27, 1866, to Cornell.
[5] Woodward, Eau Claire, June 25, 1866, to Cornell; *id.*, Vail's Gate, March 3, 1867, to Putnam.
[6] Cornell, Albany, February 27, March 4, 11, 1867, to Woodward.

Falls, while Thorp was promised that any such legislation would not harm Eau Claire. Thorp was also reminded that at the time the Cornell lands were being entered certain tracts had been conceded to him despite the prior claim the Cornell agents had on them.[7] Governor Lucius Fairchild promised his support, though he thought the bill ought to include a provision requiring sale of the Cornell land to settlers at $2.50 an acre.[8]

The support of men like Barron, Fairchild, Thorp, and Pound was encouraging, but it had been gained only by logrolling arrangements which fell to pieces before the bill came to a vote. Cornell and Woodward were accused of promising aid to the Eau Claire lumbermen, then seeking the privilege of constructing a great dam and boom on the Chippewa which would have played havoc with the interests of Chippewa Falls.[9] Furthermore, the lumbermen of the Chippewa, despite all blandishments, could see little advantage to them in a bill which would increase their taxes by granting exemption to Cornell. It was their opposition which defeated the exemption bill, opposition which for some time created mutual dislike and distrust between the absentee institution and the resident operators.[10] A few years later a reconciliation was brought about by the appearance of a common enemy, the land-grant railroads.

Still another effort to secure exemption for the Cornell lands was made in 1877, when several Wisconsin railroads were trying to persuade the legislature to exempt their land grants from taxation for an additional period. A powerful lobby functioning in behalf of the railroads was bitterly fought by numerous local interests and by the representatives of Cornell. To discredit the railroad move, a bill was introduced in the assembly to exempt the Cornell lands from taxation.[11] There it made little progress, but in the north woods it fanned the flames of anti-monopoly feeling and intensified the dislike of Cor-

---

[7] Woodward, Vail's Gate, March 3, 1867, to Putnam.
[8] *Id.*, Vail's Gate, February 25, 1867, to Cornell; *id.*, March 3, 1867, to Putnam.
[9] *Id.*, Vail's Gate, March 15, 18, 1867, to Cornell.
[10] *Id.*, Vail's Gate, March 19, 1867, to Putnam, and *id.*, March 20, 1867, to Cornell.
[11] *Wisconsin Assembly Journal,* 1877, pp. 165, 383, 446; *Barron County Shield,* March 9, 1877, and November 3, 1882; S. Robertson, Eau Claire, February 3, 1877, to J. W. Williams.

nell University. The *Barron County Shield* expressed this feeling as follows:

The monstrous combination of land speculations, land monopolists and land bulldozers of the Northwest, have consummated their plans to victimize the new counties of the Northwest; and in Senate bills 208, 209, 210, in the Cornell University exemption bill and in one or two others, the wolf's claws are hidden and disguised under familiar titles; it was expected to slip them through without comment. With doleful voices these men proclaim themselves the friend of the settler in their opposition to the railroads, and cry out let there be no exemption, no railroads. Having selected the most valuable lands in the country at a cost of less than one dollar an acre these monopolists of all monopolies would now debar the honest, industrious settlers from raising a tax on their immensely valuable claims.[12]

The *Eau Claire Free Press,* on the other hand, argued that there was as much justice in exempting the Cornell lands as those of the Wisconsin Central Railroad. It added, "Let's have a law exempting everybody's land."[13]

Having failed to secure tax exemption for the university's land, Cornell's representatives were left with the task of guarding against high assessments, making certain that taxes were paid on the correct tracts and that payments were properly recorded, utilizing county orders for tax payments when they could be secured at a discount, and raising funds to meet taxes as they came due annually. The administration of these tax matters was the most complex feature of the land business and gave many a headache to the Cornell representatives in Wisconsin and to those in charge of the lands at Ithaca.

The closest possible scrutiny was necessary to ensure payments on the correct descriptions of land. Errors might mean tax titles, disputed claims, timber stealing on tracts of doubtful ownership, and eventual loss of equity. It was necessary, therefore, to establish a system of tax and land administration in which the Wisconsin agents would pay the most careful attention to detail and the Ithaca supervisors would check with equal care all land descriptions and payments of taxes. Only by a complete and constant check on the western

[12] *Barron County Shield*, February 23, 1877.
[13] *Eau Claire Free Press*, February 8, 1877.

agents, even though they were undoubtedly reliable, was it possible to assure a fair degree of accuracy, never complete accuracy. Unfortunately, during the first few years the administration of the land and tax matters was handled in a lax manner. Woodward's plan to carry the tax burden from the proceeds of land sales failed, and he and Cornell lacked adequate funds to make payments promptly. Furthermore, Woodward and Cornell could not come to terms as to the compensation to be paid the former, and Cornell gradually turned to Putnam, in whose hands he placed responsibility for the lands. He did not, at the same time, withdraw authority from Woodward, and there was a conflict of jurisdiction which worked havoc in tax matters. When Cornell finally broke with Woodward and placed full management of the payment of taxes in the hands of Putnam, he was unable to provide him with funds as they were needed, and failed to supervise the work of the new agent adequately. There was, therefore, a period of ten years during which the tax matters became badly tangled. Costly errors were committed, lands were permitted to become tax-delinquent, heavy penalties accumulated, and some lands were lost forever.

Responsibility for this state of affairs must be attributed in part to Ezra Cornell's ignorance of the complex problems involved in western land speculation and in part to his neglect to prescribe the terms of Woodward's agency. That neglect led to bitterness and ill-feeling between the two, and embarrassed the tax business. Putnam, too, early developed a sense of grievance because he was inadequately compensated for his services in selecting the land, and this caused him to use his position as agent to advance his personal interests. Both Woodward and Putnam were land speculators operating for themselves and for others as well as for the university. Although the Cornell business was their heaviest undertaking, it was not always their first concern, and there was sometimes a conflict of interest between their responsibility to Cornell and to other absentee holders whose lands they managed. Not until 1877, when Smith Robertson took over the Cornell agency in Wisconsin, was a disinterested person placed in charge of the lands and adequate supervision provided for them. Until then there was a good deal of neglect and unnecessary expense. The unsatisfactory way in which the lands were administered was, however, a matter of small importance compared with the rapidly rising taxes assessed on the Cornell property. In combating this increase in taxation it may be said that Putnam was fully as effective as his successors.

Settlement was sparse in the counties in which the Cornell lands were located at the time the entries were made. Here and there a venturesome pioneer had located, but most of the area was still unsettled. During the years immediately following 1865 the best stands of timber were selected by Cornell, Francis Palms, Knapp-Stout, and other lumbermen and speculators in timberlands who were anticipating needs of mill operators for a generation. Private ownership did not bring settlement at once. Slowly the lumber gangs pressed up the Chippewa, the Flambeau, the Jump, the Thornapple, and the Red Cedar Rivers, and following them came a small sprinkling of settlers seeking the hay meadows and the patches of hardwood land. Their hay, potatoes, grain, and other vegetables found a ready market in the lumber camps.

These settlers soon began to ask for roads, schools, and county government. Unlike the owners of pine land, they were interested in opening up new areas to settlement. They demanded the organization of new and smaller counties, constantly pressed for local subsidies to bring in railroads, and wanted costly school buildings, permanent and expensive bridges, and numerous public buildings. The pine-land speculators frowned upon expenditures for these purposes and tried to keep them to a minimum. Their attitude brought them into conflict with the settlers, who resented the blighting effect of the pine owners' policy and took revenge by placing the major share of the tax burden on their land.

"Let's go for the speculators," was the cry of the homesteaders in the Chippewa counties who owned no land and paid no taxes.[14] They boasted that they would force the absentee owners to throw their

[14] H. C. Putnam, Eau Claire, April 15, 1873, to Ezra Cornell; *id.*, April 5, 1875, to J. W. Williams; *Barron County Shield*, December 8, 1876.

land on the market at any price it would bring, and urged that their assessments be increased by 100 per cent. Since the homesteaders controlled the local governments they had their way.[15] Discrimination against the property of non-residents became the usual thing. In Chippewa County, for example, the bulk of the absentee-owned land was in the north, and there assessments were at nearly full value, while in the southern part, where homesteaders lived on farms to which they already had title, property was assessed at 33 per cent of value. Similarly, the assessments in Barron County were anything but uniform.[16] In Chetek the Cornell agent reported that the taxes were "outrageously high in some school districts," where "the Homesteaders have piled it on to non-residents." [17]

Had the pine-land owners been forced to pay only legitimate expenses honestly incurred by settlers, there might have been little conflict, except over excessive valuations placed upon absentee-owned land. Unfortunately, the extension of local government into northern Wisconsin was accompanied by abuse of authority, mismanagement, and extravagance, if not corruption. Pioneer life on the frontier was harsh. It blunted the finer susceptibilities, fostered disregard for the law where the law worked unfairly, as it frequently did, and it placed great emphasis upon the accumulation of property. Stealing of timber from land owned by an absentee or by the government, for example, was not considered reprehensible, nor was it thought improper to assess the land of absentees at a higher rate than land held by residents. Settlers felt that it was their improvements that gave value to the speculatively owned land, and they were determined to get something from those who benefited. As for county mismanagement and extravagance, so long as they had to be paid for largely by absentee speculators, they could easily be made to conform to frontier morals. They were merely a means of forcing the absentees to pay for the unearned increment in the value of their property.

[15] Putnam, Eau Claire, April 6, 1875, to J. W. Williams; *id.*, June 26, 1874, to County Board of Supervisors, Barron County; *Oshkosh Times* in *Wisconsin River Pilot*, March, 16, 1872; *Phillips Times*, January 2, 1886.
[16] D. P. Simons, Eau Claire, January 3, 1878, to H. W. Sage & Co.
[17] *Chippewa Herald*, April 2, 1875; S. Robertson, Eau Claire, January 29, 1878, to J. W. Williams.

The creation of new counties offered the greatest opportunity for extravagant expenditures, and the business of carving up existing counties became a flourishing one in northern Wisconsin. The first counties of this section were large in size, with a sparse population in the southern part only. The county seat was properly located near the center of population, but when settlers moved farther north they found the distance from the center of local government a handicap to them. Naturally they bethought themselves of establishing new counties with a county seat which would be easier of access. More important were the numerous offices to be had—treasurer, judge, superintendent of schools, district attorney, register of deeds, and clerk of courts. Salaries of county officers were by no means niggardly in these communities, and the pioneer saw no reason why they should be, so long as they were provided for out of taxes paid by non-residents. The salaries paid their officers by two pinery counties, Lincoln and Price, organized in 1874 and 1879 respectively, are shown in Table 7.

TABLE 7

SALARIES OF COUNTY OFFICERS [18]

	Lincoln	Price
Treasurer	$1,300	$900
Judge	200	400
Superintendent of Schools	200	150
Clerk	1,000	900
District Attorney	400	—
Clerk of Circuit Court	200	—
Register of Deeds	—	175

It was probably not necessary to establish all these local offices at the outset, so sparse was the population and so limited was the public business of these new counties.[19]

In addition to the spoils of office there were contracts to be let for the construction of roads and for the erection of school and county

[18] *Lincoln County Advocate*, December 25, 1875; *Phillips Times*, March 22, 1879.

[19] The *Chippewa Herald*, commenting upon the salary of $1000 paid by Burnett County to its district attorney, said that there were not ten cases which he had to attend to, and that the most important part of his business was in looking after the tax matters and advising the county board. Despite the small amount of work, he received what was at that time a generous salary (*Chippewa Herald*, January 2, 1880).

buildings, and a county farm for the indigent had to be purchased. Moreover, there was a considerable amount of county printing to be done, enough, in fact, to support a small press and weekly newspaper. Finally, county orders, or tax anticipation warrants as they are called today, and tax titles were to be dealt in, and shrewd insiders could manipulate them to great personal advantage.

The whole question of county organization was intimately related to the tax problem. Citizens of the older parts of a county opposed division because they did not want to lose the tax income derived from any section of their county. Owners of pine lands and the Chippewa lumbermen opposed division when they were relatively satisfied with existing taxes, but if they could be persuaded that the creation of a new county would result in lower taxes they promptly supported the proposal. Thus Knapp-Stout, who had great possessions on the Red Cedar, were said to have caused the division of Polk County in 1859 in order that the company's land should not be taxed so heavily.[20] Similarly, in 1871, when it was proposed to create "Pine County" out of Chippewa County, two prominent lumbermen of Oshkosh and Walworth, one of whom owned 10,000 acres in the county, supported the move.[21] It was more common, however, for lumbermen and pine-land owners to favor a conservative policy of county organization.

Opponents of new counties charged that it was a group of "carpet-baggers" who moved into an unsettled area and began to "talk about a county, and whine about having to go so far to the county-seat." [22] The carpetbaggers were accused of being interested only in the new offices, the contracts, and the printing which the new county might have for distribution, and of disregarding the added burden of taxation which would rest largely upon non-resident landowners. They were called "a hungry horde of county seat hangers around, leeches on the property they do nothing to make," [23] a "pack of hungry ravenous creatures" who were "worse than the Tweed Ring," a "hand-

---

[20] *Barron County Shield*, October 12, 1877.
[21] *Chippewa Herald*, April 8, 1871.
[22] *Chippewa Herald*, February 23, 1877; *Waupaca Republican* in *Lincoln County Advocate*, January 19, 1878.
[23] *Eau Claire Free Press*, February 8, 1879.

Felling a pine in Sawyer County, Wisconsin, 1895.

Ezra Cornell.

Henry W. Sage.

A vast log jam on the Chippewa River, 1869.

Loggers and their families at table: Antigo, 1888.

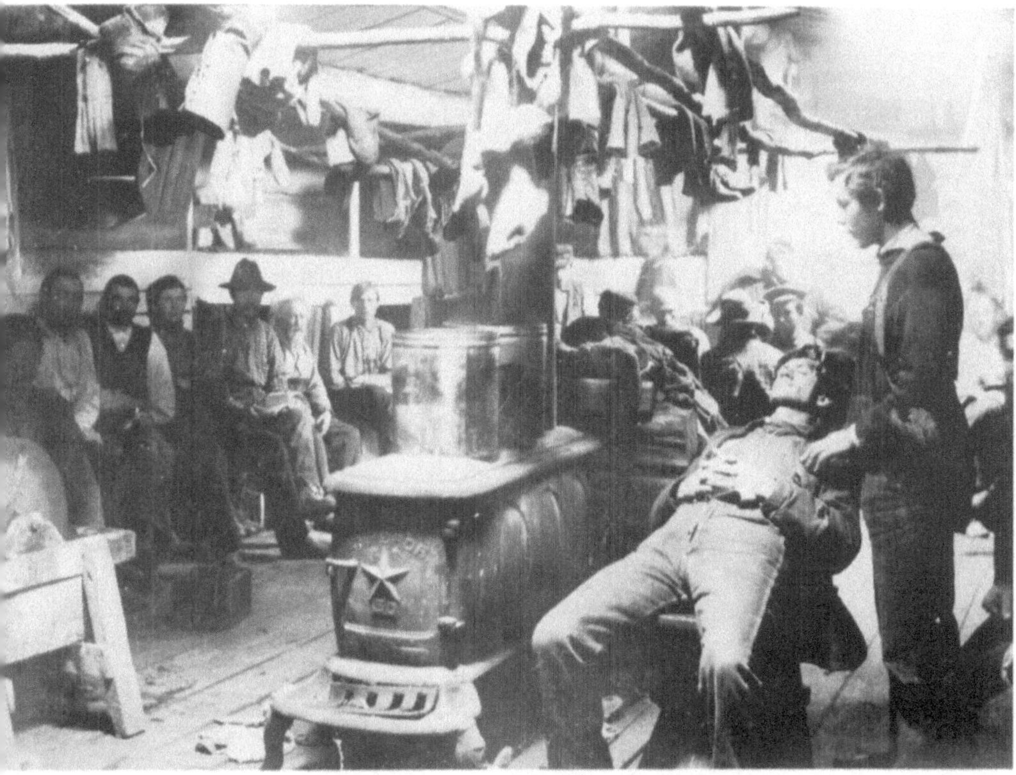

Sunday morning in a lumber camp bunkhouse in Chippewa County.

Blacksmith shop at a lumber camp in northern Wisconsin.

Loggers dining alfresco in the Rusk County pinery, 1907.

Dismembering a fallen pine in heavy brush.

Hauling a log out of the woods in Bayfield County.

Loading logs on a railroad flatcar at Marshfield, c. 1888.

Sleigh-load of logs bound for the mill. Note the snowballs splattered on the log-ends.

Logging crew in a quiet backwater on the Chippewa flowage, 1902.

Driving logs past the dam at Big Falls, Wisconsin.

Log trains departing from the pinery at the turn of the century.

Burnt-over pine lands in northern Wisconsin.

ful of settlers . . . [who] revel like brigands in the spoliation of honest wealth, until they have become a terror to men who sigh for relief, . . . lice of the human family," [24] an "organized gang of boodlers, . . . as graceless a set of scamps as ever flourished in the South when the carpetbaggers were in their glory."

All such accusations were boldly denied by the advocates of new counties. The *Phillips Times*, which was working for the erection of a county out of Chippewa and Lincoln, said:

We desire all parties owning taxable property to understand that we are not a set of scavengers, come up here to enrich ourselves at their expense, but that we came here to settle up and develop this wilderness. We desire to protect tax-payers and relieve them from the enormous burdens they are compelled to bear and exclusively for the benefit of the southern part of the county.[25]

The same journal, speaking of the area which it hoped to have included in the new county, said:

This section is bled this year to the tune of $86,000 in taxes, the most of which goes into the pockets of men at Chippewa Falls. Not one cent of this immense tax is expended in this part of the county. Have we not a right to complain? We have helped Chippewa Falls build a $60,000 court house, with a $10,000 water-closet, and in fact any and everything for which an excuse could be made to use up the money, and yet the barnacles of the Falls are not content but wish to bleed us yet more on some imaginary needed water-closet. . . . One half of the tax raised in this territory is stole direct by the thieves of the Falls, and the other half is indirectly stole by men from the same place. For example, a drunken tool of Chippewa Falls who claims to be an attorney but who never had a case in his life was paid $4,000 this year for legal advice.[26]

In this instance there was some justification for the demand for a new county. The new community developing around Phillips was far removed from Chippewa Falls and from Jenny, the county seats respectively of Chippewa and Lincoln Counties, and its population, estimated at 400 in 1877 and 785 in 1880, was rapidly increasing. Chippewa and Lincoln, which would lose a considerable amount of

---

[24] *Northwestern Lumberman*, February 24, 1877.
[25] *Phillips Times*, February 24, 1877.
[26] *Phillips Times*, February 10, 1877.

taxable property by the proposed change, looked upon division with disfavor. The official papers of these counties, which would be deprived of a part of their advertising patronage, likewise opposed division, and so did the large property owners, including Cornell University. The issue was important for the university. Almost one-fifth of its land was located in the proposed county, and since the Wisconsin Central Railroad also owned a great deal of land in the same area and the railroad's land was tax-exempt, the cost of local government was certain to fall heavily upon the university's land.[27]

Opposition by the large taxpayers and the official papers of Lincoln and Chippewa Counties defeated the proposal in 1877 and 1878, but by 1879 enough support had been obtained to bring about the erection of Price County. Success came only when the large taxpayers had become reconciled to the change as a result of the exceedingly high taxes in Lincoln and Chippewa Counties. They hoped that in the new county, which would be debt free, taxes would be lower than in Chippewa and Lincoln counties, then saddled with heavy debts as a result of long mismanagement.[28] True to predictions, Fred Sackett, a "carpetbagger" who had been the chief advocate of the new county, received numerous political plums. He became county clerk at a salary of $900, treasurer of the town of Worcester, justice of the peace, and court commissioner; his newspaper published annually the lucrative list of tax-delinquent lands; he was given the contract for the construction of the courthouse, and he was employed to make an abstract of tax titles and to perform other jobs for the new county.[29]

Meantime, efforts were being made to create a new county at the expense of Clark and Marathon Counties. The area proposed for the new county was sparsely settled and remains so today, but it was distant from Neillsville and Wausau, and this made it possible for its inhabitants to argue that division and a new county seat were justified. Chief support for division came from the Wisconsin Central Railroad,

[27] *Lincoln County Advocate,* January 27, 1877; *Chippewa Herald,* February 23, 1877.
[28] *Taylor County Star* (Medford), February 23, 1878; *Phillips Times,* January 20, February 3, December 22, 1877, March 1, 1879; *Lincoln County Advocate,* February 15, 1879; *Wisconsin River Pilot,* February 22, 1879.
[29] *Chippewa Herald,* March 14, 1879; *Phillips Times,* March 22, 1879, June 5, 1886.

which was projected through the center of the area. A new county, bisected by the proposed railroad, would surely aid it with a generous subsidy.[30] Furthermore, the Wisconsin Central, like all land-grant railroads, planned to lay out towns along its line at regular distances and to sell lots to incoming settlers. One of the railroad towns would become the county seat and this would assure its growth and a profitable land business. For these reasons the Wisconsin Central vigorously supported the move for the new county.[31] It was opposed by the large landowners, including Cornell University and the Wisconsin Valley Railroad.

This latter railroad was a rival enterprise paralleling the Wisconsin Central and to it Marathon County had granted 200,000 acres of land as a subsidy. Two newspapers, the *Colby Phonograph* and the *Ashland Press,* supported the proposal to divide Clark and Marathon Counties and denounced J. M. Smith, agent and part owner of the Wisconsin Valley Railroad. Smith, they said, was prepared to spend $5000 to prevent the creation of a new county, a change which would increase the taxes of his railroad for the benefit of the rival line. These newspapers, which were doubtless subsidized by the Wisconsin Central, also paid their respects to Cornell University for its share in opposing the new county. Sam Fifield, a bitter enemy of Cornell, argued in the *Ashland Press* that it was simply "the clamor of wild land speculators, such as the Cornell University," who were responsible for the opposition.[32]

Putnam and W. F. Bailey, Cornell's tax attorney, did not let the grass grow under their feet when measures were being considered which might increase the tax burden on the university and on other large owners whom they represented. The *Colby Phonograph* sarcastically related how Bailey appeared before a legislative committee considering measures for the creation of new counties and explained "how . . . the University . . . had euchered the towns out of a portion of their taxes." Bailey presented numerous remonstrances "signed by persons living completely out of the . . . territory pro-

[30] H. C. Putnam, Eau Claire, January 27, 1873, to Ezra Cornell.
[31] *Madison Democrat,* February 1, 1877.
[32] Quoted in the *Colby Phonograph,* February 17, 1879.

posed to be set off," a portion of which he had secured by "misrepresenting the facts." If the move to create new counties were defeated, said the *Phonograph,* it would be a victory for the "land sharks that beat the towns out of their lawful taxes" and who were opposed to the development of the area "unless it can be improved without costing them anything. . . ." [33]

Further opposition to the proposed county was expressed by the *Wisconsin River Pilot* of Wausau, official paper of Marathon County, on the grounds of inadequate population, the heavier taxation which would follow, and the small "rings" in the areas affected which were promoting a new county for personal reasons.[34] Similarly, the *Clark County Republican* of Neillsville, which, like the *Pilot,* would lose important advertising patronage if a new county were erected, declared that its supporters were "scattered homesteaders" owning no property who would create an enormous debt through extravagance and mismanagement and ruin the non-resident taxpayers.[35]

Some support for the proposal to divide Clark and Marathon Counties doubtless came from those who were distressed at the defaults of the county treasurers of the former county. Three successive treasurers had defaulted, producing a total loss for Clark County of $50,000.[36]

Frequent efforts were made to get bills through the legislature for the division of Clark and Marathon Counties, but the combination of the Wisconsin Valley Railroad, the Cornell agents, other large owners of pine land, and the official papers of the counties was invincible. Marathon remains today the largest county in the state.

Two other large counties in which Cornell University owned pine land were Chippewa and Ashland. The scattered settlers made several attempts to have these counties divided, aided sometimes by owners of pine land who came to feel that new counties might actually provide

---

[33] *Colby Phonograph,* February 26, 1879.
[34] *Wisconsin River Pilot,* January 30, 1874. In 1879, when the *Pilot* had lost the county printing to its rival, it favored the creation of new counties if the local residents desired them (*id.,* February 22, 1879).
[35] *Clark County Republican,* February 1, 1878.
[36] Wm. T. Hutchinson, Neillsville, September 25, 1876, to J. W. Williams; *Clark County Republican,* December 2, 1876, July 21, 1877.

some relief from the growing tax burden. Both Chippewa and Ashland had been extravagant in granting railroad subsidies and had wasted large sums by issuing county orders at less than their face value. H. C. Putnam, who represented a number of the large pine-land owners, either favored or opposed the creation of new counties according to his judgment of the effect that such action would have upon taxes. In 1875 he procured the division of the towns of Anson and Eagle Point in such a way as to make possible a control of the new communities. He had two "good men" elected as chairmen of the town boards, as a result of which "we can control town taxes." To make doubly sure that no unfriendly acts would be done, he hired two men to visit the new towns on election day to see that big taxes were not voted.[37] Division was secured, he wrote, by threatening the Chippewa County board of supervisors with a division of the county unless the members agreed to the town division. He admitted in private that he did not want the county itself divided then, as it had already issued about all the scrip it legally could and had built a "fine court house," a jail, and several bridges.[38] Subsequent dissension in the ranks of the pine owners over county and town organization made somewhat easier the creation of Sawyer County in 1883 out of Chippewa and Ashland, and of Gates County, later Rusk, in 1901, out of Chippewa.[39]

Although the pine-land owners optimistically expected better things of the new counties, their expectations were uniformly unrealized. Numerous and ingenious were the devices used to mulct the counties and through them the absentee owners. The general procedure seemed to be for the first settlers to form a "ring," establish a newspaper, agitate for a new county by playing upon the alleged need for a county seat easier of access than the old one, and the desirability of having the taxes from the area proposed to be included in the new county spent in the vicinity. Once the new county was organized, the numerous offices were dispensed among members of the ring.

The official newspaper, supported or subsidized by the county,

[37] H. C. Putnam, Eau Claire, April 4, 1876, to J. W. Williams.
[38] *Id.*, Eau Claire, November 17, 1875, to *id.*
[39] Louise Phelps Kellogg, "Organization, Boundaries and Names of Wisconsin Counties," Wisconsin Historical Society, *Proceedings*, 1909, pp. 184 ff.

was used to maintain the ring in control. An independent paper in Chippewa Falls had this to say about the "ring":

> Who takes from three to ten thousand dollars out of the county treasury for printing the tax list, year after year? "The Ring."
> Who in times past have gobbled up the county orders at a discount, and then paid them into the treasury dollar for dollar, in settling with the county? "The Ring."
> Who gobbled up all the land that reverted to Chippewa county, 110,000 acres, divided it up among the band and sold the balance at 20 cts. per acre on speculation? "The Ring."
> Who dictates to the voter who he shall vote for at all times and under all circumstances? "The Ring."
> Who lets the contract for highways, bridges and public buildings, and accepts the work when not half done or according to contract? "The Ring."
> Who abuses every honest man who dare raise up his voice against these dishonest practices? "The Ring."
> What has cost the tax payers hundreds of thousands of dollars in years past? "The Ring."
> Who is to blame for the Cornell University folks demanding and obtaining a compromise on their taxes, year after year? "The Ring."
> Who voted to sell the county lands at twenty cents an acre, and then bought up all of them they could raise the means to? "The Ring."
> Who says there has been or is no ring? "The Ring."
> Who has destroyed the receipts from the builders of the courthouse, who are now getting a judgment against the taxpayers? "The Ring."
> Who compromised a shortage of $4,187 with a defaulting county clerk, for $1,500? "The Ring."
> Who spirited away the plans, specification, and bond when the court house steal was perpetrated? "The Ring."
> Who carried $3,800 of cancelled redemption certificates to the credit of a defaulting county clerk, in order to balance his shortage? "The Ring." [40]

Lands on which the taxes were not promptly paid were advertised for delinquency in the official paper, and, as taxes were paid in a very dilatory manner in all Chippewa counties, there was a long list to be published annually. In older counties, where there was more than one newspaper, the possession of the contract for printing the list of tax-

---

[40] *The Independent* in *Bloomer Workman*, September 28, 1882.

delinquent land was much sought after. At a time when journalistic ethics were those of the gutter, more space was devoted by rival papers to haranguing successful opponents for their monopoly of the county tax lists than was given to local news. As one Wisconsin paper frankly declared: "The tax list . . . is . . . to the printer . . . what the grain harvest is to the farmer, and the 'log drive' to the logger." [41]

In larger counties like Chippewa the publication of the tax list netted the official paper between $3000 and $8000 annually, and in smaller counties it might bring in from $1000 to $4000. Such sums, with other amounts for miscellaneous printing, gave official papers subsidy enough for a sure profit even though they had little circulation.[42] No wonder it was said of the editor of the official paper of Price County that "he would publish a paper in a desert if there was a tax list in prospect." [43] While the tax list was being published it crowded out of the columns practically all local news. Historians may regret this, but it should be remembered that it was the tax list which made it possible for newspapers to be published in little frontier hamlets long before they could obtain enough advertising and subscriptions to support them.

For years the printing of the annual tax lists remained an expensive item in county costs. As late as 1895 the *Chippewa Current* published

[41] *Clark County Republican*, April 4, 1872.
[42] The printing patronage of Chippewa County, the bulk of which was for the tax list, was as follows: 1870, $2946; 1871, $3522; 1872, $2251; 1873, $3200; 1874, $4372; 1875, $4965; 1876, $6035; 1879, $8000. The figures for 1870–1872 are compiled from the reports of the board of supervisors of Chippewa County, as published in the *Chippewa Herald* for those years. The figures for 1873–1876 are from the *Chippewa Herald*, October 20, 1876. The figure for 1879 is from the *Taylor County News*, May 3, 1879. Lincoln County paid $13,316 for printing for 1877–1879. Both Chippewa and Lincoln Counties then contained land since given to other counties. The printing costs of Clark County were $2154 in 1873, and $3175 in 1876 (*Clark County Republican*, 1873–1876). Ashland County paid $1131 for printing in 1877 (computed from *Ashland Press* for 1877). Marathon County paid $2745 for printing in 1871 (*Wisconsin River Pilot*, September 16, December 23, 1871). Even Sawyer County, newly organized in 1883, was able to pay its official newspaper $948 for printing in 1885. Phillips County paid for 1881 $2058 and for 1882 $2045 (compiled from *Phillips Times*). St. Croix County paid for printing in 1867 $2208 (*Hudson Star and Times*, January 16, 1867). For printing the tax list Barron County paid $1332 in 1877 and $1418 in 1878 (*Barron County Shield*, June 15, 1877, November 12, 1878).
[43] *Eau Claire Free Press*, February 1, 1877.

an editorial under the caption "County Robbing" in which it demanded reform at the county seats and at Madison. Setting up and printing the lists cost from $6 to $15. The newspapers of Chippewa County, said the *Chippewa Current*, had entered into a "regular combine to . . . divide up the plunder," one newspaper putting in the bid, "and the others are kept quiet by nice fat wads of the people's money." The chairman of the board of supervisors of Chippewa County is quoted as calling the printing racket "the worst robbery ever I saw. We have tried to stop it every way in our power, but no use. The only plan we have not tried is to start a printing press of our own in the basement of the county building at Chippewa Falls and run off our own tax lists." [44] Another critic called the two papers of Chippewa Falls which shared the official printing "Ringsters." [45]

Efforts at reform in Madison were equally futile. Naturally the pine owners resented extravagance in printing as in other items of county expenditures, and when the counties spurned their advice to be economical they tried to get a bill through the legislature requiring counties to let the tax lists to the lowest bidder. This was one of the numerous measures which the Cornell representatives in Madison championed vigorously. They also urged upon the legislature a bill to reduce the cost per insertion from 25 cents to 10 cents.[46] The opponents of these measures argued that the cost of the tax list rested largely upon absentee owners and therefore the custom of charging 25 cents an insertion should not be changed.[47] All such reforms were defeated by the "ring of tax list printers, who summarily squelch every such bill before it gets through one branch of the legislature," said one paper which was denied its share of the patronage.[48]

Another complaint made by property owners was that cut-over lands whose value was little or nothing and on which no one cared to pay taxes were assessed and certificates issued on them year after

[44] *Chippewa Current,* March 25, 1895.
[45] *Chippewa County Independent,* November 2, 1882.
[46] J. W. Williams, February 2, 1878, to Smith Robertson.
[47] *North Wisconsin News* (Clear Lake), January 29, 1878, February 12, 1878; *Taylor County Star and News,* April 18, 1885.
[48] *North Wisconsin News,* January 29, 1878.

year to the sole advantage of the printer. The county held the certificates, paid for the advertising, but could not take a tax deed as private individuals could.[49]

Extravagance in letting contracts for the construction of roads and sidewalks and the building of schoolhouses, sometimes called "palaces" by those opposed to such expenditures, was quite general in the pinery counties. As early as 1860 a Stevens Point land agent remarked about the "exorbitant contracts for making roads. . . ."[50] In the town of Anson the board of supervisors was accused of contracting for the construction of a road at $3.50 a rod, which, when completed, was not worth 75 cents a rod. Another contract was given to the father of a member of the board at $5.50 a rod which, it was said, was not worth $2 a rod.[51] In Ashland County the officials were accused of spending $30,000 for highways in four years, but outside the towns of Ashland and La Pointe they had not completed twenty miles of passable road. Money intended for road construction elsewhere was used in these towns without authority.[52]

Roads were often laid out in such a way as to damage the property of absentees. The law provided that towns might construct roads on section lines and that if any road benefited the property through which it was built as much as the value of the timber which was cut the owners had no claim for compensation. This allowed for numerous cuttings on absentee-owned property, although it was remarked that the roads thus laid out were entirely impassable. Furthermore, the cutting was done at county expense.[53]

In Oneida County, where Henry W. Sage's holdings were large, the Land, Log & Lumber Company of Milwaukee led a campaign against local expenditures. In 1883 this company brought action against the board of supervisors to void the board's action in employing 131 men

[49] *Chippewa Herald*, March 20, 1874.
[50] B. Brett, Stevens Point, March 13, 1860, to Charles Mason (Mason MSS).
[51] *Chippewa Herald*, March 13, 1874.
[52] *Eau Claire Free Press*, February 8, 1879; W. F. Bailey, Eau Claire, March 29, 1881, to Smith Robertson.
[53] K. W. Ingham, Colby, Wisconsin, September 8, 1875, to J. W. Williams; *Northwestern Lumberman*, February 24, 1877.

and women at an expense of $4 to $6 a day each to make valuations of the land in the county, claiming that the proceeding was a corrupt scheme to mulct absentee landowners.[54]

There was an element of *opéra bouffe* about the finances of a school district in the town of Luddington. An election in 1888 brought in new officers who accused their predecessors of misappropriating school funds. The accusation was disproved and the retired officers then brought suit against the district for false arrest and defamation of character. The suit was compromised, the district agreeing to pay each of the contestants $500 for the damage to their feelings and $2000 to their attorneys. Since there was no money available for the payments it was necessary for the district to borrow. That in turn called for an election to determine whether the district should sell bonds to the amount needed. Since there were only seven or eight voters in the district, five of whom were involved in the matter, it was a foregone conclusion that the vote would be favorable. To the jaundiced eye of the large landowners, including Cornell University and the Omaha Railroad, the whole affair reeked of collusion, and action was taken to invalidate the bonds.[55]

Construction of the courthouses gave insiders the chance to secure lucrative contracts. Despite the sparseness and poverty of population in the pinery counties, large and elaborate buildings were erected. Putnam relates the action of Barron County, where the "thieves," as he called them, advertised to let the building of the courthouse. Only $2000 was available for this purpose, but the building was to be started on a $50,000 plan and subsequent requests for additional funds were to be made. Putnam opposed the plan on the ground that an elaborate and massive courthouse was not as yet necessary and that its cost would be an unduly heavy burden upon the taxpayers.[56]

Most counties found it desirable to have poor-farms, regardless of the number of paupers for whom they had to provide, and the purchase of farms for this purpose gave an additional opportunity for

[54] *Id.,* April 14, 1883.

[55] J. T. Barber, Vice-President, Northwestern Lumber Company, October 2, 8, 1888, to W. H. Phipps.

[56] H. C. Putnam, Eau Claire, March 10, 1876, to J. W. Williams.

graft. Shortly after its organization the board of supervisors of Lincoln County bought an 80-acre farm from one of its own members for $4000 at a time when it was questionable whether the county could boast more than one pauper.[57] Some felt that double the value of the farm was paid and that the cost of maintaining it would be ten times the cost of keeping one pauper. Buffalo County paid $5000 for a poor-farm only to sell it within a few years for $700 because it was such a heavy expense.[58] The action of Dunn County in purchasing seven and a half acres of land for $2000 was so widely criticized that the board of supervisors reversed itself, cancelled the contract, and determined to study the situation further before acting.[59]

Mismanagement, extravagance, corruption, and tax delinquency combined brought the finances of the pinery counties to a deplorable state, yet additional burdens were placed upon them. These counties went to great lengths to secure railroads, giving them large financial subsidies, land grants and rights-of-way, while the state legislature was induced to exempt their land grants from taxation for long periods. The financial and land subsidies and the tax-exemption privileges, details of which will appear in the following chapter, combined to make an already chaotic stiuation intolerable. But if the plight of the counties was desperate, that of the taxpayers was worse. With extravagance and mismanagement so widespread and the resulting taxes so burdensome, it was natural that property owners should revolt against what they considered great injustices.

Putnam, Smith Robertson, D. P. Simons, and other members of the Chippewa Valley Lumbermen's Exchange met in Eau Claire in 1876 to discuss the high taxes in Chippewa County. There devolved upon Putnam the leadership of the group and he was requested to contest the taxes, which were regarded as unfair. The resulting investigation brought out sufficiently damaging information to arouse the pine owners to fight fire with fire. In an election in Flambeau the

---

[57] *Lincoln County Advocate*, August 5, 1876; *Barron County Chronotype*, August 19, 1876.

[58] *Lincoln County Advocate*, September 29, 1879, quoting the *Buffalo County Journal*; *Dunn County News*, April 21, 1877.

[59] *Dunn County News*, April 1, 1877; March 8, 1879.

group brought into the town thirty of their own men "who were legal voters, at a good deal of trouble & expense . . . but the scoundrels had gone into Min[nesota] & took 3 loads of men . . . and all voted." Having lost the election the pine owners resorted to the courts.[60] They also presented the facts to the Chippewa County board of supervisors and urged it to dissolve the town of Flambeau and unite it with Anson.[61] A subsequent examination by the board "struck a mine of rottenness which astonishes outsiders," and its airing of the case, together with the injunctions secured by the pine owners to restrain the local officers from collecting taxes and selling tax-delinquent land, forced reform.[62]

Meantime, Cornell's tax attorney, W. F. Bailey, had investigated the affairs of Chippewa County, the management of which he found to be "fearfully rotten." County fees had exceeded the legal limit by $2500; orders to the amount of $15,000 had been issued illegally for the construction of bridges, and worse still, a means had been found to permit certain holders of illegal orders to collect from the county upon them. So widespread was the corruption in Chippewa County that Bailey was moved to write:

The whole body politic is permeated with the corruption growing out of these infernal stealings & almost every official & merchant is tainted. They resort to every species of fraud and chicanery to prevent investigation & exposure. We find rascality at every step & it requires constant vigilance & nerve to checkmate it.[63]

In a letter to the *Minneapolis Lumberman* he branded the Chippewa county and town officials as thieves who came from all parts "for the purpose of manipulating all tax matters, so as to pile the largest possible amount of taxes upon land owners, that they may gloat over and fatten upon what they have come to regard as their legitimate prey."[64]

More costly to the taxpayers in the pinery counties than the numer-

---
[60] S. Robertson, Eau Claire, April 11, 1877, to J. W. Williams.
[61] *Chippewa Herald*, May 11, 1877; *Chippewa Times*, April 16, May 16, 1877.
[62] *Chippewa Herald*, July 4, 1879; *Eau Claire Free Press*, July 17, 1879.
[63] Quoted in letter of S. Robertson, Eau Claire, June 1, 1877, to J. W. Williams.
[64] Quoted in *Chippewa Times*, March 5, 1879.

ous and well paid officials, the extravagant contracts, or the tax-list business was the loose manner in which the finances were conducted. When a county was organized it was divided into towns, each of which had a town board and town treasury. Salaries, roads, public buildings, and schools had to be provided for the new counties and towns shortly after organization. To meet these expenses the boards of supervisors of the counties and the local officials in the towns issued orders on the treasury, redeemable when the taxes began to come in. Large amounts of these orders were put in circulation and they immediately depreciated in value, in some instances by as much as 40 per cent.[65]

Depreciation in county orders induced contractors, salesmen, and others to charge the counties higher prices in proportion to the decline in value of the orders, thus further burdening them. Even this might not have become intolerable, but taxes were paid slowly, many of the larger owners of land delaying payments for years, and the county and town orders could not be taken up. Landowners were permitted sometimes to pay their taxes with these depreciated orders, but the income of the counties never seemed to catch up with the outgo of the orders. Illegal issues of orders were made, the holders of which went to the courts and secured judgments against the counties and thus obtained priority for their orders over those which might have been legally issued. In Bloomer, Big Bend, and Ashland special judgment taxes were levied to provide for these orders.[66] Huge debts accumulated which sooner or later had to be funded. Bonds issued under such circumstances naturally brought less than par value and carried high interest rates, and the annual burden of interest contributed to the further demoralization of local finances. County and town orders and the judgments against the counties fluctuated in value and became an important medium of speculation. They were bought and sold by the local treasurers, who also advertised in eastern

---

[65] Lincoln County voted to sell orders in 1877 for 60 cents on the dollar (*Lincoln County Advocate*, May 12, 1877); S. Robertson, Eau Claire, October 23, 1877, to J. W. Williams. In 1873 Chippewa County orders were selling at 70 to 75 cents on the dollar (H. C. Putnam, Eau Claire, October 13, 1873, to Ezra Cornell).

[66] W. F. Bailey, Eau Claire, January 27, 1879, to S. Robertson.

and western papers that they would pay taxes, using the orders, and give the savings thus made possible to the landowners.[67] It was said that speculation in the orders and judgments was carried on as far away as New York.[68]

Abuses in issuing orders were general in the northern counties, but probably nowhere were they as bad as in Chippewa County. In the town of Anson it was reported that there was "an organized system of robbing" the town treasury through road contracts which were let to insiders at exceedingly high rates. The responsible officers were subsequently prosecuted, found guilty of issuing orders illegally, and fined heavily. A year later Anson was divided and the towns of Flambeau and Big Bend were created, and in 1876 Worcester was cut out of Flambeau. A few scattered settlers inhabited these towns, which became the worst administered communities in the state. Road contracts at extortionate rates, illegal and fraudulent issues of county orders, thefts of orders, orders which were retired and cancelled and then reissued, these and other frauds were committed. In 1876 the treasurer of Anson defaulted with a net loss to the county of $1400, which induced the *Chippewa Herald* to say: "Anson is afflicted worse than the grasshopper regions." [69] D. P. Simons, agent of Sage & McGraw, had an announcement in the *Chippewa Herald* warning persons not to buy orders of the town of Flambeau dated after January 1, 1877, as all were issued illegally.[70]

Sawyer, one of the last of the Chippewa counties to be formed, went through all the experiences of the older counties in financial mismanagement. As late as 1903 it was said there was "an organized gang of boodlers who have been robbing the . . . county for years, and they are getting even bolder and now do not hesitate to issue fictitious orders for any amount from two to five thousand dollars; besides all this, the corruption extends down to the remotest parts of

---

[67] Advertisement of Thomas P. Mathews, treasurer of Lincoln County, in *Lincoln County Advocate*, July 7, 1875.

[68] W. F. Bailey, Eau Claire, January 20, 1879, to Smith Robertson.

[69] H. C. Putnam, Eau Claire, April 2, 1874, to C. H. Pratt; *Chippewa Herald*, March 13 and July 3, 1874, and June 23, 1876.

[70] *Chippewa Herald*, January 23, 1877.

the town district so that the result is the tax payers are paying four times as much taxes as they ought to pay." [71]

The large owners of pine lands were not above criticism in the methods they used to minimize their tax burdens. They opposed expenditures for necessary buildings, roads, and schools, they swore that their lands were worth less than $5 an acre when they were refusing to sell for less than $10.[72] They made constant attacks upon the assessments and the officials responsible for them which shook the confidence of people in local government and further demoralized an already bad situation. They came to control some of the most important pinery newspapers, through which they exerted a not altogether wholesome influence on local politics.[73] They employed agents who fought corruption with corruption.[74] They sold or stripped their land of the valuable pine and then refused to pay taxes on cutover areas. They opposed public subsidies to railroads which they thought would be of no benefit to their tracts, while on the other hand they urged subsidies to lines which would aid them in getting out their timber, regardless of the value of such lines once the timber was gone. They delayed payment of their taxes as long as possible and in some cases they never met their taxes. The *Ashland Press* declared that their refusal to pay

> increases the tax levy one-half every year, as the county board is obliged to levy a tax sufficient to cover delinquencies, cost of advertising, interest upon interest, litigation and other expenses incurred in the collection of

---

[71] E. P. Arpin, Secretary, Arpin Lumber Company, Grand Rapids, Wisconsin, January 21, 1903, to Daniel Shaw Lumber Company (Eau Claire Public Library).

[72] *Northwestern Lumberman*, March 2, 1879, pp. 4–5.

[73] The *Chippewa Herald*, known in the eighties as a Weyerhaeuser paper, was also accused by its Greenback competitor of being a "ring" organ, as was also the *Chippewa Times* (*Chippewa County Independent*, November 2, 1882). Large advertisements by the various Weyerhaeuser companies in numerous other newspapers assured no unfriendly attention. The *Barron County Chronotype* was obviously dominated by Knapp, Stout & Co. The *Eau Claire News* roundly condemned excessive taxes and then requested Cornell to give it advertising patronage (S. Robertson, Eau Claire, January 17, 1878, to J. W. Williams).

[74] In describing the efforts he had made to secure a reduction in taxes from Ashland County the Cornell agent said: "We shall pay a certain party about 2 per cent fees on the Am't we pay out. I was pretty sure I could make the deduction when I hit the right party to do it." Again he wrote in 1875 that he was "pulling more strings that I think will win. I had one prominent Lincoln Co. man here yesterday all day—took

taxes, besides an amount sufficient to cover the sum bulldozed out of the county board and officials in the shape of rebates, etc.[75]

In the conflict between the pine-land owners and the settlers there was right and wrong on both sides. The *Chippewa Independent* and the *Bloomer Workman,* pinery Greenback papers, were justified, one must conclude, in condemning both the local "rings" and the great landowners, for whether they worked together or in opposition to each other they succeeded in demoralizing county affairs.[76]

As the largest non-government owner of pine land in Wisconsin, Cornell University was forced to take an active part behind the scenes in fighting tax assessments. Henry C. Putnam had full charge of the Cornell tax matters until 1874. In the struggle over taxes his interests were identical with those of the university, since he owned a large quantity of pine land. Through his efforts numerous schemes to place unduly heavy burdens upon the Cornell lands were frustrated. Even after his resignation as agent in 1876 he continued to work closely with his successors in the fight for fair taxes.

Putnam's first method in dealing with high assessments was to urge upon the county boards that Ezra Cornell and the university for which Cornell held the land were not speculators in the western sense, but that the lands were entered "for the good of the children of the U.S." and should not be treated like the property of speculators.[77] It is doubtful if this line of argument was effective. Westerners could not but feel that Cornell University, no matter how worthy, was an eastern institution which hoped to profit from what was as much a speculation as if a private individual had entered the land for himself. Harder and more realistic arguments were necessary to keep taxes within bounds.

In fighting the "tax thieves" Putnam relied heavily upon William F. Bailey of Eau Claire and D. P. Simons, at this time agent of Henry

him home to stay, to the theatre, drove him out, etc. & he has gone home & will take hold for me. I have also had some of the Ashland people around. . . . I may use a little money on something else but will treat the matter judiciously & as my own."

[75] Quoted in *Chippewa Times,* March 5, 1879.

[76] *Bloomer Workman,* September 28, 1882; *Chippewa Independent,* November 2, 1882.

[77] H. C. Putnam, Eau Claire, September 8, 1870, to Ezra Cornell.

W. Sage. Bailey was the ablest and most successful tax lawyer in Wisconsin. For years he was retained by Cornell to handle all legal problems concerning taxation, during which time he saved his employer many thousands of dollars. His opponents called him the "chief tax bulldoser of the Cornell University," so effective was his work.[78] "Rebate Simons," so called because of the numerous occasions on which he demanded rebates on unfairly assessed taxes, was an able associate of Bailey and Putnam. These men came to represent many of the large owners of pine in the Chippewa Valley, such as Henry Hewitt, D. M. Peck, S. A. Jewett, Hersey, Staples & Co., Schulenberg & Co., Knapp, Stout & Co., and the Weyerhaeuser interests.[79] Their chief client was Cornell University and the aggressiveness of their attack upon local taxes was due to the persistence of that institution's leaders. The university did not always appear in the controversies, however, because its leaders preferred to work behind the scenes.[80] Yet its board of trustees instructed the university treasurer "to resist the illegal assessments . . . and to cooperate with other large taxpayers . . . in the proposed combination against tax thieves." [81]

In common with most owners of western pine lands, Cornell's representatives were in no hurry to pay taxes. Delay in making payments might induce local officials to compromise the taxes, especially where they were badly in need of money to bolster their credit. According to long-standing custom, owners permitted their lands to become tax-delinquent, knowing that the tax certificates issued by the county could later be purchased for less than the tax itself. The huge tax lists published by the official newspapers of the pinery counties each year attest the large amount of land on which taxes were unpaid. Putnam, Bailey, and Simons scrutinized tax rolls carefully, and if they were convinced that the assessments were unfair, or that there had been corruption and mismanagement in local

---

[78] *Chippewa Times,* February 26, March 5, 1879.
[79] S. Robertson, Eau Claire, December 23, 1885, and December 31, 1886, to E. L. Williams; *Dunn County News,* May 8, 1875; *Phillips Times,* February 23, 1878; *Barron County Shield,* November 3, 1882.
[80] J. W. Williams, Ithaca, February 4, 1879, to Smith Robertson.
[81] Action of the executive committee of the board of trustees, February 2, 1878 (*Proceedings, Board of Trustees, Cornell University, 1865–1885,* p. 161).

finances, they refused to pay taxes either on the Cornell lands or on those of other large holders whom they represented. When tax certificates were subsequently issued they tried "to dicker" with the county officials for the purchase of them and on numerous occasions secured them at substantial reductions.

Putnam's first major victory was gained in 1868, when he succeeded in inducing the board of supervisors of Chippewa County, after a delay of more than a year, to sell the certificates on Cornell University land for 50 cents on the dollar. In 1876, after a long controversy, the Ashland County officials were persuaded to permit the redemption of the Cornell lands for two-fifths of the face value of the certificates.[82] In Barron County the large owners of land refused to pay their taxes in 1872, 1873, and 1874 because the assessments were "outrageous," and as a result the county finances were badly demoralized.[83] Even the partisans of the local board admitted that there had been gross mismanagement. In 1875, when Putnam offered to pay 25 per cent of the face value of the certificates, the board countered with a demand for 50 per cent, but the county was so badly in need of money that its officials finally agreed to accept 35 per cent.[84] Other compromises in which Cornell University was involved were with Marathon County, which agreed to accept 50 per cent for its certificates;[85] Price County, which accepted 58.5 per cent; Taylor County, which accepted 78 per cent, and Lincoln County, which accepted 25 per cent.[86]

The pinery counties also had sharp controversies with the land-grant railroads which claimed exemption from taxes. The North Wisconsin Railroad was finally able to buy the tax certificates on its Burnett County lands in 1877 for 10 cents on the dollar, and those

[82] *Ashland Press,* February 5, 1876.
[83] *Chippewa Herald,* June 4, 1875.
[84] H. C. Putnam, Eau Claire, January 25, 1874, to Ezra Cornell; *id.,* May 26, June 14, 1875, to Cornell University; *Dunn County News,* May 29, 1875; *Chippewa Herald,* June 4, 1875.
[85] *Wisconsin River Pilot,* May 25, 1878.
[86] *Phillips Times* in *Chippewa Herald,* July 29, 1881; *Chippewa Herald,* December 2, 1881; *Hudson Star and Times,* February 13, 1880.

on its Barron County lands in 1879 for 20 cents on the dollar.[87] To settlers who had made improvements on their lands Barron County offered to sell certificates for 50 cents on the dollar.[88]

There was a risk in permitting tax certificates to be issued on one's property. Because the title was clouded, the land could not be sold until the owner of the certificate had been satisfied, and it was never certain at what price the certificates could be secured. Sometimes the certificates were bought by speculators who held them for their full value together with the heavy interest the law allowed. Not infrequently small loggers bought tax titles which gave them a color of title to tracts of land, and then stripped the timber from the land before the owners of the patent titles knew of their operations. The possible profits in the tax-certificate and tax-title business induced many people to speculate in them, some on a large scale. Wayne Ramsay and George B. Burrows of Madison, John L. Gates of Milwaukee, and the Comstock Land Company of Hudson were the largest dealers in tax titles, their purchases frequently including all the outstanding certificates and titles of one or more counties.[89] It was through the operations of the dealers in tax titles, large and small, that numerous absentee owners lost their equity in Wisconsin property. One of these disappointed investors composed the following bit of doggerel which, together with the reply, appeared in the *Chippewa Herald:*

Following Postal received few days ago & answered by Dan Seymour of C. F.

Postmaster to hand to the most wide-awake real estate man, Chippewa Falls, Chippewa County, Wis. Recipient acknowledge receipt.

[87] *Barron County Shield,* June 29, 1877, May 15, 1879; *Hudson Star and Times,* May 23, 1879.
[88] *Barron County Shield,* June 29, 1877.
[89] The Comstock Land Company bought tax certificates comprehending 20,000 acres in Price County in 1882 (*Phillips Times,* May 20, 1882) and 64,000 acres of Lincoln County (*Chippewa Herald,* June 23, 1882). Henry Corwith bought tax titles to 169 parcels of land in Marathon County in 1864 at prices ranging from 40 to 80 cents an acre (I Deed Records, Lincoln County). Captain Tainter of Knapp, Stout & Co. in 1876 bought tax certificates on 26,000 acres in Barron County (*Barron County Chronotype,* January 8, and February 12, 1876). The Ramsay Land Company offered for sale 8,000 acres of tax-deed land in Clark County in 1885 (see *Lands owned by Ramsay Land Co. of Madison, Wis. in Clark County,* 1895). Some of the land deals of J. L. Gates are described in the final chapter of this study.

I wrote to Town Clerk at Cadotte;
As yet, no answer have I got.
Mailed the P. M., too, at the Falls,
In all three letters, cards or calls—
Started from Brooklyn February first.
Answers to none—"silence be cursed."
Poor property owners must suffer tremendous,
Legislative enactments and taxes stupendous.
Please, somebody, write—this is really well meant,
Bid, bid, for the land ere is gone the last cent.
NW ¼ NE 28 29 6W 120 acres sold for taxes
SWNE 26, E ½ SWNE 27, SENE 27, 29, 6W
All this also sold for taxes
Sold to different parties.

Get a bid so as to save something out of the wreck, and write me quickly.

    Please, whoever gets this card,
    If they think the job too hard,
    Keep it moving—hand it round—
    Some smart fellow can be found;
    If he sells, and job is done,
    We shall count him number one.

Do not let this rest. Shove it round till somebody bids for each parcel. Direct me F. D. Thorne, 16 Lee Ave. Brooklyn, N. Y.

ANSWER

F. D. Thorne, 16 Lee Ave., Brooklyn, N. Y.
DEAR SIR:

    I have your card about the land;
    And, if I rightly understand,
    You wish some one to buy the lot
    Before the whole is gone to pot.
    I wonder if you ever came
    Up here and bargained for the same?
    Or if you were acquainted well
    With these said lots you wish to sell?
    If so, 'tis needless to relate
    Their quality or present state.
    But, tell me truly, neighbor mine,
    Did you suppose these trees were pine,
    Or that a bargain you had got
    In those waste-barrens near Cadotte?
    Long years ago, old settlers tell,
    'Tis like a dream remembered well,
    Some scanty saplings, miscalled pine,
    Grew up, in height eight feet or nine;

And, they assert upon their souls,
Boys used them up for fishing poles;
So at the present time there's not
A single pine to mark the spot.
The land is stony, poor and rough,
The timber scrawny, twisted, tough;
The brush is fearful to get through—
But for description this will do.
Don't whine—you are a lucky man;
Be thankful for the tax-deed plan
That kindly comes to your relief
Before you're overwhelmed with grief.
Although your land is gone, 'tis gain;
You have no reason to complain—
The loss falls on the other man
Who took them on the tax-deed plan.[90]

To prevent their land from falling into the hands of dealers in tax titles and tax certificates, the large landowners, when they had reason to question the assessments, protested to the county and town boards and demanded a reduction in their taxes. Putnam, Bailey, and Simons met frequently with the boards of supervisors of Chippewa, Lincoln, Clark, Taylor, Barron, and Ashland Counties, and on numerous occasions induced them to compromise the taxes of Cornell University and of other property owners. To such a session Bailey explained the policy of Cornell respecting taxes as follows:

The University desires to pay its proper share of the legitimate burdens of government and only objects to such taxes as are levied in excess of what is authorized by law, and where there is an evident discrimination in the county against the University; and whenever the authorities are willing to meet us in a spirit of fairness and adjust difficulties upon an equitable basis they will always find the University prompt and willing to pay, and without taking advantage of any legal technicalities.[91]

Since the membership of the county boards was constantly changing, owing perhaps to the principle of rotation in office, little experience was acquired by them. One is not surprised then to note how inexpertly such important matters as the making of assessments and the equalizing of taxes were handled. Numerous errors were made, sometimes mere technicalities, and shrewd attorneys like Putnam

[90] *Chippewa Herald,* February 2, 1877.
[91] *Barron County Shield,* October 4, 1878.

and Bailey would seize upon them and, contrary to the above statement, threaten to upset the entire tax schedule unless a reduction were granted their clients. If the reduction were not granted they would challenge the assessments in the courts, sue out a restraining order to prevent collections or sales, and try to have the tax set aside. All the Chippewa counties were exasperated by Putnam's readiness to pounce on their errors and by Bailey's persistent opposition. Year after year Bailey came back to them demanding economy in expenditures and reduction in taxes. He was frequently accused of harassing the county and town officials by his numerous threats, suits, injunctions, and decrees.

Perhaps the most prolonged fight was with Chippewa County. The towns of this county had issued large amounts of orders, sometimes fraudulently, and Putnam bought up these depreciated orders and insisted that the county accept them at face for taxes. The county at first refused but threats of legal action forced it to change its decision.[92] In 1870 and 1871 assessments on the university's land in Chippewa County were so "enormously" high that Putnam employed William P. Bartlett of Eau Claire to investigate their legality.[93] Bartlett was able to find flaws in the assessments and his threat to take them into court induced the board to compromise and saved the university $8000.[94] Similarly Bartlett attacked the Flambeau taxes in 1873, 1874, and 1876, and was able to secure reductions. In 1875 Putnam induced the county to reduce its assessments on 4000 acres of Cornell lands which he called "cutover or worthless."[95] Two years later Bailey brought a number of suits against the county to set aside its assessments and secured an injunction restraining it from advertising for sale the university's lands. Since the injunction threatened to reduce sharply the advertising of the official newspapers their proprietors employed counsel to set it aside. The injunction was dissolved and the lands were then advertised for sale, but prior to the date of

---

[92] H. C. Putnam, Eau Claire, April 8, 1876, to J. W. Williams.
[93] *Id.*, Eau Claire, December 30, 1870, to Ezra Cornell.
[94] W. P. Bartlett, Eau Claire, July 31, 1877, to D. Boardman.
[95] J. W. Williams, Ithaca, August 18, 21, 1877, to S. Robertson; *Chippewa Herald*, November 19, 1875, April 7, 1876.

the sale the county board compromised the taxes, so pressing was its need of money. The county not only allowed Cornell an abatement of 40–50 per cent on the taxes but agreed to pay Bailey's bill of $700 for his services in fighting the assessments. In addition it had to pay the cost of printing, which ordinarily was saddled upon the owner of the delinquent lands.[96] In 1881 Bailey was again in Chippewa County investigating "unjust assessments" in Big Bend, Flambeau and Anson. This time he secured rebates ranging from 20 to 35 per cent.[97]

Other counties were compelled by Bailey to reduce their taxes on Cornell lands. Scrutiny of the proceedings of the board of supervisors of Lincoln County revealed that reductions as high as 40 per cent had been granted to some taxpayers. Bailey promptly demanded that the same concessions be made to Cornell. Four years later he won a reduction of 60 per cent from Lincoln County.[98] After inspecting the assessment rolls of Clark County in 1878 the Cornell agent became convinced that the university's lands were assessed at a higher rate than other tracts of equal value. When his offer to compromise was spurned he brought suit in the United States Circuit Court to set aside the taxes and secured an injunction restraining the treasurer from selling land for taxes. Subsequently the injunction was dissolved and the lands were offered for sale, but a large proportion of the tax certificates were not purchased and remained in the hands of the county. The county was no better off, however, for it had no funds for its efforts and, when another offer was made to compromise, it agreed to accept $1878 for the $2678 originally assessed.[99]

Bailey had perennial conflicts with Ashland County over taxes. One such fight he pressed vigorously because he felt that an important principle was involved. The town of Ashland, which included a large area outside the village proper, levied heavy taxes in 1886 for the

---

[96] *Chippewa Herald,* October 24, 1879, November 28, 1879; *Chippewa Times,* December 3, 1879; *Bloomer Workman,* September 7, 1882; W. F. Bailey, Eau Claire, November 30, 1879, to Smith Robertson.

[97] *Chippewa Herald,* March 11, 1881.

[98] S. Robertson, Eau Claire, October 25, 1877, to J. W. Williams; W. F. Bailey, Eau Claire, March 29, 1881, to Robertson; *Chippewa Times* in *Barron County Shield,* February 20, 1879; *Chippewa Herald,* April 25, 1879.

[99] *Clark County Republican,* May 17, July 26, 1878.

construction of waterworks, a gas plant, and other municipal improvements which would not benefit the rural area. Doubting the legality of the taxes, Bailey refused to pay them, enjoined the treasurer from selling the land for taxes and refused to compromise because he wished to carry the issue through the courts. His action put the town authorities in a more conciliatory mood. When an agreement was finally reached it provided that the university should pay 67 cents on the dollar of assessed taxes and that the town should incorporate as a city and eliminate much of the surrounding area from its limits.[100]

Numerous other suits were brought by Putnam, Bailey, Robertson, and Simons to restrain officials of the pinery counties from selling university land for taxes and to set aside assessments. In such ways did the agents of Cornell University attempt to influence the internal affairs of the northern Wisconsin communities.

The Chippewa lumbermen and pine owners found that coöperative action was essential for their mutual protection. The common method was for the lumbermen to meet at Eau Claire, Menomonie, or Chippewa Falls, agree upon the program they wished to press at the county seats or at Madison, and send representatives to advocate it. Costs were allocated in proportion to the amount of land individual members owned. Such *ad hoc* groups had been brought together by Putnam on frequent occasions prior to 1876, but they were most effective after that year. In 1876 the Chippewa Valley Lumbermen's Exchange met at Menomonie to consider the rapidly rising tax burden. The association condemned the high taxes, arguing that they forced owners to strip their lands of pine whether there was a demand for it or not, with the result that the market was frequently glutted, the cut-over lands were abandoned by their owners, and the taxing jurisdictions could expect no further revenue from them for years to come. A similar association of owners of pine lands in Lincoln County met the same year at Oshkosh to protest against tax assessments.[101] In 1878 an anti-tax meeting was held at Eau Claire in the office of Smith Robertson, to which came representatives of many of the largest

---

[100] W. F. Bailey, Eau Claire, March 5, 1887, to Smith Robertson.
[101] A. Haight, Oshkosh, January 26, 1877, to J. W. Williams.

lumbering firms on the Mississippi and its tributaries, including W. J. Young of Clinton, Iowa, Daniel Shaw & Co., the Valley Lumber Company, Porter, Moon & Co., William Starr, John S. Owen, and Sage & McGraw. Promises of support were also received from Hersey, Staples & Co. of Stillwater, Minnesota, Cameron & Losey of La Crosse, and Philetus Sawyer of Oshkosh. The group proposed the abolition of the township school system and amendments to the assessment laws to provide for thorough examinations and assessments of forest and wild lands every five years.[102] At the same time the Wisconsin Central Railroad, which had waged a bitter fight against the pine owners' lobby during the previous year, agreed to join hands with its erstwhile enemy in an effort to secure legislation to protect their common interests.[103]

The Cornell agents, the Chippewa lumbermen and pine owners, and the Wisconsin Central Railroad continued to struggle against extravagance and unfairness on the part of local officials by refusing to pay their taxes, instituting court proceedings, and obtaining injunctions. But these were cumbersome methods at best, and it was not long before the pine-land owners saw that the only thoroughgoing remedy was to strip the counties of some of their spending and borrowing power by limiting the amount of taxes which the counties and towns could raise for highways, buildings, and incidental purposes. It was necessary also to make the organization of new counties more difficult and less profitable by requiring them to have a minimum number of inhabitants and by limiting the amount of county orders they could issue. In this way county governments and the spoilsmen who intended to establish new counties would be effectually brought under control. If in addition the sale of tax certificates on tax-delinquent lands, which afforded insiders a chance to profit at the expense of landowners trying to clear their titles, could be strictly regulated, pine-land owners would secure much relief.[104]

The fight to curb the taxing and bonding power of local govern-

[102] S. Robertson, Eau Claire, January 17, 1878, to J. W. Williams.
[103] H. W. Sage & Co., New York City, January 7, 1878, to J. W. Williams.
[104] Copy, letter of W. F. Bailey, Eau Claire, January 25, 1879, to Senator George B. Burrows.

ments reached its climax in the sessions of 1877, 1878, and 1879. Members of the legislature were "besieged" for relief by the pine owners, who formed numerous strange combinations with groups fighting the creation of new counties and opposing bills to extend the period of tax exemption on railroad lands.[105] The landowners' lobby, called by the *Barron County Shield* the "infernal combination," tried to have adopted "snake laws . . . under different titles, forms and guises, cunningly devised and adroitly handled by a large lobby of skillful lawyers on the floor of both houses."[106] Judicious use of "champaign, cigars and fine suppers" aided in getting some measures adopted, but not until they were shorn of what their opponents regarded as their most obnoxious features.[107] One of these acts prohibited town officers from issuing orders until the voters had approved taxes to provide for their retirement.[108] Another provided that no town officer should be interested, directly or indirectly, in any contract made by the town, nor should any officer purchase or deal in orders issued by the towns, and heavy penalties were authorized for violation of the law.[109] These measures were to strike at the corruption which had made the towns of Flambeau, Anson, Sigel, and Worcester, in Chippewa County, so notorious. A third act placed limitations on the amount of debts counties could incur in aiding railroads, but it applied only to narrow-gauge lines.[110] Bailey was unsuccessful in securing legislation to change and regulate the size of road and school districts and to reduce the compensation paid printers for the tax-delinquent list.[111]

The achievements of the landowners' lobby in the sessions of 1878

---

[105] Sam Fifield in *Ashland Press*, March 31, 1877.

[106] The same issue of the *Shield* described the mismanagement in Cedar Lake, Barron County, where civil and criminal action had been brought against the secretary of the town board for "fraudulent and corrupt exercise of his office . . . in the issue of certain school orders," apparently without realizing that instances of this sort had obliged the landowners to organize in self-defence (*Barron County Shield*, May 4, 1877).

[107] *Id.*, March 16, 1877. The share of Cornell University in maintaining a lobby in Madison in 1878 was $261.65 (D. P. Simons, Eau Claire, August 20, 1878, to Daniel Shaw Lumber Company, Eau Claire Public Library).

[108] Act of March 8, 1877, *Laws of Wisconsin*, 1877, p. 598.

[109] *Id.; Barron County Shield*, April 20, May 4, 20, 1877.

[110] Act of February 7, 1877, *Laws of Wisconsin*, 1877, pp. 9–10.

[111] *Chippewa Times*, March 5, 1879.

and 1879 were meager. In the latter year an act was adopted which stated that the tax sale certificates of Chippewa County were not to be appropriated for any purpose.[112] Also the new county of Marinette was restricted to a tax of $1000 annually for five years for the construction of public buildings, except for the cost of a county jail.[113] Price County, created in 1879, was prohibited "from voting any bonds in aid of any railroad." [114] Restrictive legislation, or "snake bills" to curb powers of local governments, were not popular, and landowners were forced to resume their fight against taxes and assessments at the county seats and in the courts.

There was one development that brought some comfort to the large taxpayers in northern Wisconsin. In the older pinery counties the homesteaders were slowly acquiring title to their farms and beginning to take an interest in the costs of local government. At this point the Cornell agent noted that the settlers became tax-conscious and joined hands with the larger landowners in reducing expenses.[115]

Increasing tax consciousness on the part of the homesteaders helped the large landowners in Price, Chippewa, Barron, and Lincoln Counties, but in the extreme northern counties there was no relief from oppressive taxation until after the turn of the century. In the nineties, the Weyerhaeuser companies, Knapp, Stout & Co., Cornell University, and other large owners again asked the legislature for protection from the "tax wolves." A representative was sent to Madison to demand that the borrowing power of the towns and counties be limited and that a state tax commission with the power of review over local assessments and taxes be created. The latter measure was defeated, but the legislature did place a tax ceiling of three per cent on the assessed valuation of towns and counties. Unfortunately, there was a loophole in the measure which permitted communities with a heavy debt to escape from the restriction.[116]

The persistent interference of absentee landowners in county and

[112] Act of March 4, 1879, *Laws of Wisconsin*, 1879, p. 336.
[113] Act of February 27, 1879, *id.*, p. 116.
[114] Act of February 26, 1879, *id.*, p. 101.
[115] Smith Robertson, Eau Claire, April 22, 1879, to J. W. Williams.
[116] $1025 was expended by the lobby in behalf of these measures (C. O. Law, April 29, 1895, to Smith Robertson).

town affairs and their failure to pay taxes aroused a great deal of feeling in northern Wisconsin.[117] The official newspapers, whose proprietors had smarted under the lash of Putnam and Bailey, struck back in a series of bombastic editorials wherein absentee owners, especially Cornell University and its attorney, W. F. Bailey, were castigated in the severest of terms. One of these editorials, written by Sam Fifield, who owned the official papers of Ashland and Bayfield Counties and against whom the Cornell agents were arrayed in frequent battles, was printed in the *Ashland Press,* the *Bayfield Press,* the *Lincoln County Advocate,* the *Chippewa Times,* and the *Barron County Shield.* It was as follows:

The Cornell University owns over a million of acres of land in Northern Wisconsin, and there is nothing that stands in the way of the progress, development, improvement and settlement of the portion of the State where those lands are situated as this unfortunate situation.

The lands are managed upon the most narrow, selfish and miserly principles, and every dollar realized from the sale of the lands or the timber standing thereon, goes into the long sock of that institution. It does not expend one dollar in establishing a single enterprise in the country where the lands are situated, nor aids a single improvement, nor offers an iota of inducement to a settler.

The institution annoys and harasses towns and counties with all manner of law suits, involving sometimes only the insignificant sum of five dollars. The institution hires men to slander and abuse the people in the country where their lands are situated, and to blacken and injure every enterprise that is begun in spite of it.

The institution, through its agents, browbeats, threatens and bulldozes town and county officers into compromises of taxes, where honest enterprising men pay promptly and without grumbling. More suits have been brought by that concern than by any other corporation in the State of Wisconsin in the same length of time.

It is time towns, counties and municipal officers ceased being driven and browbeaten into compromises with Cornell University, and the State will do a real service when that eating sore is cut out by the roots. It is a fungus on the State that is absorbing the lifeflow of the upper portion.

Every dollar realized from the great domain held by the institution goes

[117] *Hudson Star and Times,* February 13, 1880. When the large owners finally paid their taxes there was much rejoicing in the pineries (*Chippewa Herald,* May 9, 1879; *Phillips Times,* December 10, 1881).

to the State of New York. The State of Wisconsin receives no benefit, and a large portion of the State is blighted in consequence of its wealth being held by such a selfish and narrow contracted concern. Let a remedy be devised.[118]

Bailey was castigated with equal severity. "This false citizen," the *Chippewa Times* said, who writes "dirty, lying communications in the newspapers, that get their living and are fed by pine land monopolists . . . spends his winters sneaking around legislative committee rooms trying to steal through legislation what would ruin every frontier settlement in the state." [119] The *Barron County Shield* said of him:

There is no man in Northwestern Wisconsin, who by his persistent fighting year after year of the taxes against non-residents, has shifted so many thousands of dollars of the burdens of just taxation, through the merest technicalities of the law from the shoulders of the large land owners to those of the settler, as has Mr. Bailey.[120]

Ironically, Bailey, the representative of Cornell, Sage, McGraw, Jewett, Knapp-Stout, and the Weyerhaeuser companies, who together came near to acquiring a monopoly of pine lands on the Chippewa, was the "antimonopoly" candidate for Congress in 1882. The county in which some of his most successful fights had been conducted gave his opponent a large majority.[121]

It is clear that Cornell University and other large landowners had much to complain of in the matter of assessments and administration of local government in the pinery counties of Wisconsin. Yet, on examining the taxes the university paid, one is amazed to find that in proportion to the price for which its lands were held the taxes were exceedingly light. For example, lands were sold in 1882 for $16.80

[118] *Ashland Press,* June 15, 1878; *Bayfield Press* in *Lincoln County Advocate,* July 13, 1878; *Barron County Shield,* June 14, 1878. S. Robertson, Eau Claire, June 15, 18, 28, 1878, to J. W. Williams. Robertson called Sam Fifield, who was responsible for the "villainous article," one of the "three great political bummers of Wis." "Whoever questions their right to live on unjust taxes," he said, "must expect all their rage and vengeance, in any way their fiendish ingenuity can invent."

[119] *Chippewa Times,* March 5, 1879.

[120] *Barron County Shield,* November 3, 1882. See also the *Chippewa Times,* February 26, 1879.

[121] *Barron County Shield,* November 10, 17, 1882.

an acre which were taxed the previous year only seven cents an acre. Other lands which were sold at the same time and at the same price were taxed from one cent to 50 cents an acre. The latter rate was high, the former low, but neither was typical. The records indicate that assessments were increased much more slowly than the asking price for the land. The Cornell authorities kept confidential all information concerning their land prices, and county boards had to levy taxes without this information. When there was little demand for land and consequently few sales, as between 1873 and 1879, there was little positive information to use in making assessments. The financial problems involved in meeting the rising tax burden were heavy upon Cornell University, but the total cost of taxes cannot be regarded as excessive, if one considers the profits the university made. Although the bulk of the sales were made in the eighties and nineties, and taxes were paid on these lands for twenty-five and thirty years, the total tax cost was less than one-tenth of the gross income from sales.

CHAPTER NINE

Cornell Against the Railroad Lobby

IN THE twentieth century the State of Wisconsin has enjoyed an enviable reputation for good government, but in the nineteenth century it was as badly administered and as boss-ridden as any state in the Union. The two groups which dominated the politics of the state in the seventies and eighties were the railroads and the lumbermen. Their spokesman in Madison was "Boss" Elisha Keyes while in Washington Philetus Sawyer and John C. Spooner watched over their interests. The most notable persons who rose to be governors, senators, or representatives served an apprenticeship in either the railroad or the lumbering industry, among them being Cadwallader Washburn, Thaddeus C. Pound, Isaac Stephenson, and William T. Price. Except for the unsatisfactory Granger legislation, little Federal or state action was taken which was harmful to these interests. Their control of the press of the state made crusades against them difficult, and their ability to assess members for political purposes gave their leaders an ever ready and highly necessary campaign chest on which to draw. Favorable state and Federal land laws, liberal railroad charters, tax exemption, and legislation to authorize the construction of booms, dams, and other improvements in the log-driving streams were the principal objects for which they worked. Efforts to achieve some of these aims brought the railroads and lumbermen into head-on collision with Cornell University, the largest owner of pine land in Wisconsin.

Wisconsin's earliest settlers were quick to request railroad connections with the East, and later comers supported their insistent demands. Within half a century the southern part of the state had become well gridironed with lines of steel and the northern part could boast at least seven north-south lines and a number of transverse lines. In the more heavily populated areas of southern Wisconsin the railroads were built for the most part by private capital. In northern Wisconsin the proportion of land suitable for settlement was small and most of that small proportion was held by speculators. Settlers who would have welcomed an opportunity of homesteading in that section after 1862 found that speculators had anticipated them and that they would have to go farther afield in their search for free grants. By preventing compact settlement these speculators had made the task of financing railroads in northern Wisconsin difficult, since private capital was not prepared to build railroads where settlement was sparse. If railroads were to be built in this area government assistance was necessary, and local governments, the state, and the Federal government were all solicited for aid.

In the mid-nineteenth century representatives of all the public-domain states in which there remained unentered lands joined in the demand for Federal aid to railroads, and a responsive Congress gave way to their importunities. In 1850 Congress made the first grant to aid in the construction of a railroad to extend from Chicago to Mobile. Six sections, or 3840 acres, were given for each mile of railroad in the public-land states of Illinois, Alabama, and Mississippi.[1] In 1852 and 1853 similar grants were given for railroads in Missouri and Arkansas, and in 1856 Florida, Alabama, Mississippi, Louisiana, Iowa, Michigan, and Wisconsin received like donations for railroads which they were projecting. These grants were given to the states and were by them donated to corporations which undertook to build the lines.

Wisconsin received grants for the construction of three lines through the pinery counties of the north. The first line thus aided was to connect southern Wisconsin with Minneapolis and St. Paul by way of the pineries of the Black, the Eau Claire, the lower Chippewa, the Red Cedar, and the St. Croix Rivers. Another line was projected from some point on the St. Croix near Hudson to Superior,

---

[1] Paul W. Gates, *The Illinois Central Railroad and Its Colonization Work* (Cambridge, 1934), pp. 21–43.

with a branch to Bayfield. The third road was to run from Fond du Lac northerly to the Michigan-Wisconsin line. Some 2,400,000 acres were given the state for these three lines.[2]

For a time the government's bounty produced little railroad building in northern Wisconsin. In 1864 Congress renewed the grants and enlarged them to ten sections or 6400 acres for each mile of railroad. At the same time a new line to extend through central Wisconsin to Ashland was given a similar grant.[3] The increased donations and the rapid development of lumbering on the Wisconsin, Black, and Chippewa Rivers gave courage to capitalists, who now undertook to construct these lines. The promoters were aware that the land grants would not provide immediate funds for construction, and not being able or willing to risk much capital themselves they tried to obtain other government subsidies to supplement the Federal grant.

After numerous experiments with state construction and state financing of internal improvements in the lush period prior to 1837, and again before 1857, several of the western states, including Wisconsin, had become strongly opposed to any further ventures of this sort. Consequently the promoters of the pinery railroads could get no financial assistance from the Wisconsin legislature, but they were able to secure the enactment of much friendly legislation, including a series of measures authorizing towns, cities, villages, and counties to give aid to local railroads. In 1869 the legislature authorized the local governments in the region through which the Milwaukee & St. Paul and the Wisconsin Central Railroads were projected to subscribe to the stock or bonds of the companies engaged in constructing these lines.[4] The following year a general law was adopted which authorized counties to exchange their bonds for the stock of local railroads to the amount of $5000 for each mile of railroad located therein. In lieu of taxes the railroads were to pay a license fee of six per cent of their gross earnings to the state, which would apportion the receipts among the counties

---

[2] Act of June 3, 1856, 11 *U. S. Stat.*, p. 20.
[3] Act of May 5, 1864, 13 *U. S. Stat.*, p. 64.
[4] Acts of March 8 and 9, 1869, *Laws of Wisconsin*, 1869, pp. 107 and 125.

to aid in retiring the bonds.⁵ Two years later the legislature provided that local governments might extend aid to railroads to the extent of ten per cent of the assessed valuation of their taxable property, and that special taxes might be imposed for the interest and amortization of the bonds.⁶ In 1875 this act was broadened by a provision which permitted counties to levy a special tax of five per cent on their assessed valuation for a donation, not a loan.⁷ Finally, in 1876, municipal corporations were authorized to guarantee the interest on first-mortage bonds of narrow-gauge railroads for a period of ten years. A special tax was to be levied for this purpose and the railroads were to exchange their first-mortgage bonds for the amount of interest thus paid.⁸ The backwoods communities of Wisconsin thus received a dangerous liberty which permitted them to hazard their financial future in competition with one another for railroad connections.

During the period from 1850 to 1880 local governments everywhere were being badgered into giving aid to railroads. Altogether well over $200,000,000 was subscribed by them, and no small share of the mileage of branch lines and even of the main lines of many railroads was made possible by their assistance. These subscriptions were given in two ways: the local government either exchanged its bonds for the stock or bonds of the projected railroads or made them outright gifts of cash, bonds, or tax exemption privileges.⁹ In Wisconsin there were few counties or municipalities which were not induced to subsidize one or more railroads.

The conflict between actual settlers and the non-resident owners of land in the pinery counties flared up fiercely over the question of aid to railroads. Settlers, whether farmers, merchants in the logging towns, owners of sawmills, local speculators in land, or carpetbagging politicians, were united in their advocacy of local subsidies to rail-

---

⁵ Act of March 4, 1870, *Laws of Wisconsin*, 1870, pp. 35–42.
⁶ Act of March 25, 1872, *Laws of Wisconsin*, 1872, p. 260.
⁷ Act of March 3, 1875, *Laws of Wisconsin*, 1875, p. 290.
⁸ Act of February 16, 1876, *Laws of Wisconsin*, 1876, p. 35.
⁹ Federal Coordinator of Transportation, *Public Aids to Transportation* (4 vols., Washington, 1938–1940), vol. ii, "Aids to Railroads and Related Subjects," investigates this question of local aids to railroads in detail.

roads. They were well aware that if the companies which were aided proved to be financial failures the cost of the subsidies would come out of the taxes paid by the landowners. Indeed, it was commonly argued that the local subsidy policy forced absentee owners to pay their rightful share of the cost of local improvements. The *Chippewa Herald*, in supporting the proposal that Chippewa County grant $75,000 to the Chippewa Falls & Western Railroad, observed that a large proportion of the property in the county was held by non-residents who lived in Pennsylvania and New York and elsewhere, and added: "Let them pay their share for improvements. It raises the value of their property as well as those living here." [10]

Lumbermen of the Chippewa Valley did not need railroads as much as the lumbermen of the Wisconsin River Valley, where there were more serious obstacles to log driving. Despite their more favorable position, the loggers and owners of sawmills on the Chippewa wanted railroads. Supplies could be transported by railroad more economically than by ox teams. Furthermore, if railroads were constructed into the logging areas they would free the loggers of the necessity of building their own roads and would pass on the cost of such improvements to others. For these reasons lumbermen did not oppose local subsidies to railroads, even though this policy meant higher taxes, unless the projected lines were laid out in parts of towns and counties remote from their own land.

Opposition to railroad subsidies came from the absentee owners of pine land and their Wisconsin agents. Land suitable for farming was likely to be increased in value by the construction of railroads, but pine land adjacent to drivable streams was not. It might even decrease in value. Railroad locomotives frequently set fire to standing timber and caused great damage. Settlers who were brought in by railroads stole timber from absentee-owned land and increased taxes by their demands for schools, roads, and public buildings. With little or no taxable property of their own, the settlers in charge of local governments would, as experience had proved, be extravagant with the public money and grant railroad subsidies right and left,

[10] *Chippewa Herald*, August 1, 1873.

subsidies which would have to be financed by taxes on other people's property. Better then, the absentee owners argued, to fight the movement for local aid to railroads at the outset.

Cornell University and Sage & McGraw naturally looked with disfavor upon any move which might increase their taxes. Yet they did not at the outset oppose local aid to railroads, principally because their Wisconsin agent, Henry C. Putnam, was so closely identified with the development of the Chippewa Valley that he found himself on both sides of the question. Putnam was primarily a real-estate dealer. He laid out towns, sold town lots, dealt in farm property, and bought and sold great tracts of pine land. He worked closely with various groups who were interested in promoting the growth of Eau Claire by bringing railroads to the city. Heavy taxes on the land of those whom he represented Putnam naturally deplored, but for the time being his interest in the agricultural and commercial development of the Chippewa Valley exceeded his fear of high taxes. Since Ezra Cornell expected to sell to settlers part of the land which Putnam had entered for him, he was not averse to giving aid to railroads which might make it easier to attract immigration. Sage, McGraw, and Dwight were also induced to favor railroad construction in the Chippewa Valley.

The first railroad to reach Eau Claire was the West Wisconsin, which was building from Elroy to Hudson to connect Chicago and St. Paul. With the aid of a liberal grant of land and subsidies from the counties and cities through which it was projected, this railroad was built as far as Eau Claire by 1870.[11] Connection with the outside world was thus established, but the powerful group of lumbermen in Eau Claire and Chippewa Falls was not satisfied. They wanted a railroad parallel to the Chippewa River to enable them to get supplies into their logging camps. Sage, McGraw, and Dwight, whose land was located for the most part north of Chippewa Falls, were ready to aid them in such an enterprise, as was also Ezra Cornell. Under the leadership of Putnam this group conceived the plan of building a railroad from Wabasha, near the

[11] H. C. Putnam, Eau Claire, September 1, 1870, to Ezra Cornell.

mouth of the Chippewa, to Bayfield on Lake Superior. To build a line 200 miles long through the heart of the Chippewa pinery would call for more capital than these men were prepared to invest, and there was little prospect of securing a new grant of land from the Federal government, so strong had opposition to such use of the public lands become. Fortunately, there was a grant which had been going begging for years and the group laid plans to secure it.

The Federal land grant for the construction of a railroad from the St. Croix River to Lake Superior had been given by the State of Wisconsin to the St. Croix & Lake Superior Railroad. No progress had been made in building the line, and although the grant had been renewed in 1864 it expired again in 1869. Its status then became a subject of dispute. Some thought that it had reverted to the Federal government, while others maintained that a grant, once given, could not revert without positive action by Congress or by the courts.[12] There was some justification for the latter view, as the Secretary of the Interior had sanctioned the action of the State of Wisconsin in policing the lands to prevent timber stealing upon them and in collecting damages for pillaging. The St. Croix grant lay in an area which bore a great stand of choice white pine. Since the lands had been withdrawn from entry they had not been picked over by speculators nor had much plundering been committed on them. They were, therefore, the largest and most valuable body of land in public ownership in Wisconsin. Various groups, aware that the prize was too choice to be permitted to revert to the public domain, moved to secure it. Among those interested were the West Wisconsin, the Wisconsin Central, the Milwaukee & St. Paul, and the Sheboygen & Fond du Lac Railroads and a combination of St. Paul and St. Croix lumbermen and capitalists. Putnam saw in the St. Croix grant an opportunity to finance the construction of a railroad through the Chippewa Valley which would aid Eau Claire and at the same time increase the value of the Cornell land. He urged Ezra Cornell and his New York associates to join with him in an effort to secure at least a share in this grant for a railroad through the Chippewa Valley.

[12] Putnam expressed the latter view in a letter of April 2, 1872, to Ezra Cornell.

Ezra Cornell and John McGraw were not averse to participating in railroad promotion, being already deeply involved in a number of lines centering at Ithaca. The pine on the St. Croix grant, together with that already held by Cornell and McGraw, would give them a powerful hold over the lumber industry of the upper Mississippi, and the railroad for which the grant was desired would certainly increase the value of their holdings. It would make it possible for lumber to be shipped from Eau Claire and Chippewa Falls at any time of the year and would enable these mill towns to compete with the lower Mississippi mill communities on easier terms. Furthermore, it would improve the position of some of their town-lot speculations in Eau Claire, Brunet Falls, and elsewhere. They therefore fell in with Putnam's plans.

In 1870 and 1871 the Chippewa Valley & Lake Superior Railroad Company was organized with a board of directors including Ezra Cornell, his son Alonzo, John McGraw, his brother Thomas, Henry W. Sage and his two sons, Dean and William H., Jeremiah W. Dwight, Henry C. Putnam, "Jim" Thorp of the Eau Claire Lumber Company, and John H. Knight, register of the Bayfield land office.[13] The company planned to build its line from the junction of the Chippewa with the Mississippi, by way of the Chippewa Valley to Bayfield. Dwight, president of the road, proposed to bond all the localities between Wabasha and Chippewa Falls, for which distance there would be no land grant.[14] The St. Croix grant, it was hoped, could be secured to build the line north of Chippewa Falls. The necessary steps to carry out these plans were, first, to secure from Congress an extension of the life of the St. Croix grant and, second, to have the Wisconsin legislature give to the Chippewa Valley & Lake Superior Railroad a share if not all of it. To attain these objects Putnam brought to bear on the Wisconsin legislature and on Congress the full influence of those New Yorkers, like Cornell, Sage, McGraw, and Dwight, whose lands he managed, and of such Eau Claire and Chippewa Falls lumbermen as he could persuade to help him.

[13] *Chippewa Herald,* September 16, 1871.
[14] J. W. Dwight, Dryden, October 9, 1871, to H. C. Putnam.

Putnam's attempt to unite the Eau Claire and Chippewa Falls lumbermen in support of his railroad plans was made difficult by the bitter rivalry among these groups over the Dells bill. The Eau Claire millmen were trying to get from the legislature the right to dam the Chippewa at the Dells, just above the city of Eau Claire. The slack water provided by the dam and the natural setting at the Dells would permit the construction of a boom and of separating devices to take care of the logs destined for Eau Claire, but, since the dam would also obstruct navigation, Chippewa Falls opposed it. Thaddeus C. Pound, lieutenant governor, ardent fighter for Chippewa Falls and vigorous opponent of the Dells bill, was at swords' points with "Jim" Thorp of Eau Claire, an equally strong supporter of the measure. Both put forth their utmost energies to strengthen their positions in the legislature and were prepared to make almost any compromise to that end. They thoroughly approved of the Chippewa Valley railroad, but it was not as vital to them as was the Dells fight, or "the miserable Dells bill," as Putnam called it because it had crossed up so many other issues he was pushing. Thorp and Pound both supported Putnam, but he could not but feel that their support was weakened by their other interests.[15]

Putnam had little finesse as a lobbyist, but, like Senator Dillworthy, he believed that all men were motivated by personal interests and could be influenced by promising the support of their pet measures, agreeing to let them share in some choice speculations, offering them outright cash, or by otherwise buying off their opposition. When he was unsuccessful in winning support he assumed that the enemy, Jay Cooke, the Northern Pacific Railroad, or some other rival group, had influenced members of the legislature by more lavish promises than he could afford to make. His campaign in Washington to win extension of the St. Croix grant shows that he was thoroughly familiar with the Washington atmosphere and could match the tricks of his opponents. By calling to his assistance Cornell, Sage, and McGraw he was able to give an air of respectability to his doings, but all to no avail. His failure to secure an extension of the grant was due to

[15] H. C. Putnam, Eau Claire, December 25, 1871, to Ezra Cornell.

the strong anti-railroad sentiment in Congress and the disagreement among those who wanted a share in the grant.

Defeat in Washington in 1872 did not end the matter. Hoping that the courts would shortly uphold Wisconsin's right to the grant, regardless of its expiration, Putnam brought together in Madison all possible assistance to get the grant divided in such a way as to assure the Chippewa railroad a share. The session of 1873 was a notorious one in which railroad lobbyists were reputed to be as "thick as fleas." The disposition of the St. Croix grant, now judicially recognized as belonging to the state,[16] was one of the major questions, and, after a campaign marked by the bitterest feeling and by charges of outright bribery, the legislature gave the grant to the Milwaukee & St. Paul Railroad. Putnam did not lose all, however, for he succeeded in having the measure concerning the grant amended to provide that, in order to earn it, the Milwaukee & St. Paul Railroad must build a number of lines, including the Lake St. Croix & Bayfield, a branch to Superior, a line into Dunn and Barron Counties, and another line from Wabasha *via* the Chippewa Valley to Chippewa Falls.[17] This last, of course, was the route of Putnam's railroad. With this arrangement Putnam had no ground for dissatisfaction, but, unfortunately for him, the Milwaukee & St. Paul subsequently decided that the branch mileage was too great to undertake and the grant was thrown back upon the state.

Still another conflict ensued over the St. Croix grant, and this time the coveted prize was obtained by the North Wisconsin Railroad. This company was closely identified with the West Wisconsin and with the aid of capital provided by the latter was enabled to complete the line to Bayfield with a branch to Ashland in 1883.[18] Putnam and the officials of Cornell University did not obtain a share in the land

---

[16] Decision of 1872 by the United States Circuit Court for the Eighth Circuit (John F. Dillon, *Cases Determined in the U. S. Circuit Courts, for the Eighth Circuit*, 2, 398, affirmed by the United States Supreme Court in 1874, 21 *Wallace*, 44.

[17] H. C. Putnam, Eau Claire, January 27, 1873, to Ezra Cornell; *Railroad Gazette*, 5 (March 22, 1873), p. 119.

[18] W. H. Stennett, *Yesterday and Today: A History of the Chicago and North Western Railway System* (Chicago, 1910), p. 169.

grant, but the completion of the railroad opened up some of their inaccessible land and enhanced its value.

As representative of the Eau Claire and Chippewa Falls lumbermen and the Cornell interests, Putnam was not satisfied with the disposal of the St. Croix grant, because it made difficult the construction of a railroad up the Chippewa River. He would not give up his favorite project, and when he found that the West Wisconsin was planning to build a branch to Chippewa Falls he fought it, as he feared it would defeat his valley road. The West Wisconsin appealed to Chippewa Falls to aid the new line to the extent of $75,000. The city wanted railroad connections with Eau Claire very badly. Its chief citizen, Thaddeus C. Pound, and its chief paper, the *Herald*, warmly supported the move, but they were opposed with equal warmth by Putnam.[19] At the expense of Cornell University, Putnam distributed 2000 circulars condemning the subsidy and overwhelmingly defeated it.[20] The following year the town of Anson also defeated a proposal to give $10,000 to the same road.[21] However, in 1874, Chippewa Falls did vote a $30,000 subsidy to connect the town with Eau Claire by railroad, perhaps by then despairing of the success of the valley road.[22]

Putnam continued to plan for pinery railroads. In 1875 he attempted to get Eau Claire County to vote $100,000, Chippewa County to vote $150,000, the city of Menomonie to vote $50,000, and other towns in the Chippewa Valley similar amounts for a railroad to cut through the Chippewa and Red Cedar Valleys.[23] Apathy among all but the lumbermen associated with him delayed the enterprise and meantime other issues intervened to absorb their attention.

Once the movement for local aid to railroads reached the pinery

---

[19] *Chippewa Herald*, August 1, 1873.
[20] H. C. Putnam, Eau Claire, September 3 (and accompanying circular), and September 10, 1873, to Ezra Cornell (Cornell MSS); *Chippewa Herald*, September 12, 1873; *Eau Claire Free Press*, September 10, 1873; *Railroad Gazette*, 5 (September 27, 1873), p. 388.
[21] *Chippewa Herald*, September 4, 1874.
[22] *Id.*, July 17, 1874.
[23] H. C. Putnam, Eau Claire, July 10, 1874, to C. H. Blair, and *id.*, July 14, 1875, to Capt. Wm. Wilson.

counties of Wisconsin it seemed to run wild. Counties, towns, and municipalities vied with each other in offering subsidies to railroads. By presenting alternate routes to competing communities and playing counties and towns off against each other, the promoters were successful in securing generous subsidies. As early as 1874 the Wisconsin railroad commissioner reported that bonds to the amount of $7,515,186 had been authorized to aid railroads. Considerable additional assistance was subsequently to be given them.[24] The Green Bay & Lake Pepin Railroad alone received $800,000 in local subsidies. Other railroads which obtained local aid were the Wisconsin Valley, which was being pushed up the valley of the Wisconsin River; the Wisconsin Central, projected to connect Ashland with Portage and Stevens Point; the West Wisconsin and the North Wisconsin. With the exception of the Green Bay & Lake Pepin and Wisconsin Valley Railroads, all of these projects had received a share in the Federal lands granted to the state by the Acts of 1856 and 1864.

The Wisconsin Valley Railroad, ultimately to be united with the Milwaukee system, was being pushed by James F. Joy, "railroad king" of the Burlington. It was designed to open up a portion of the north Wisconsin woods and was to parallel a major log driving stream. The line was to run from Tomah east to the river and thence north to Stevens Point and beyond. Joy sent his son into the state to enter lands for him and to secure local aid for the enterprise.[25] Marathon County gave a ready response in 1873 by voting a donation of 200,000 acres of tax-deed land and $25,000 in notes on condition that the road should go direct from Wisconsin Rapids to Wausau and thus avoid Stevens Point.[26] This assistance was sufficient to complete the line to

---

[24] Wisconsin Railroad Commissioner, *Fifth Annual Report*, 1879, p. xxxiv.

[25] James Joy, Tomah, Wisconsin, August 7, 1873, to his father (Joy MSS, Burton Historical Collections, Detroit Public Library).

[26] Cyrus Woodman, Cambridge, Massachusetts, March 31, 1873, to James Hinman, Kilbourne City, Wisconsin (Woodman letter book, 36, Woodman MSS); *Eau Claire Free Press*, September 17, 1873; *Oshkosh Times* in *Wisconsin Lumberman*, 2 (July, 1874), p. 364. Apparently the railroad received only 140,500 acres, for which it exchanged $25,000 of its stock (conveyance of April 28, 1875, in 7 Lincoln County Deed Records). See also the *Milwaukee Times* in *Ashland Press*, August 21, 1875. The railroad advertised 170,000 acres of land in Marathon and Lincoln Counties for sale in 1879 (see advertisement of J. M. Smith in *Hungerford's Real Estate Journal*, June 15, 1879). Marathon County was reported to have voted 40,000 acres of swamp land

Wausau by 1874.[27] The company then offered to extend the road to Jenny (Merrill) if Lincoln County would exchange $50,000 in cash and $60,000 in bonds for $110,000 of railroad stock.[28] This proposal, when submitted to the people, was ratified by a vote of 307 to 10. Lincoln County was still sparsely settled, most of its permanent residents being homesteaders who had not as yet acquired titles to their claims. Taxes meant little to them for they would be borne for the most part by absentee owners, chief of whom was Cornell University.[29]

Cornell's officials determined to fight the bonding project. They induced Senator George B. Burrows, of Madison, a large dealer in tax titles, to oppose "the robbery," and with others joined in sending William F. Bailey to Jenny to begin legal proceedings against the county. Bailey sued to restrain the board of supervisors from issuing the bonds on the ground (1) that the amount was in excess of the maximum allowed by law, (2) that a large amount of taxable property would receive no benefit from the railroad, (3) that the railroad had no authority to make the proposition to the county, and (4) that of the seventeen miles of railroad to be built with the aid of the bonds only five were in Lincoln County.[30] The suit was instituted in the name of Henry W. Sage, also a large landowner in the county, as it was not deemed advisable to let the university's name appear. Bailey secured an injunction restraining the officials from issuing the bonds. At this point Lincoln County was divided by the legislature, and that part containing the Cornell and Sage lands became Price County. Bailey then let the matter drop and the injunction was dissolved because no one appeared in its behalf. Subsequently, another combination of large landowners of the reduced

---

to the Milwaukee, Lake Shore & Western Railroad in 1882 (*Colby Phonograph,* July 28, 1880; *Phillips Times,* July 15, 1882).

[27] *History of Northern Wisconsin,* p. 551.

[28] *Railroad Gazette,* 10 (October 4, 1876), p. 487.

[29] *Lincoln County Advocate,* September 21, October 12, 19, 1878; *Phillips Times,* October 5, 26, 1878.

[30] S. Robertson, Eau Claire, September 24, 1878, and January 13, 1879, to J. W. Williams (Cornell MSS); *Lincoln County Advocate,* December 28, 1878, February 15 and 22, 1879; *Eau Claire News* in *Phillips Times,* December 28, 1878, and January 18, 1879; *Barron County Shield,* January 2, 1879.

Lincoln County resumed the fight against the bond issue and the special railroad tax imposed to raise the $50,000 cash.[81] The contest delayed the enterprise and the officials of the railroad, discouraged by the heavy expenses incurred in defending their case, gave up the subsidy.[82] The people of Lincoln County were not to abandon the project so willingly, however, and they subsequently adopted by a vote of 322 to 36 a plan to exchange $55,000 of county bonds for the same amount of railroad stock.[83]

The officials of Cornell University had nothing more to fear from the Wisconsin Valley Railroad. They had safeguarded their interests by securing the establishment of the new county of Price, which was prohibited from issuing bonds to aid railroads. With the Wisconsin Central Railroad, on the other hand, they were to have a prolonged conflict.

The Wisconsin Central Railroad was a bold enterprise to build through the least developed section of Wisconsin so as to connect Portage and the Lake Winnebago area with Lake Superior. The only business the railroad could expect for years would be the shipment of lumber southward and the movement of supplies northward for the lumbering camps. It was hoped that at Ashland, the northern terminus, sufficient through traffic in wheat, ore, and lumber would be provided, together with way freight, to make the enterprise a success. As events were to show, a large part of the country through which the railroad was to build was not suitable for farming, and few industrial communities, except small lumbering towns, were to develop. From Stevens Point, the focal point of the southern branches, to Neenah, Portage, and Ashland, a total distance of 320 miles, there are today only three towns with a population in excess of 2500.

The Wisconsin Central was given a valuable land grant, a considerable portion of which was lost by delay in construction, for when the railroad was completed and the lands were selected it was found

---

[81] *Eau Claire Free Press* in *Barron County Shield*, January 10, 1879; *Oshkosh Northwestern* in *Lincoln County Advocate*, March 24, 1879.
[82] *Lincoln County Advocate*, March 31, 1879.
[83] *Lincoln County Advocate*, June 9, July 7, August 4, 1879; *Chippewa Herald*, August 15, 1879; *Phillips Times*, August 9, 16, 1879; *Colby Phonograph*, August 20, 1879.

that only 839,275 acres were available instead of the 1,800,000 promised. Despite the loss of more than half of its grant, the Wisconsin Central was the largest private landowner in the state and, next to Cornell University, the greatest holder of pine stumpage. Because its lands could not be selected as the Cornell lands had been, they included many barren tracts and others on which hardwood predominated. Furthermore, as the lands had been inadequately protected by the state, some of their more valuable pine had been stolen. Yet they contained much desirable lumber, part of which was located on drivable streams though the bulk of it was not. Financial exigencies forced the company to offer its grant for sale as soon as it was earned, but sales were slow because there were no lumber mills in the vicinity of the land. Quick and profitable exploitation of its land grant through the rapid settlement and speedy economic growth of northern Wisconsin were essential for the welfare of the railroad. These considerations led it to undertake an emigration promotion campaign in Europe.[34] New towns, expensive county buildings, elaborate systems of roads, well constructed school houses—all would aid in advertising northern Wisconsin and in selling land. The railroad favored all these new developments, of which the officials of Cornell had to disapprove, having in mind the prudent management of their land investment. A clash between the two greatest owners of land in Wisconsin over such questions as county organization, management of local government, town and county aid to railroads, taxation, rights-of-way, and timber cutting was unavoidable.

Local promoters first undertook to build the Wisconsin Central, but, lacking capital, they were subsequently displaced by Gardiner Colby and his son Charles, who came to control the road.[35] Through the Colbys sufficient funds were secured so that construction could

---

[34] Kate Asaphine Everest, "How Wisconsin came by its large German Element," *Wisconsin Historical Society, Collections,* xii (1892), p. 329; Wisconsin Historical Society, *Proceedings,* 1907, p. 270 n.; Theodore C. Blegen, "The Competition of the Northwestern States for Immigrants," *Wisconsin Magazine of History,* iii (September, 1919), pp. 22–23.

[35] Roy L. Martin, *History of the Wisconsin Central* (Railway and Locomotive Historical Society, *Bulletin* No. 54, Boston, 1941) is a sparkling piece of railroad history dealing with construction, management, finances, personalities, and locomotives.

be started. The Colbys doubtless recognized that there would be little profit in operating the finished railroad, and in common with many promoters of western lines they planned to make their profit from construction rather than operation. Actual construction was turned over to the Phillips & Colby Construction Company, reminiscent of the Crédit Mobilier and the Union Pacific Railroad. The intervention of the construction company produced a struggle for local aid, as the profits of Phillips & Colby would be increased in proportion to the amount of assistance they could secure. Heavy pressure was exerted in Madison and in the counties and towns through which the line was projected, and a number of subsidies were made available.

Ashland and Douglas Counties voted the largest subsidies for the Wisconsin Central. In 1871 the people of Ashland County were asked to vote on a proposal to exchange $200,000 of county bonds for $200,000 of stock in the railroad. The county was then in its infancy, having a population of only 300 and a gross income less than the interest would be on the bond issue. Obviously such a proposal would largely increase taxes. On behalf of Cornell University and other absentee owners of land, Putnam attempted to defeat the bonding proposal. He was outwitted, however, for the "Ashland & Bayfield Shysters" brought over from a nearby stone quarry 70 Irishmen whose residence was in Chicago and they were made to vote for the subsidy. The result was 85 votes for the proposal and none against.[36] Interest on the bonds was not to begin until the road was completed, which was in 1877, but in the three previous years the county levied special taxes to meet the interest. The large landowners, including Cornell University, refused to pay the special tax because they were convinced that the bonds had been issued illegally. As a result, the delinquent tax list swelled alarmingly and there was talk of repudiation. Eventually a compromise was worked out, the holders of the county's bonds agreeing to take securities bearing lower interest.[37]

During the seventies the Wisconsin Central pushed actively in the legislature bills to provide for the establishment of new counties,

---

[36] *Chippewa Herald,* July 22, 1871; H. C. Putnam, April 3, 1875, to J. W. Williams.
[37] *Ashland Press,* February 16, 1884, August 18, 1886.

expecting that local aid could be acquired more easily from them than from the older counties. It was the main force behind the move to carve "Luddington" out of Chippewa and Lincoln Counties and "Forest" or "Webster" out of Clark and Marathon. The Central still had a considerable gap to fill in between the two railheads building from Ashland and Stevens Point, and was finding it difficult to raise sufficient funds for this purpose. Opponents of new counties claimed that the railroad was pushing the move in order that it might secure $250,000 in county bonds to aid in bridging this gap.[38] It was instructive to witness the Wisconsin Valley Railroad, which had been so liberally subsidized by Marathon County, oppose division for fear that its rival would be aided in a similar fashion.[39] Government extravagance and the cost of subsidies to railroads were not a matter of any significance to the Wisconsin Central, since its own lands were exempt from local taxes. Not only might the new counties and even the straggling towns contribute to the cost of finishing the railroad, but their establishment would facilitate the sale of town lots, always a profitable source of revenue to land-grant railroads.

The chief issue in the conflict between the Wisconsin Central and Cornell University was taxation. When the first land-grant railroad was chartered by Illinois in 1851 all its lands were exempt from taxation. Until they were sold and the title conveyed, the railroad lands contributed nothing to local or state government.[40] Complete exemption from taxes made it unnecessary for the Illinois Central to sell its lands immediately, and under the sales policy adopted the grant was disposed of so slowly as to arouse resentment. Wisconsin was only slightly less generous in 1866 when it turned over the lands that it had received from the Federal government to the railroad companies which were consolidated into the Wisconsin Central, tax exemption being granted for ten years. Unfortunately, the railroad could not get title to the lands until they had been earned

[38] *Lincoln County Advocate*, February 5, 1876; *Wisconsin River Pilot*, February 12, 1876; *Madison Democrat*, February 1, 1877.
[39] I have described the efforts to divide these four counties in the previous chapter.
[40] The Illinois Central Railroad was given exemption from all taxes but was required to pay into the state treasury seven per cent of its gross earnings annually (*Incorporation Laws of Illinois*, 1850–1851, pp. 61–74; Gates, *op. cit.*, p. 65).

by construction, and as the route from Ashland to Stevens Point
was not completed until 1877, part of the lands became taxable as
soon as they were acquired. Since traffic over the completed line
was disappointing and the returns were meager there was no profit
in railroad operations. Nor could the lands be sold advantageously
in 1877, or indeed for some years to come, so greatly had the depression following 1873 affected pine-land values. If the lands were
to be taxed as heavily as were those owned by Cornell University or
other speculators, the added burden, amounting to $60,000 to
$100,000, would surely throw the company into bankruptcy.[41] With
this situation in mind, Charles L. Colby and those associated with
him in the management of the Wisconsin Central went to the legislature and asked for an extension of the period of exemption.[42]

Colby's request precipitated the sharpest legislative fight in Madison since the conflict over the Dells bill.[43] Against the plan were
arrayed all the large landowners, local and out-of-state, the settlers
of northern Wisconsin, many newspapers, and some rival railroads.
Most active in opposition were the Cornell agents, who sought to
arouse all landowners to the dangers of extending exemption. In support of the plan were the "minions" of the Wisconsin Central, "Boss"
Elisha Keyes, "representatives of all the prominent daily papers
save the *Milwaukee Sentinel*, . . . judges, politicians, and ex-members, all urging its passage on the grounds of great results to
the state." [44]

Well organized, well led, and, indeed, well financed were the forces
contending for exemption. It was said that the Wisconsin Central
was prepared to spend $100,000 for votes necessary to carry the
bill.[45] Colby was in charge of it, ably assisted by Keyes, Sam Fifield, and other members of the powerful railroad bloc. They
argued that the Wisconsin Central was contributing to the development of northern Wisconsin, from which it had thus far received

[41] *Lincoln County Advocate*, January 20, 1877.
[42] The fight to extend exemption was begun in 1875 but the heaviest pressure was exerted in 1877–1879. See the *Ashland Press*, February 20, 27, March 13, 1875.
[43] *Langlade Enterprise* (Colby), February 24, 1877.
[44] W. F. Bailey, Eau Claire, March 17, 1877, to J. W. Williams.
[45] E. S. Shepard, New London, Wisconsin, February 16, 1877, to Cornell University.

no dividends, and that to tax its lands so soon after they were earned would be grossly unfair. Capital for the completion of the road and its further improvement would be difficult to procure if the lands were taxed; local development would be stopped and the railroad might cease to operate. Fifield attempted to picture the issue as a conflict between an impoverished railroad company, which had extended its line into the wilderness for the benefit of settlers, and a combination of land speculators who were doing their utmost to retard the development of the state. He spoke of the "pine kings" opposing exemption not in the interests of the "poor settler" but to protect themselves against taxation by settlers which the railroad brought into the country.[46] The fight was conducted, he said, by "the Milwaukee Sentinel, Cornell University, through its paid attorneys, backed by a heavy lobby from the Mississippi and the Chippewa Vallies [sic]. . . ."[47]

In the most effective speech in behalf of exemption, a speech charged with emotion, Charles Colby dealt effectively with the argument that the "poor settlers" along the line were opposed to his bill:

Who are the "poor settlers" along the line of our road? . . . You know that these homesteaders are the ones who levy the taxes in that country, who every year want to build roads on every section line, and school houses on every forty, and who even assess property in order to build roads which are projected, but never built at all; who receive the benefit of all the work that is done; who do the necessary work themselves at prices which they themselves fix, and then assess the non-residents to pay for it. I don't think that, in a matter of this kind, this class of "poor settlers" require much consideration at your hands.[48]

It could easily be foreseen that further exemption of the lands of the Wisconsin Central from taxation would be a serious blow to Cornell University and other large owners of land in the pinery counties who had been carrying the cost of local government. In Ashland, Chippewa, Lincoln, Marathon, and Clark Counties, where

[46] *Ashland Press*, March 3, 1877.
[47] *Id.*, February 24, 1877.
[48] *Speech of Charles L. Colby . . . in favor of the bill to extend the time in which the Wisconsin Central Railroad Company is exempted from taxation on its lands* (1877), p. 11.

the railroad lands were concentrated, exemption had already substantially increased taxes on other land. Furthermore, as long as exemption was continued the railroad would have no incentive to foster prudent financial management by the counties. Putnam urged that if exemption were extended it would almost result in confiscation of the Cornell lands that were adjacent to the road, as the railroad company would urge the residents to lay out their highways, build their schoolhouses and county courthouses and bridges during the time exemption was in operation. The added burden on Cornell would be crushing, he declared.[49]

J. W. Williams, treasurer of Cornell University, put the matter even more strongly when he said:

You may be assured that in case they succeed . . . we might as well give away our land contiguous to their line, as there would be no scheme, however bad, but would receive their support provided it promised to increase their prospective profits. New Counties & towns would be formed, hosts of new officials created, beautiful structures for public purposes (and for the purpose of selling town lots owned by said R.R.) would be built.[50]

To the claim that the railroad had improved the country, the *Eau Claire Free Press* replied that so also had the settlers, and at greater hardship. If the railroad was poor, so were the settlers. Colby and others tried to make it appear that if exemption were granted the burden of taxation would fall on absentee landowners, but the *Free Press* replied that the stockholders of the Wisconsin Central were also non-residents and they might with equal justice be asked to contribute their share to the support of local government. The editor held that the lumber business was already staggering under a ruinous load of taxation and could not stand more. Exemption, he argued, instead of inviting settlers and capital into the state would have the effect of repelling them.[51]

The counties affected by exemption naturally opposed further extension of the privilege, although some settlers living on the line of the Wisconsin Central who were anxious to have the road com-

---

[49] H. C. Putnam, Eau Claire, January 22, 1877, to J. W. Williams.
[50] J. W. Williams, Ithaca, January 22, 1877, to Smith Robertson.
[51] *Eau Claire Free Press*, February 1, 8, 15, 1877.

pleted and who, in most instances, were under obligations to Phillips and Colby, supported extension. Marathon County, which the Wisconsin Central tried to divide, was so much aroused by the proposal that its board of supervisors appointed four men to go to Madison "to use their influence and work against the passage of the bill," [52] and appropriated $500 for their expenses. The official paper of Marathon County had this to say for the Wisconsin Central:

The influence of these railroad companies throws the proverbial brazen jackass completely in the shade. They start out first with an immense and valuable land grant; they then secure local aid in as large sums as possible, and in case of the Wisconsin Central Railroad as fast as the road could be built through this great wilderness . . . they have organized new counties, and then voted the bonds of those counties in aid of the road, voted these bonds, while they with their employees had control of the vote.

It spoke of the exemption measure as an effort to "rob the people" which "Boss Keyes, with his little whip in the role of lion-tamer" is pushing.[53] The *Shawano Journal* called further exemption "a gross injustice and an outrage upon the hardy pioneers." "Despite the hundreds of thousands of dollars voted for the railroad it still refused to pay taxes which the homesteaders must meet." It held that rich railroad corporations had been exempt from taxation too long, and it hoped for the defeat of the exemption bill, notwithstanding the clamor of certain subsidized newspapers along the line of the railroad.[54]

The leadership in the fight against further exemption was in the hands of Putnam, Bailey, and Robertson, assisted by Williams and Sage. Williams wrote to at least one member of the Wisconsin legislature calling the exemption bill "a great outrage" and urging him to defeat it. He asked Robertson to fight "to the bitter end" against the bill.[55] Sage contended that the owners of the Wisconsin Central were "rich men" who had pocketed at least one-third of the amount

---

[52] *Wisconsin River Pilot*, February 3, 1877.
[53] *Id.*, February 3, 1877.
[54] Clipped in *id.*, February 3, 1877.
[55] J. W. Williams, Ithaca, February 12, 1877, to Hon. David Hammel, Madison, and *id.*, January 22, 1877, to Smith Robertson.

received from the sale of bonds and that it was this factor which had delayed completion of the road. "Nothing," he said, "could be more monstrously selfish" than the exemption bill.[56] When it was announced by Charles W. Colby that Sage was in favor of exemption the latter telegraphed hotly that he was strongly opposed.[57]

Robertson marshalled the forces in opposition in Eau Claire and vicinity, and Putnam and Bailey took up the cudgels against the bill in Madison. Finding that the "most powerful lobby" of the Wisconsin Central was making progress with their bill in committee, they attempted to amend it to reduce its worst dangers, and to get the legislature tangled up in other controversies so as to break up the supporting group. They tried to have the bill provide that the state should assume payment of the taxes from which the railroad was exempted; they added an amendment to provide that the railroad should pay taxes on all platted towns and lots; they had other exemption bills introduced, including one—alluded to above—which would provide for exempting the Cornell lands from taxation.[58] Despite these efforts to defeat the railroad lobby, in which Cornell's representatives were for the first and perhaps the only time joined in a common fight with the settlers, the bill passed, although the period of exemption was reduced from five years to three.[59]

The fight between Cornell and Colby had engendered much rancor and ill feeling that did not die down immediately. The university and its representatives were castigated for their temerity in opposing the railroad lobby. In his *Ashland Press* Sam Fifield published a series of attacks upon Cornell and its agents which were widely copied. One of them, which appeared just after the exemption bill was approved, included the following:

Among the active opponents of the Central Railroad this winter was Esquire Bailey, of Eau Claire, the attorney and representative of the Cornell University. He is a smart, shrewd, active lobbyist, and handled his case

---

[56] H. W. Sage, New York, February 6, 1877, to J. W. Williams.
[57] Smith Robertson, Eau Claire, February 3, 1877, to J. W. Williams.
[58] Smith Robertson, Eau Claire, February 3, 7, 16, 1877, to J. W. Williams; W. F. Bailey, Eau Claire, March 17, 1877, to J. W. Williams.
[59] *Madison Democrat*, February 15, 16, 17, 1877; *Laws of Wisconsin*, 1877, pp. 39–40.

ably, earning his fees with compound interest and when he presents his bill, if the Treasurer of that pine land institution of learning should "kick," we will furnish him with abundant testimony that he ought to handle their filthy lucre to the utmost farthing demanded—blood and all. It is such land grabbers as the Cornell University, owning as it does the best belt of pine land in the State, the profits from which go to enrich a college located in the wealthy State of New York, that seek retard [sic] the settlement and progress of Wisconsin. They don't want a railroad built through the country because, as one of their "friends" expressed himself to us the other day, "it will fill the woods full of poor devils who will tax us to death, besides their locomotives set fire and burn up *our* timber." Selfish to the last. This institution can afford to let the "New Wisconsin" remain a wilderness, as their pine trees can be ran down the rivers, and their lands be stripped of their wealth without the aid of a railroad. They can afford to hold their lands for better prices too. Originally costing less than *ninety cents* an acre, they are now worth ten times that and as the pine is consumed on other lands, theirs increases in value. Many an acre that is assessed on the Ashland Co. tax roll at $2.50 per acre, would "stump" today for $100. And yet they growl at our taxes of less than four per cent. upon less than an average quarter valuation.[60]

Fifield and other subsidized editors, though fighting for one "monopolistic" institution against another, did their best to arouse and make use of the West's inherent prejudices against eastern capitalists who invested in western lands. They had no love for Cornell University, which spent in the state only the minimum amount required for taxes, salaries, and fees for agents and attorneys. Like the Wisconsin settlers in general, they preferred to have lands held for speculation in the hands of residents. The Wisconsin Central was not an alien institution to the same degree that Cornell was. Its principal officer, Charles W. Colby, was a resident of Milwaukee, it employed many local people in construction and operation, it liberally subsidized the press, aside from the tax question its policy with respect to lands and sales was not under attack, it was actively working to attract immigration to northern Wisconsin, it was promoting the growth of cities and towns along its line, and its purse strings were loose. Fifield pressed the fight against Cornell further

[60] *Ashland Press*, March 3, 1877. See also *id.*, February 24, 1877, and June 15, 1878.

in connection with another issue which had in the meantime come to the fore.

No owner of pine lands in Wisconsin—or indeed anywhere in the West—could expect to be free from the annoyance of timber stealing by small operators, unless he employed timber cruisers to watch his land. Cornell University never worked out a completely satisfactory system of timber protection and suffered considerably from petty pilfering. It had more serious difficulties with influential loggers who contracted to buy land or stumpage on the understanding that payments were to be made in advance in proportion to the amount of timber to be cut during the ensuing season. Such contracts, except when made with Knapp-Stout and the Weyerhaeuser companies, inevitably led to bickering over interpretation and resulted in frequent lawsuits between the university and the purchasers of its lands or logs. With John S. Owen and William A. Rust, important persons in the lumber industry on the Chippewa, ill feeling over timber contracts and land purchases came to a head in 1877 and 1878, when Cornell brought suit for damages of $10,000 for trespass on its lands. Owen, in reply, denied that Cornell could legally hold title to the lands on which the trespass had allegedly been committed, as the statutes of Wisconsin said that no seminary, academy, or other institution of learning could acquire title to more than 40 acres of land.[61] Judgment in the suit was given for Cornell, but meantime the attack upon the title to the Cornell lands had been carried to the legislature. Owen, Rust, and other lumbermen who had been at odds with the Cornell officials over contracts, and a combination of "tax plundering thieves and every other hostile element," including Fifield and the press subsidized by the Wisconsin Central, all joined in the campaign against Cornell.[62] The part personal feeling played in the matter is shown in a letter of Smith Robertson in which he said:

"Billy" Rust . . . swears he will in every possible way attack and injure C. U. interests as well on account of the Owen suit as on acc't of his failure

[61] Clipping dated November 28, 1877 (scrap book, Cornell MSS).
[62] S. Robertson, Eau Claire, February 9, 1878, to J. W. Williams.

to secure that quarter section on the North Eau Claire on which his dam is located. He has been very active about Madison and everywhere in blowing against C. U. . . .[63]

The attack upon the Cornell title was opened by the speaker of the state assembly, who introduced a resolution instructing the attorney general to commence proceedings in the courts to determine by what right, if any, a foreign corporation could hold real estate in Wisconsin, and to secure the forfeiture of the lands if no such right existed.[64] The resolution was rushed through without printing or reference to the appropriate committee and was kept off the journal, being discovered by the watchful Cornell agents only by chance.[65] Robertson hurriedly telegraphed news of the action to Ithaca, where it was decided that the matter was so serious that Henry W. Sage, chief member of the trustees' land committee and the person most responsible for the administration of the Cornell lands, should rush to Wisconsin to oppose the resolution in the senate.[66] No man in America knew pine-land values any better than Sage, and no man was more respected by his associates. His prestige was high in Wisconsin, and when he arrived in Madison to appear in opposition to the resolution it was decided to hold open hearings. Sage held the floor of the senate committee for half an hour while he sought to allay the feeling against Cornell University by describing its origin and progress and its objectives in entering the land. His efforts were successful, and the senate voted overwhelmingly to postpone the resolution.[67]

This attack upon Cornell may be considered as part of the Mid-West's growing revolt against the ownership of extensive areas of land by absentees. In Wisconsin, as in Illinois, Kansas, and other states, the antimonopoly movement accomplished little. It is safe to say that had the legislature given way to the enemies of Cornell

[63] S. Robertson, Madison, February 22, 1878, to J. W. Williams.
[64] A copy of the resolution is enclosed in a letter of W. F. Bailey, Eau Claire, February 16, 1878, to J. W. Williams.
[65] S. Robertson, Eau Claire, February 16, 1878, to J. W. Williams.
[66] Telegram of H. W. Sage, New York, February 19, 1878, to Wm. C. Russell, Ithaca, and copy of telegram of J. W. Williams, Ithaca, February 19, 1878, to W. F. Bailey.
[67] Telegrams of Sage, March 1, 1878, to Robertson and Williams.

the courts would not have decided against the university, and apparently the trustees were more fearful that the attack would retard sales than that it would lead to forfeiture of the land.[68]

In 1879 the Wisconsin Central returned to the fray to secure further extension of exemption. At the same time the North Wisconsin Railroad was seeking an extension of tax exemption for its lands. Since the North Wisconsin was unfinished, there was some justice in its request for further liberal treatment. Its parent, the West Wisconsin, with which Philetus Sawyer and John C. Spooner were closely identified, had urged extension of tax exemption upon the legislature as early as 1870, when railroads were still popular in northern Wisconsin, and had secured the enactment of a measure which exempted its lands from taxation until 1884.[69] In subsequent years this law became highly unpopular and numerous efforts were made to have it repealed or modified.[70]

If the appeals of both the Wisconsin Central and the North Wisconsin Railroads were to be granted, nearly 2,500,000 acres of land in the northern counties would be withdrawn from taxation for years to come. In some of these counties the railroads owned as much as one-fourth to one-half of the entire area. Exemption naturally meant that the privately owned land would have to pay substantially higher taxes, and was not in keeping with the intention of the authors of the land-grant policy, who hoped to have railroad lands sold and developed quickly. Without exemption the railroads would be forced to sell their land speedily; with exemption they could afford to hold them for high prices and the development of the northern counties would be retarded. True, there was no great movement of population into northern Wisconsin during the years 1877 to 1879. True, also, the pine-land business was not flourishing. Yet, if the railroad land were granted further exemption, the taxes on other land would continue at the high level they had already reached, the hardships

---

[68] J. W. Williams, Ithaca, February 18, 1878, to Smith Robertson.
[69] *General Laws of Wisconsin*, 1870, pp. 163–164.
[70] John H. Knapp, Menomonie, Dunn County, Wisconsin, January 24, 1872, to D. A. Baldwin (Keyes MSS); Thomas E. Randall, *History of the Chippewa Valley*, pp. 148–155; *Madison Democrat*, January 18, 24, 30, February 2, 4, 1877.

of the pioneer farmer would be increased, the lumbermen might be forced by unduly heavy taxes to dump their stumpage on the market and thus further depress prices; the logger would be induced to overcut and flood the market in order to strip everything of value from his overburdened lands before permitting them to go to tax sale. In short, the financial condition of the pinery counties, already bordering on a state of bankruptcy, would become deplorably chaotic.

Strengthening the claim of the railroads for further exemption was their weak financial position. The long depression following 1873 had reduced traffic, lowered earnings, and made it difficult for the roads to meet their fixed charges. In fact, the Wisconsin Central was, fortuitously, forced into bankruptcy while the movement for further exemption was getting under way, and this circumstance gave support to the arguments of the railroad lobby that the companies needed the relief the exemption measures would give them. Sage's counter argument that any reduction in taxes for the Wisconsin Central would simply benefit the bondholders who, with few exceptions, lived in the East or in Europe, was an effort to play upon western prejudices.[71]

As in 1877, strong assistance was given the exemption move by the *Madison Democrat*, which held that the Wisconsin Central could not earn one per cent on its invested capital during the next five years because of the slow development of the country. It was folly, argued the *Democrat*, to attempt to force the railroad to pay taxes under such circumstances, since, if the lands were assessed, they would become delinquent and would be sold to purchasers of tax titles who would strip them of timber and then abandon them.[72] "Nearly all the large land owners and heavy tax payers throughout the entire length of the road favor this bill," declared this newspaper, except for Cornell University "an interest that is outside of and foreign to this state," and the bitterest enemy of the proposal.[73] A similar argument in support of the bill was made by Senator William

[71] H. W. Sage, New York, February 26, 1879, to J. W. Williams.
[72] *Madison Democrat*, February 26, 1879.
[73] *Id.*, February 19, 1879.

T. Price, himself a prominent lumberman of Black River Falls.[74]

Price and the *Democrat* were quite unwarranted in their assertions concerning opposition to exemption. In an open letter to the *Democrat* W. F. Bailey pointed out that the Eau Claire Lumber Company, the Valley Lumber Company, Knapp, Stout & Co., Henry W. Sage, the Wisconsin Valley Railroad, and the counties of Lincoln, Taylor, Marathon, and Chippewa were all opposed to further exemption.[75] Bailey might also have mentioned Thomas Irvine of the Beef Slough Company, Jesse Spaulding of Chicago, and Artemas Long and Frederick Weyerhaeuser of Rock Island, who were all opposed to further exemption.[76] Irvine, Lamb, and Weyerhaeuser, whose interests on the Chippewa were already large, were shortly to join in the purchase of a substantial portion of the remaining Cornell lands. Sage, whose land business kept him travelling between Bay City, Michigan, the Chippewa Valley, and the numerous lumberyards which he operated in the East, added his weight to the opposition. Bailey worked hard to get Senator Burrows to oppose, but found him undependable.[77] The chief aid that Bailey had in the legislature came from Senator Kellogg, of the Clark-Marathon district.[78] Despite his Republican predilections, Kellogg was elected in 1878 in a strongly Democratic district because he had pledged himself to oppose exemption.[79]

The claims of the North Wisconsin for further exemption were from the first conceded as being more valid than those of the Wisconsin Central, and early in the session a bill to exempt its land from taxes for ten years was enacted.[80] The fight over the Wisconsin

---

[74] *Id.*, February 20, 1879.
[75] *Madison Democrat*, February 21, 1879.
[76] *Id.*, February 12, 1879.
[77] W. F. Bailey, Madison, February 12, 1879, to Smith Robertson.
[78] Bailey was a busy man at the 1879 session of the legislature, what with fighting the Wisconsin Central exemption bill, supporting a measure to repeal the law allowing counties to vote aid to railways, opposing the bill for the division of Clark and Marathon Counties, and opposing a bill to permit a group of lumbermen to build a dam and charge tolls at Fork Red Cedar Lake, Barron County. He was also conducting a case before the Supreme Court (W. F. Bailey, Madison, February 21, 1879, to Smith Robertson.
[79] *Colby Phonograph*, February 26, 1879.
[80] *North Wisconsin News* (Clear Lake, Polk County), February 7, 21, 1879; *Madison Democrat*, February 8, 18, 1879; *Barron County Shield*, February 20, 27, 1879; *Laws of Wisconsin*, 1879, pp. 21-24.

Central measure was much sharper and more prolonged, and, like the battle of 1877, left much ill feeling in its wake.

Effective in support of the exemption measure were Charles L. Colby and his attractive wife, whom he brought to Madison for the occasion. Her charms were used so effectively that Smith Robertson complained because she was "lobbying sharply" with her husband. Colby, Robertson said, made "most desperate and plausable [sic] efforts" to win support by calling "to his aid by telegraph & by rail every influence he can from all parts of the state."[81] There is plenty of evidence, however, to show that the same methods were employed on both sides. Votes were swapped, compromises were arranged, promises were made, and talk of monopolies and corruption was common. If the railroad lobby, the subsidized press, and the express and telegraph companies were on the side of the Wisconsin Central, on the other were land speculators, large lumbermen, the Wisconsin Valley Railroad, and other special interests, in addition to Cornell University.[82]

As introduced, the bill provided that the lands of the Wisconsin Central be exempted from taxation for five years. The opposition was so keen, however, that the measure was changed to make it somewhat more palatable to northern Wisconsin and, as one opponent said, to make it easier for some members under obligation to the railroad to vote for it. As passed by the senate, where its support was strongest, the bill would have extended exemption for five years but would have required the Wisconsin Central, in return for this privilege, to sell all land suitable for farming north of Medford for not over $2.50 an acre and to pay, in addition to the excise tax, $13,000 a year to the state to be distributed to the counties in proportion to the amount of Wisconsin Central land they contained.[83] This payment of $13,000 a year was only a slight concession to gain votes, a "sop," as Smith Robertson called it.[84] Opposition was stronger in the assembly, but even here the railroad lobby was well

[81] S. Robertson, Madison, February 17, 1879, to J. W. Williams.
[82] *Id.* to *id.*, Eau Claire, March 5, 1879.
[83] *Colby Phonograph*, February 19, 26, 1879.
[84] S. Robertson, Madison, February 20, 1879, to J. W. Williams.

entrenched. Three members of the senate who had voted for the bill lobbied openly in the assembly to line up members in support of it. Smart manoeuvring by the opposition defeated their efforts, and the measure failed of adoption by a vote of 45 to 52.[85] Cornell could well feel that its agents had won a notable victory over the Wisconsin Central Railroad.

Another point at issue between Cornell University and the Wisconsin Central related to the right-of-way. Because the university's lands were selected before the line of the railroad was surveyed, the Wisconsin Central had to acquire a right-of-way through them. In northern Wisconsin it was the usual practice for landowners to donate the right-of-way or to sell it for a small consideration because the railroad when completed would enhance the value of their tracts. The Cornell agents regarded the matter differently. They considered railroads an additional hazard to their property because forest fires were frequently started by sparks from the locomotives. Since much of the university's land was close to the main logging streams the railroad was not so essential to it as it was to more remote land. Sage maintained that the railroad should pay full value for all land it needed for its right-of-way, a position from which he refused to withdraw regardless of the railroad's threats to take the matter into the courts and have the land condemned.[86] Sage doubtless took the view that Colby and other financiers associated with him in the Wisconsin Central were wealthy, could afford to pay full value for the land, and should be allowed no charity. Roy L. Martin, in his entertaining *History of the Wisconsin Central,* has characterized Cornell's policy toward the railroad and the right-of-way question in this manner:

Cornell agents were highly mercenary in the disposal of their lands, and unlike the Wisconsin Central, were not interested in local improvements and developments, thereby retarding the growth and settlement of that particular area.

[85] Telegram of S. Robertson, Madison, February 27, 1879, to J. W. Williams.
[86] E. B. Phillips, Milwaukee, September 25, 1876, to H. W. Sage; W. F. Bailey, Eau Claire, December 25, 1878, to Sage (copy); *Chippewa Herald,* April 1, 1881.

Despite the bitterness engendered by the struggle over tax exemption, amicable relations were soon established between the officials of the Wisconsin Central and of Cornell University, for now both groups were deeply interested in keeping down local government expenditures.[87] Furthermore, the railroad was completed in 1877 from Stevens Point to Ashland and could expect no further county aid, save for any branch lines that it might project. There was to be rivalry in the future over sales of land, rights-of-way, and the location of station sites, but nothing comparable to the fight over tax exemption.

Cornell University was involved in a final controversy over local aid to railroads in 1885. Sawyer County, newly created two years before, wished to have railroads constructed through it. When a proposal was submitted for a county subsidy of $70,000 to aid a railroad connecting Hayward with the Lac Court Oreilles Indian Reservation, the people approved it. Knapp, Stout & Co., who had large holdings in Sawyer County, were disturbed at the prospect of higher taxes, the chief benefit of which would go to a rival lumbering company logging in the vicinity of the proposed line.[88] They informed the Cornell people of the impending move and Bailey secured an injunction to restrain the county from issuing the bonds. For his action Bailey was again accused of working for non-resident taxpayers against the settlers.[89]

Cornell's chief conflicts over taxation, expenditures of local governments, local aid to railroads, and the creation of new counties took place in the seventies, when its agents provided the leadership for the opposition. In the eighties its lands were being sold to other interests which took its place in these matters. Its period of prominence in the development of Wisconsin was over.

[87] S. Robertson, Eau Claire, March 5, 1879, to J. W. Williams.
[88] Knapp, Stout & Co., Menomonie, July 13, 1885, to E. L. Williams.
[89] S. Robertson, Eau Claire, August 1, 1885, to E. L. Williams; *Taylor County Star and News*, August 8, 1885.

CHAPTER TEN

Sales of Pine Land

IT IS now clear that when Ezra Cornell undertook to buy the New York land scrip and to enter with it some 900,000 acres of land in the West for the benefit of Cornell University he had little conception of the magnitude or complexity of the burden he had assumed or of the risks involved. He was assured by Woodward that almost from the outset the income from the land would be sufficient to carry the investment and that there would be little drain on his private resources. Woodward and Cornell apparently expected that timberland values would rise quickly after news of their land entries became known and that within a comparatively short period the demand for pine would be sufficient to enable them to sell at prices ranging from $5 to $25 an acre.[1]

These optimistic expectations were not to be fulfilled. Pine lands, save those close to mills and the main drivable streams, became a drug on the market, so rapidly did the Federal Government offer its land in Michigan, Wisconsin, and Minnesota at auction sale. Lumbermen like Knapp-Stout and the Eau Claire Lumber Company bought sufficient pine land to meet their needs for ten or fifteen years; the down-river millmen were supplied by independent loggers until well into the seventies; and numerous speculators who had rashly bought quantities of pine land anxiously awaited a chance to unload at a profit. There was, therefore, little prospect of disposing of the bulk of the university's land for years to come. On top of this situation came the financial crash of 1873 and a long period of industrial inactivity. The western market for pine lumber

[1] Ezra Cornell, New York City, September 19, 1870, to A. D. White (White MSS); W. A. Woodward, Vail's Gate, December 20, 1870, to Cyrus Woodman (Woodman MSS).

contracted at once, loggers and millmen reduced their cuts drastically, and pine land became unsalable.

Meantime, taxes were increasing and the costs of management, including the numerous suits necessary to protect the land against depredators, were mounting. At Ithaca the university was desperately in need of money. Furthermore, Ezra Cornell had taken an active part in promoting a number of railroads centering at Ithaca, all of which were absorbing his capital. These various demands on his purse made it imperative for him to sell a portion of the land even if in doing so he sacrificed future chances for profits.

To provide some ready money for the university and for the taxes on its land, Cornell and Woodward attempted to organize a land company, to be financed by friends of the university, which should take over 100,000 acres of land at $5 an acre. A charter was secured from the New York legislature for the organization of the New York Lumber, Manufacturing & Improvement Company, the capital stock of which was to be $600,000. The objects of the company were "the purchase, improvement, and sale of timber and other lands, the manufacture and sale of lumber, the improvement of a town-site and water power, and the sale, renting, and leasing thereof in the State of Wisconsin." [2]

Anticipating such a venture, Cornell had arranged through Woodward and Putnam for the purchase of the water-power site at Brunet Falls, some little distance above Chippewa Falls on the Chippewa River. This site was to be taken over by the new company. A city called Cornell was to be laid out, mills, houses, and other improvements were to be constructed and leased or sold, and pine lands in the neighborhood were to be acquired to supply the mills. The prospectus of the company contained some highly optimistic assertions, such as that lumbermen in the Green Bay area made a profit of $50 an acre on cutting their pine lands, and the following description of the property acquired for the company:

The property is constantly increasing in value. It cannot fail to yield a profit greater than simple interest. The dividends must be large, and there can be

[2] Act of April 23, 1867, *Laws of New York*, 1867, Chap. 663.

no loss. The property is not speculative; is not put in at high prices; there is no party behind the curtain to realize and pocket large profits at the expense of others; there is no expectation of remuneration by a turn of good luck; no game of chance; no hope of making large dividends by speculation. It is an investment in good substantial property, worth double its cost, and sure under good management to pay large dividends. . . .[3]

Water power was certainly available at the site of the proposed metropolis, but it could only be used at that time for sawmills, and of these there was an abundance at Chippewa Falls and Eau Claire, each of which was being promoted aggressively by able leaders. Cornell and Woodward had no experience in lumbering, lacked the capital and entrepreneurial skill for such an undertaking, and were too old for new enterprises. The proposed city of Cornell was as visionary a scheme as numerous other paper communities laid out by land speculators, and it was fortunate for the university that Cornell failed to induce capitalists to risk funds in the project.

Sales of Cornell land in the first decade after they were acquired were confined to small purchases except for the large contracts arranged with Sage, McGraw, and Dwight—described below. Between 50,000 and 100,000 acres of farm land had been selected and from the outset there was some demand for it. These sales were made on time and brought in little immediate cash, but they promised well for the future and helped to stiffen Ezra Cornell's resolution to retain the land until the higher prices that Woodward and Putnam promised could be obtained. Furthermore, these contracts called for interest on delayed payments of seven and in some cases ten per cent, which was a better return than the university could get on other investments.[4] To compete with other land companies, Cornell did some advertising in the seventies to attract settlers, but with little effect.[5]

During this period of dull sales the university was troubled by depredations upon its timber that threatened to reduce if not to

---

[3] *Prospectus of the New York Lumber, Manufacturing and Improvement Co.* (Albany, 1867), pp. 15–16. Cf. *Ithaca Journal*, October 22, 1867.

[4] J. W. Williams, Ithaca, April 20, 1877, to Smith Robertson.

[5] *Id.*, Ithaca, May 1, 1877, to *id.*; S. Robertson, Eau Claire, February 25, 1890, to E. L. Williams; W. Dahlke, Reserve, Erie County, New York, August 13, 1879, to J. W. Williams; *Lincoln County Advocate*, February 22, 1879.

destroy the value of its land investment. In the Wisconsin pineries no man's land was safe from timber thieves if it contained valuable timber. Land owned by absentees or speculators was the more commonly attacked, and the pinery newspapers, generally controlled by the "county ring," most of whose members were land agents, frequently warned absentee owners that their property would soon become worthless unless they employed local agents to protect it.[6] Constant supervision was necessary and that entailed keeping men in the woods much of the time. Cornell University sustained considerable losses from timber depredations, but its land holdings were so large and its investment so great that, unlike many other land speculators, it found it practicable to keep agents in the woods on the watch for timber thieves.

There were many refinements in timber stealing, as the Cornell agents soon discovered. It was a common practice for individuals to acquire a quarter section in the vicinity of a heavy stand of pine and then to strip off the pine from bordering tracts. When haled before the court the offender could swear that the corners were difficult to find and that he had inadvertently cut over the line. His timber might be seized but the owner then had the trouble either of selling it in the woods or of driving it to the mill towns. Cornell took both courses when Putnam was in charge, but returns were meager and not very satisfactory from either. Another practice was for some small logger who operated "on a shoestring" to buy from Cornell a few hundred acres of pine land on several years' credit. The logger would then quickly strip off the timber and dispose of it while the agents were busy elsewhere. The university found it extremely difficult to deal with such cases, for the Wisconsin law seemed to favor the logger against the landowner. Cornell's treasurer, exasperated at the constant failure to secure damages from trespassers, observed:

It appears that the Laws of Wisconsin throws [sic] its arms about and around the loggers in such an effectual and intimate fashion that nothing but "perjury" which must be proved in open court, will suffice to penetrate the legal armor of the poor logger. A contract may be violated in the most shame-

[6] *Wisconsin River Pilot*, February 6, 1869, and April 24, 1874.

ful manner, the logs removed and sold without the least security, and a payment may be deferred for nearly a year after it is due, for the reason that the Law is so intricate upon the point that a grave question presents itself whether the payment is due upon the date mentioned in the contract.[7]

During the seventies the university made a number of contracts with such shoestring loggers out of which it acquired an almost endless series of disputes, court actions, and long-delayed payments. It naturally preferred, thereafter, to deal with responsible parties like Knapp-Stout, the Eau Claire Lumber Company, or the Mississippi River Logging Company and its numerous associates.

Another hazard associated with investments in timber lands which made owners wish for early sales was that of the windstorms which swept through the pineries. Sometimes the blow would affect only a few thousand acres; at other times it would range over ten townships or more, like the tornado which struck Chippewa County in 1872. This storm blew down an estimated 200,000,000 feet of pine, not over fifteen per cent of which could be salvaged.[8] In 1874 and again in 1875 Putnam hired loggers to cut the down timber on a number of hundred acres of Cornell land, and in the former year, because of the absence of buyers, he drove the logs down the Chippewa to find a purchaser.

When Putnam first began to sell the Cornell land he followed the Wisconsin practice of selling stumpage when the land itself was not wanted. It was the custom for the buyer of timber to pay the taxes on the land until cutting was done, at which time it was abandoned by both buyer and seller. In 1875 the officials of the university decided to make no further sales of stumpage but to insist upon selling both the timber and the land. By this means it was presumed higher prices could be obtained than from sales of stumpage alone. Against this decision Putnam appealed with the most telling argument that it was contrary to custom and that no lumberman in Wisconsin could be induced to pay for land for which he had no use after the timber

[7] J. W. Williams, Ithaca, June 19, 1876, to H. C. Putnam.
[8] *Chippewa Herald*, November 2, 1872; *Ashland Press*, October 5, 1872.

was cut.⁹ At that time he protested in vain, but later he had the satisfaction of seeing the university reverse itself. This reversal of policy, which was put into effect in 1880, was most fortunate for Cornell, since it made it possible for the university to sell timber off many tracts several times over as rising stumpage prices made marketable what was previously regarded as of no value. Under the new policy the purchaser was required to pay the taxes on all the land involved in a stumpage contract until the timber was cut and the contract fulfilled.¹⁰ This shifted the burden of taxes to purchasers even though they had no equity in the land and made it easier for the university to carry its land until the hard woods and second growth, as well as the land itself, came into demand.

Cornell University derived little income from the sale of its land until 1871. Woodward's promise that the property would carry itself soon proved absurd, and the costs of administration and taxes threatened to exhaust all resources. Ezra Cornell's own funds were stretched to the limit to meet these obligations. Relief came from two friends of the university, Henry W. Sage and John McGraw.

Henry W. Sage, a former resident of Ithaca, had been elected a trustee of Cornell University in 1870. Like John McGraw, Hiram Sibley, and Ezra Cornell himself, all early trustees of the new university, Sage was a man of large business interests. He orginally engaged in the lumbering industry in a small way in New York State. Later he built great mills on the Saginaw River in Michigan, where he sawed the logs floated down from his tracts on the headwaters of that important logging stream. The supervision of his logging operations, his giant sawmills, the marketing of lumber, and the cruising and purchasing of pine lands made him a busy man with little time for leisure. In 1880 he returned to Ithaca and lived there for the remainder of his life. From the outset of his connection with Cornell University Sage devoted many hours and days each year to its needs.

⁹ J. W. Williams, Ithaca, March 30, April 8, 1875, to Putnam; Putnam, Eau Claire, November 20, 1875, to J. W. Williams; E. L. Williams, Ithaca, February 5, 1880, to Abner Gile, La Crosse.
¹⁰ E. L. Williams, Ithaca, May 1, 1893, to Smith Robertson.

He thoroughly sympathized with the kind of program Ezra Cornell and Andrew D. White were carrying out and gave to it liberally his time and his money. Sage College for Women, the Sage School of Philosophy, Sage Chapel, Sage Library, and other gifts testify to loyal support of the university by himself and his family.

John McGraw, another wealthy lumberman, whose residence was in Ithaca, but whose lumber interests stretched from Albany through Ontario to the Saginaw Valley, and into Wisconsin and Iowa, was Sage's partner in numerous enterprises. At a time when the affairs of Cornell University seemed to have reached their lowest point, Sage and McGraw decided to come to its assistance.

When the pressure for funds threatened to swamp him, Cornell inserted in the *Ithaca Journal* an advertisement for the sale of the lands.[11] Shortly afterwards, Sage and McGraw, who were buying a good deal of pine land in the Chippewa Valley, offered to purchase 100,000 acres of pine land at $4 an acre provided they might choose the area in which the land was to be taken and within that area select only those 80-acre tracts on which the merchantable pine averaged at least 4000 board feet to the acre. Cornell assured Sage and McGraw that practically all the land would prove to have a greater amount of pine than 4000 feet, basing his statement on the assertions of Woodward and Putnam. No careful examination of the land had as yet been made, but Putnam was one of the smartest judges of pine in Wisconsin and there was good reason for Cornell's confidence.

Woodward was extremely jealous of his position as intermediary between Cornell and Putnam and was fearful that the two would sooner or later come to realize that his position was expensive and useless. He was then pressing for a settlement of his account, and meanwhile did not want the land business to get out of his hands, nor did he want Sage and McGraw to intrude themselves into it. He therefore opposed the sale, arguing that the land would soon be worth $25 an acre and should not be sold for less than $5.[12]

---

[11] *Ithaca Journal,* June 28, 1870.
[12] Ezra Cornell, New York City, September 19, 1870, to A. D. White; W. A. Woodward, Vail's Gate, December 20, 1870, to Cyrus Woodman; *id.,* December 30, 1870, to Cornell.

Cornell was better advised and the sale was made. At the same time Cornell arranged for a sale of 50,000 acres on the same terms to John McGraw and his brother Thomas, both of Ithaca, and Jeremiah W. Dwight of Dryden. Both contracts provided that payments were to be extended over a period of ten years with interest of 6 per cent. The following year Sage and McGraw offered to take an additional 100,000 acres at $5 an acre. Cornell was reluctant to sell more land at the time, for he still hoped for the promised $25 an acre. Pressure by the members of the board of trustees, however, induced him to consent.[13] In these three contracts about one-half the land that Cornell had acquired was sold for $1,100,000, which was an excellent profit for the short time it had been held. An additional income of $66,000 seemed assured to the university which would more than cover the cost of carrying the remaining lands.

Sage, the two McGraws, and Dwight were all shrewd lumbermen who were familiar with timber values and business methods. They drew up contracts which gave them the right to select the choicest of the land and to reject all poor tracts. They sent a crew of skilled examiners to cruise the lands for the purpose of ascertaining which tracts contained the minimum amount of merchantable pine stipulated in the contracts. A careful and systematic examination was conducted and for the first time fair estimates as to the amount of standing timber on many of the tracts were obtained. These estimates were disconcerting, for they showed that much of the land had little merchantable pine and that even more of it did not have 4000 board feet to the acre. Sage was discouraged and persuaded Cornell to revoke the two contracts with Sage and McGraw for 100,000 acres each. Later Sage and McGraw agreed to buy 50,000 acres at $4 an acre.[14]

Subsequent examinations and logging experience were to show that Sage's land examiners had greatly underrated the Cornell land.

[13] Petition of October 11, 1871, signed by Horace Greeley, Andrew D. White, Hiram Sibley, Alonzo B. Cornell, and others (White Papers); statement of Francis M. Finch, December 20, 1873, "Testimony in investigation of the College Land Grants, etc.," New York, *Senate Document*, 103, January, 1874, p. 275.
[14] Henry W. Sage, New York, September 16, November 27, 1872, to Ezra Cornell.

In buying timber it was doubtless good business practice to set a conservative estimate on one's intended purchase, but Sage's timber cruisers seem to have been much too cautious. The explanation seems to be that Sage's men, like Sage himself, were accustomed to Michigan pineries, where the pine was generally thicker and of better quality than in the Chippewa Valley. They disregarded the Norway pine, spruce, hemlock, and hardwoods, all of which were subsequently to come into demand, and they also failed to evaluate the smaller pines, which, within a few years, when the larger trees were exhausted, were to be cut commercially. It should be pointed out that at a later time Sage changed his mind with regard to the amount of pine on a substantial part of the Cornell land and was the one who held out for high prices in the eighties.

Sage & McGraw and McGraw & Dwight proceeded with the selection of their 100,000 acres of land under the two contracts, which were carried through. That they secured choice land is shown by its subsequent resale at high prices.

Shares in the McGraw & Dwight purchase were taken by Douglass Boardman, a legal associate of McGraw, and by Henry C. Putnam. The latter was in charge of the McGraw & Dwight land while serving at the same time as agent for Cornell University. Since the university's lands were not selling, because of the high price for which they were held and because the more accessible lands had been taken by Sage, McGraw, and Dwight, Putnam was eager to find a purchaser for the McGraw & Dwight tracts. When he learned that some of the Mississippi River millmen needed more pine he courted them assiduously. He offered to join with them if they would buy the 50,000 acres from McGraw & Dwight, and although he was employed by the university to get the best possible prices for its land he undertook to persuade it to sell them an additional 31,000 acres at the lowest price obtainable. Putnam had come to have grievances against the university officials, who were keeping a tighter rein on him than Ezra Cornell had. He disliked the restraints placed on his authority, resented the constant demands that he should exercise more care in making tax payments and in keeping his books, and felt that his compensation was inadequate for the labor and services that he performed. By 1875 he had reached a position where his other land business was more remunerative to him than the agency for the university's land and had begun to put his other interests first.

After a complicated series of negotiations, Putnam succeeded in selling the 50,000 acres to the Mississippi River Logging Company for $10 an acre. During the five years that McGraw, Dwight, Boardman, and Putnam had held the land it had cost them—in taxes, interest at 6 per cent on the investment, wages to timber cruisers, and miscellaneous expenses—$81,454, leaving them a profit of $219,192 on an investment in which their actual cash outlay was small.[15] Putnam's shrewd management accomplished this quick success.

The Sage & McGraw lands were not sold as promptly but they brought in far larger sums. Not until the eighties did Sage begin to sell his share. By that time the rapid exhaustion of pine on lands owned by lumbermen had forced them into active bidding for tracts still held by speculators. Prices went up rapidly. In Price County, where most of his lands were located, Sage made sales at prices ranging from $20 to $50 an acre. His total sales in this county of land bought from Cornell were 22,305 acres for which he received $640,907, or an average of more than $28 an acre.[16] This meant an appreciation of 700 per cent in twelve years.

It has not been possible to trace so fully the disposal of the McGraw share of the 50,000-acre purchase, but the following statistics are significant. By 1881 20,679,000 board feet of pine had been cut on 2807 acres, which was nearly double the minimum called for in the Sage & McGraw contract. At the valuation prevailing in 1880 and 1881 this timber would be worth at least $40,000, or more than $14 an acre. The pine alone on 13,783 acres, then in the possession of W. J. Young & Co. of Clinton, Iowa, a firm in which John McGraw was largely interested before his death, was estimated to be worth $290,000, or better than $21 an acre. On an additional 4680 acres,

---

[15] *Eau Claire Free Press*, October 25, 1875; H. C. Putnam, Eau Claire, October 26, 1875, to J. W. Williams; J. W. Williams, Ithaca, January 5, June 29, 1878, to J. W. Dwight.

[16] Compiled from Price County Deed Records.

from which one-half to two-thirds of the pine had been cut, the timber was valued at $38,075, or about $8 an acre.[17]

On the basis of prices received in the eighties by Cornell University one may conclude that Sage had secured some of the choicest land the university owned. The fact that he was a member of the board of trustees at the time the purchase was made gave rise to criticism later. Like other business men of the time, Sage, though annoyed and resentful at the criticism, disdained to answer it, apparently believing that his action showed his good intentions. That Sage had no thought of profiting at the expense of the university is clear from a communication of 1875, in which he stated it to be his purpose to return all the profit he made from the transaction to the university.[18] The subsequent donations of Sage and members of his family to Cornell University were, in fact, much larger than the profit which he made from the transaction in its pine lands. McGraw also planned to return the profits he made from the purchase of Cornell land. In his lifetime he gave generously to the university, and upon the death of his daughter, Jennie McGraw Fiske, the bulk of the McGraw estate was willed to Cornell. Although the will was later broken by the McGraw family and by Willard Fiske, husband of Jennie McGraw, a part of the McGraw fortune came to the university under Fiske's will.

Ezra Cornell had been much elated by the three large contracts for the sale of 250,000 acres, although they were for sums much smaller than he had hoped to receive, and he was sorely tried by the reports of the land examiners and the resulting cancellation of sales to the amount of 150,000 acres. His own resources were being strained to the limit by constant drafts for taxes and administrative expenses on the land. At the same time he was being badgered by Woodward, who had brought suit for $160,000 compensation for making the land entries, work which appeared at the time to have been badly done. Furthermore, Cornell's railroad schemes were proving unprofit-

---

[17] The data on the McGraw lands are compiled from New York Court of Appeals, *McGraw-Fiske Estate*, 5, pp. 2627–2630.

[18] *Proceedings*, Board of Trustees of Cornell University, 1865–1885 (Ithaca, 1940), p. 139.

able, for the panic of 1873 had brought disaster to them as well as to numerous other such enterprises in the country. Gloomy, indeed, was the outlook. The lands were not paying their own way nor was there any early prospect of their doing so. True, the two sales to Sage, McGraw, and Dwight were bringing in enough to meet taxes, but the needs of the expanding university were not being met nor were the costs of administering the lands covered. Furthermore, Cornell was now approaching the twilight of his career and could not be expected to continue to carry the land business. In 1874 the university trustees agreed to take over the Cornell lands and to reimburse Ezra Cornell for the outlays that he had made on them. Thereafter Sage and McGraw took active charge of land policies and of the establishment of prices, while the administrative routine was left to the treasurer of the university, to whom the Wisconsin agent was made directly responsible.

The land policy of Ezra Cornell was never clearly defined, and it was not until the lands had been taken over by the university that any well considered principles can be seen in their management. Under Sage's leadership a policy of land disposal was outlined which was clearer than anything previously in existence, but as it was based on conditions which were constantly changing it was never clearly stated to the public. The university did not establish minimum prices for its land and advertise it for sale on that basis, but did, through its agents, invite bids from loggers and millmen. All bids were carefully considered and if they seemed to represent the fair value of the property they were accepted. Usually, however, there followed a period of dickering in which Putnam or Robertson or Sage attempted to get the price raised.

Sage and McGraw were doubtless dismayed when they discovered in what a wretched condition the land titles and the records of the land business were. Even the patents were still in Woodward's hands, although he had not been employed by Cornell for three years. Taxes had not been systematically paid, some lands had been permitted to revert to public ownership because they were of little value, there was reason to believe that some tracts bearing heavy stands of pine had been sold at low prices, the books both at Ithaca and Eau Claire were poorly posted, and the information available as to the amount of timber on any tract was totally inadequate. The situation was described by Joseph W. Williams, treasurer of the university, as follows:

> You well remember how ignorant we all were at this end of the line of what had been done. That we were utterly at sea, without a rudder, whenever an attempt was made to get at past transactions, and that beyond the mere acc't of cash pd. & rec. we had nothing, not a copy of a contract, no record of deeds, nor of securities rec'd.[19]

Under the new management order was slowly brought out of chaos. A carefully devised system of bookkeeping was introduced to enable the land committee and the treasurer to keep in touch with each tract and to know when the taxes were paid on them, what the estimated stand of timber was, whether it had been damaged by windstorms or fires, and whether any depredations had been committed on it. All decisions as to prices, major expenditures, and policies concerning tax disputes were henceforth to be determined in Ithaca, and the Wisconsin agent was deprived of practically all authority.

The scattered sales made in the late sixties and early seventies by Putnam with the approval of Ezra Cornell were entered into with nothing but superficial estimates of the merchantable pine. Sage was convinced that the university could well afford to retain its land until a full and fair price was offered, and that no distress sales should be made. After he became chairman of the land committee sales were made more cautiously and never without a reasonably accurate estimate of the amount of pine on each tract. As stumpage increased in value greater caution was used in making estimates of pine, and by the late eighties the university had compiled figures which enabled it to get the fullest price for its land. Sage had to deal with some of the shrewdest judges of timber in the Lake States, like Weyerhaeuser and Knapp-Stout, and the respect which they had for his figures of stumpage and prices indicates that he was their equal in driving bargains.

By the eighties Cornell's land policy was well outlined. Stumpage

[19] J. W. Williams, Ithaca, March 13, 1875, to H. C. Putnam.

estimates were rarely given, but prospective buyers were invited to cruise tracts and form their own judgments. Bids were asked but initial prices were not announced. After the bargaining had gone on for some time and the university had decided upon its minimum demand it would sometimes let this price be known to others, but it reserved the right to change the price at any time. If there seemed to be special interest displayed in some tract by a number of competitors, timber cruisers would be despatched at once into the region to determine the reason for the excitement. Rivalry over dam sites, particularly choice clumps of superior pine, or tracts adjacent to other sections on which lumbering was then being conducted might, if judiciously handled, enable the university to obtain fancy prices. Sage kept watch over developments in the Wisconsin pineries and quickly sensed any changes which might raise prices.

Scattered sales in small lots continued to be made during the seventies. Small operators looking for a "logging chance," lumbermen who were detected cutting illegally on university land, Knapp-Stout and other millmen who found university tracts adjacent to their own which it was advisable to cut together, and settlers in the vicinity bought areas ranging from 80 to a few thousand acres. The Mississippi River Logging Company, in addition to its purchase of the McGraw & Dwight tract of 50,000 acres, bought from the university 2149 acres for $8775 in 1875 and 185 acres for $3100 in 1877. A summary for the early years is given in Table 8, on the next page.

These sales helped to meet the cost of carrying the land, but the returns they brought in were, after all, insignificant. Cornell's dream of leaving a large endowment for his university seemed unlikely to be realized unless land values went up and the demand for timber substantially increased.

In the dark days of the seventies a great potential demand for lumber was being created. Although immigration declined in this period and reached its lowest point in 1878, when fewer persons came to the United States than in any year since the Civil War, it did not come to a halt. Over a million immigrants were received in the depression years, 1874 to 1879, a larger proportion of whom went west

TABLE 8
CORNELL SALES OF LAND AND OF STUMPAGE [20]

Year	LAND		STUMPAGE	
	Acres	Price	Acres	Price
1866	800	$ 1,240	—	—
1868	1,103	6,699	—	—
1869	1,361	8,500	—	—
1870	51,338	207,168	—	—
1871	4,173	23,000	80	$ 400
1872	50,678	207,600	156	927
1873	480	2,811	1,311	4,090
1874	2,272	16,515	9,602	38,166
1875	7,327	33,846	7,051	27,577
1876	14,437	68,112	—	—
1877	4,509	25,897	—	—
1878	2,634	16,393	—	—

than probably would have done so in a period of greater industrial activity. They were joined by displaced Americans who continued to abandon the rural sections of the East and who were beginning to leave Indiana, Ohio, and Illinois for the cheap lands farther west. These people were pressing into Kansas and Nebraska, southern Minnesota, and Dakota territory, where they were building sod shanties and temporary dwellings until they could accumulate funds enough to buy lumber for frame houses and barns. Their coming added to the demand for railroads, stimulated the growth of many little towns throughout the Great Plains as well, and made possible the rapid development of such urban centers as Chicago, Milwaukee, St. Louis, Quincy, Dubuque, Des Moines, Topeka, and Kansas City. Pine lumber was the chief material with which these towns were built.

In 1879 and 1880 prosperity returned. The dammed-up needs of America burst the depression bonds and created a great era of industrial expansion. Factories reopened or enlarged their equipment; railroad construction was resumed on a large scale, and the demand for labor reached unparalleled proportions. Millions of Europeans

---

[20] The figures for 1866–1875 are taken from Letter Book "Western Lands, 1881–1883," p. 247; those for years after 1875 are compiled from "Conveyance Record" (MSS), vol. i. Statistics of land sales given in the reports of the State Comptroller and in the proceedings of the McGraw-Fiske will case are somewhat different from these. The figures used in this chapter are for calendar years.

had been waiting impatiently for this opportunity and now they grasped it. In the single year 1882 over three-quarters of a million immigrants reached our shores. No small share of these immigrants found homes in the frontier states of Nebraska and Minnesota and in Dakota Territory.

The rapid development of the Great Plains and the expanding population and rising standard of living in older frontier communities created an unprecedented demand for lumber which caught many millmen unprepared. Between 1877 and 1882 the annual cut of white pine in the three Lake States more than doubled, as is shown in Table 9. The importance of the Chippewa Valley pinery to the

TABLE 9

ANNUAL CUT OF WHITE PINE IN MICHIGAN, WISCONSIN, AND MINNESOTA, 1877–1882 [21]

Year	Board Feet	Year	Board Feet
1877	3,595,000,000	1880	5,651,000,000
1878	3,629,000,000	1881	6,768,000,000
1879	4,806,000,000	1882	7,552,000,000

lumber industry of the Lake States is indicated by an estimate of the amount of lumber cut in several regions on the Mississippi River and its tributaries in the winter of 1881–1882, as shown in Table 10.

Increasing demands for lumber sent prices upwards, mills were

TABLE 10

LOGS CUT IN THE WINTER OF 1881–1882 [22]

Region	Board Feet
St. Croix Valley	123,000,000
Chippewa Valley	475,000,000
Black River Valley	112,000,000
Wolf River Valley	140,000,000
Lake Superior Country	186,000,000
Mississippi Valley above the St. Croix	952,000,000
Area of the Wisconsin Valley Railroad	170,000,000
Area of the Wisconsin Central Railroad	175,000,000
Miscellaneous	240,000,000

[21] *Northwestern Lumberman*, February 18, 1888, p. 8.
[22] *Lumberman's Gazette* in *Phillips Times*, March 4, 1882.

forced to expand, and both loggers and millmen found their depleted stock and even their stumpage inadequate. At the same time another factor intervened to add to the growing scramble for stumpage.

For many years Americans had wastefully used their heritage in minerals, soils, and forests. European travellers, accustomed to more careful exploitation of these resources, were shocked by the careless methods of mining, the unscientific cultivation of the soil, and the reckless cutting of standing timber. Their comments brought a few Americans to realize that the country's natural resources should be scientifically managed and conserved, but not until after the Civil War was there any concerted movement to do anything about such matters.

An unparalleled onslaught upon the forests of the Lake States was produced by the great sweep of settlers into the treeless country west of the Mississippi. White pine was the preferred lumber, and whereever it could be found it was threatened with quick destruction. The timber along the drivable streams was first taken, and then, as prices rose, lumbermen found it profitable to cut at a greater distance from streams and to haul the logs to the river bank for the spring freshet. When the hauls became too long for oxen and horses, logging railroads were constructed. Withal went an increase in price, and a threatening scarcity. This situation could not but impress the East, where the white pine was already nearly exhausted and where its price had reached levels which forced building contractors to use inferior lumber. Here then is the background for the conservation movement, the purpose of which was to institute certain controls in the system of cutting timber and to set aside certain areas as forest preserves to be used when privately owned land had been exhausted.

In 1880 professional forestry was in its infancy in the United States and the conservation movement, if it were to gain headway, had to win support from other groups. True, Charles S. Sargent of the Arnold Arboretum, Bernhard E. Fernow, Franklin Hough, and other professional men organized associations, wrote numerous tracts and government pamphlets, and gave public addresses to arouse interest in conservation. Their efforts were ably assisted by the work of certain important lumbermen, notably Henry C. Putnam and William Little. Some of the lumber trade journals also supported the movement. An opinion favorable to conservation was rapidly formed which produced Arbor Day, the tree-planting crusade, the Timber Culture Act, and numerous state measures for the more conservative utilization of standing timber. But most important in winning support for the conservation movement was the creation of a fear-psychology, so effectively used in modern advertising. This method, once it was tried and found effective, induced some of the conservationists to exaggerate unduly the danger of the nation's timber being exhausted at an early date.

During the seventies and eighties Sargent and other "arboriculturists" repeatedly warned the country that the white pine of the eastern states was practically exhausted and that at the existing rate of use the pine of the Lake States would soon be gone. An example is Sargent's article in the *North American Review* of October, 1882, in which he said:

Fatal inroads have already been made into the great pine forest of the North Atlantic region. Its wealth has been lavished with an unsparing hand; it has been wantonly and stupidly cut, as if its resources were endless; what has not been sacrificed to the ax has been allowed to perish by fire. The pine of New England and New York has already disappeared. Pennsylvania is nearly stripped of her pine, which only a few years ago appeared inexhaustible. The great north-western pine States, Michigan, Wisconsin, and Minnesota, can only show a few scattered remnants of the noble forests to which they owe their greatest superiority.

Such a statement, with its "approaching exhaustion" motive clearly stated, was widely copied by the press and in the journals of the lumber trade.[23]

Sargent's prominence in the field of forestry led to his appointment by the superintendent of the census as special agent to prepare a report for the Tenth Census on the forests of North America. Sargent delegated the actual task of preparing estimates of standing timber to eight men, among whom was Henry C. Putnam. The latter had

[23] For numerous quotations see *Forest Protection and the Tariff on Lumber. Spirit of the Press* (New York, 1883), 35 pp.

become one of the largest dealers in pine lands in Wisconsin and Minnesota and possessed a fortune estimated at half a million dollars.[24] As a result of his extensive operations, which included both lumbering and the buying and selling of pine land, he had acquired a special knowledge of the location and extent of pine in these states. Putnam had reached the conclusion that the white pine was being rapidly depleted and he agreed with Sargent, with whom he had formed a close friendship, that government action was necessary to prevent fires and careless cutting.[25]

Putnam was asked to prepare estimates of the merchantable standing white pine for the four most important states, Pennsylvania, Wisconsin, Michigan, and Minnesota. Here were located the last great stands of white pine in the United States; when they were exhausted this valuable tree would be a thing of the past. With the assistance of George W. Hotchkiss, secretary of the Chicago Lumber Exchange, Putnam prepared his estimates from reports of "timber-land owners and experts familiar with the forests," actual surveys wherever available, and his own personal knowledge of the Wisconsin-Minnesota pineries.[26] But it is clear that his figures came largely from persons who were interested in having the price of stumpage and lumber rise and that he himself was no disinterested investigator. The statistics which he presented shocked the lumber trade to its very founda-

TABLE 11
PUTNAM'S ESTIMATE OF STANDING WHITE PINE AND OF THE CUT FOR 1881 [27]

State	Standing	Cut for 1881
Pennsylvania	1,800,000,000 bd. ft.	380,000,000 bd. ft.
Michigan	35,000,000,000 " "	4,397,211,000 " "
Wisconsin	41,000,000,000 " "	2,097,299,000 " "
Minnesota	8,170,000,000 " "	540,997,000 " "
Total	95,970,000,000 " "	7,415,507,000 " "

[24] *Northwestern Lumberman*, November 27, 1880, p. 16.
[25] See Putnam's article, "Forest Fires," *American Journal of Forestry*, Franklin B. Hough, editor, i (October, 1882), pp. 27–30.
[26] *Tenth Census of the United States*, 1880, Vol. 9, by Charles S. Sargent, *Report of the Forests of North America* (Washington, 1884), pp. 506, 551.
[27] Compiled from *id.*

tion, for they indicated that, at the existing rate of cutting, the pine would be exhausted within a short period (see Table 11). Although Sargent's volume, *Report of the Forests of North America*, with maps and tables, was not to appear until 1884, Putnam's estimates were published in March, 1881, and immediately became the subject of much controversy.[28]

The *Northwestern Lumberman*, most influential lumber-trade journal of the upper Mississippi Valley, took the lead in attacking the estimates. It branded the writers of the report as "scarcity howlers" who were misleading and erroneous, and termed them "timber scribbling lunatics," or "denudiacs." The *Lumberman* declared: "It looks wonderfully as if the estimates were made under some tree that protected the 'expert' from the rays of the sun while he was making copy for the government printing office." The Minnesota figures should be trebled, in its opinion, and the others should be greatly increased. For Putnam the *Lumberman* had nothing but feelings of friendship, but it went on to say that it could not expect him to be accurate in estimates, since,

by instinct, association and policy he trains with the large body of men whose pockets demand that the price of pine lands be forced to the highest possible pitch. For years he has been a pine land agent and speculator, and the advance in pine has been his bread and butter.[29]

For years thereafter the *Lumberman* continued to denounce the estimates of 1880 and to parade statistics which disputed them.[30]

The attack of the *Lumberman* and of other trade journals which

[28] The figures for the standing white pine, as published in the *Northwestern Lumberman* for March 5, 1881, are as follows: Michigan, 35,000 million board feet; Wisconsin, 40,500 million board feet; Minnesota, 6150 million board feet; total (the amount for Pennsylvania was not given), 81,650 million board feet.

[29] *Northwestern Lumberman*, August 26, 1882, p. 5.

[30] The *Northwestern Lumberman* was much nearer correct than were Putnam and Sargent about the amount of merchantable white pine in the four states of Pennsylvania, Michigan, Wisconsin, and Minnesota. In the three last-named states alone 154,000,000,000 board feet of pine were cut between 1880 and 1900, or 60 per cent more than Putnam's figure for all four states, and it was estimated that there were at least 13,000,000,000 feet remaining uncut. (Statistics are from the *American Lumberman*, January 18, 1902, as quoted in the *Twelfth Census of the United States*, 1900, Vol. 9 [Washington, 1902], pp. 830, 836, 842–843.) The compiler of statistics on the lumber industry for the Twelfth Census took obvious pleasure in disparaging the "Sargent" estimates. (*Id.*, pp. 835–836, 842–843.)

followed its lead induced Sargent to reconsider the estimates. He was forced to admit that the original estimates included only pine trees with a diameter of 12 inches at a height of 24 feet from the ground.[31] Meantime the rising price of lumber had made it profitable for lumbermen to cut the smaller trees. It follows that the estimates were already out of date before Sargent's volumes finally appeared in 1884. This was partially admitted by Sargent, but he allowed an increase of only 10 per cent for the small timber which had come into use and the original estimates were, with slight changes, permitted to stand.

The *Lumberman's* attack upon the Putnam-Sargent figures was the keener because its editors felt that they were deliberately made small in order to "bull" the market. This certainly was the effect that the estimates had. Prices went up rapidly after 1881, although it should be noted that the improvement did not begin then. For example, the *Lincoln County Advocate* of September 22, 1879, described a growing lumber boom which was sending prices upward and increasing the demand for timber land. Similarly, the *Northwestern Lumberman* of December 6, 1879, remarked about sales of timber lands at rising prices, reports of which were coming in from all parts of the country. In December, 1880, the *Lumberman* reported—still before the appearance of the Putnam-Sargent figures—that stumpage on the Chippewa had advanced during the past year from 50 cents to $1 a thousand board feet and that Cornell University had increased its prices from $3 to $3.50 a thousand.[32] It is clear, however, that prices rose most rapidly during and after 1881. That the continued upward trend of prices was caused by the census report was recognized by the *Chippewa Herald* and was claimed by Putnam himself, who wrote to Cornell University, in November, 1883:

> I know I have added thousands of dollars to values of pine since my report & work for the U.S. of 1880 & 81 on forestry pine estimates, etc., in the then timber states, Mich. Wis. & Minn. Mr. Weyerhaeuser, the Prest. of

---

[31] C. S. Sargent, Brookline, Massachusetts, March 16, 1883, to H. C. Putnam; *Tenth Census,* 9, p. 551.

[32] *Northwestern Lumberman,* December 6, 1879, pp. 2–3, and December 11, 1880, p. 6.

M.R.L. Co. claims that I "have raised the cost of stumpage on them by my efforts" over $1.00 per M.[33]

The rising price of Wisconsin pine lands may be seen in a number of sales arranged between 1880 and 1882—at prices distinctly higher than any yet obtained—by Francis Palms, then one of the largest owners of pine land on the Chippewa (see Table 12).

TABLE 12
SALES OF PINE LAND BY FRANCIS PALMS, 1880–1882 [34]

Purchaser	Year	Acres	Amount
Robert M. Forsman, Williamsport, Pa.	1880	2,800	$ 27,500
Weyerhaeuser & Denkmann, Rock Island, Ill.	1880	19,981	191,147
Mississippi River Logging Company	1880	3,309	33,093
Renwick, Shaw & Crossett } Davenport, Iowa Lindsay & Phelps	1881	2,680	40,474
Sanger, Rockwell & Co., Milwaukee, Wis.	1881	3,836	38,362
Weyerhaeuser & Denkmann, Rock Island, Ill.	1882	2,296	19,785
Whitcomb & McLaren, Chippewa Falls, Wis.	1882	3,120	31,200
Totals		38,022	$381,561

Important sales by H. C. Putnam included an unstated acreage in Lincoln, Price, Taylor, Clark, Eau Claire, Chippewa, and Ashland Counties for $137,743; David Preston of Detroit sold 10,000 acres in Lincoln County for $130,000; Milton G. Shaw of Dover, Maine, sold to Weyerhaeuser & Denkmann 5640 acres for $115,000, and Patton Sherry of Neenah, Wisconsin, sold 3420 acres for $55,500. With such prices prevailing on the Chippewa, the Cornell lands, which contained the largest block of pine not in the hands of lumbermen, were certain to attract renewed interest.

The improvement in the lumber market, and perhaps the desire on the part of some of the officials of the university to dispose of the land at an early date, led to the formation of a New York syndicate to purchase 275,000 acres of Cornell land for $1,250,000, or about $4.50 an acre. There was a division among the members of the land committee over the matter, and the resulting delay prevented action until the market firmed sufficiently to justify a higher price. Fortu-

[33] *Chippewa Herald*, September 29, 1882; H. C. Putnam, Eau Claire, November 1, 1883, to S. D. Halliday.
[34] Compiled from Deed Records of Price, Chippewa, Rusk, and Taylor Counties.

nately for Cornell University, the syndicate then postponed and finally suspended further negotiations.[35] Within a few months these same lands were to bring $10 and even $15 an acre.

Cornell University felt the upward movement in pine-land prices in 1879, when 19,816 acres were sold for $105,262. In 1880 sales were larger, 13,221 acres being sold for $84,066 and the pine on 8394 acres for $69,600. Even more encouraging than the acreage and dollar value of the sales was the fact that most of the millmen on the Chippewa and its tributaries, such as the Eau Claire Lumber Company, Knapp-Stout, Daniel Shaw Lumber Company, and the Valley Lumber Company, were being forced to turn to the university to replenish their diminishing supplies of pine. Furthermore, the Mississippi River Logging Company, whose president, Frederick Weyerhaeuser, had recognized as early as 1878 that his associates would soon have to resort to Cornell University for their pine, was now increasing its purchases.[36] Best of all was the fact that the lands which had been rejected by Sage & McGraw in 1872 as not having sufficient quantities of merchantable pine were now attracting attention. For example, the pine on 2400 acres on the Black River in Clark County, estimated at nearly 5000 board feet to the acre, was sold in November, 1880, for $10 an acre, or double the price that Sage & McGraw had agreed to pay. The land itself was reserved, and was subsequently to be sold at prices ranging from $5 to $10 an acre. This sale was made to the firm of J. S. Keator & Son of Moline, Illinois, which was a member of the Mississippi River Logging Company. Another sale of pine on 4000 acres in Clark County was made to Charles L. Colman of La Crosse for $30,500. Also Murphy & Gaynor of Chippewa Falls bought 2841 acres on the Thornapple for $22,500.

The full effect of the Putnam estimates and the resulting increase in stumpage prices was felt by Cornell in 1881 and 1882, when the scramble for pine produced gratifying sales (see Table 13).

[35] E. L. Williams, Ithaca, March 13, 1880 to Smith Robertson; Samuel D. Halliday, *History of the Federal Land Grant of July 2, 1862 . . . as Relating to Cornell* (Ithaca, 1905), p. 48. In 1881 the board of trustees considered a proposal by Arnold & Co. and James MacLaurens for the purchase of 270,000 acres at $5.50 an acre (*Proceedings*, Board of Trustees, 1865–1885, p. 305).

[36] S. Robertson, Eau Claire, April 16, 1878, to J. W. Williams.

TABLE 13

SALES OF PINE STUMPAGE AND OF PINE LAND BY CORNELL
UNIVERSITY IN 1881 AND 1882

Year	Stumpage	Price	Pine Land	Price
1881	10,260 acres	$67,491	37,347 acres	$ 534,038
1882	4,600 "	34,789	133,322 "	2,106,787

In the four-year period from 1879 to 1882 the university sold pine stumpage and land to the value of more than three million dollars. The dream of Ezra Cornell was now being realized. One can well imagine the elation with which the Cornell officials announced these sums.

The bulk of the Cornell sales in 1881 and 1882 were made to the two great combinations operating in the Chippewa Valley, namely, Knapp-Stout and those Weyerhaeuser associates who were organized as the Chippewa Logging Company. The Knapp-Stout group had bought pine lands to the amount of 135,000 acres at the government land offices and was said to own in 1877 250,000 acres of pine.[37] The group might well have regarded this extensive acreage as sufficient to last for years to come, but an accelerated rate of cutting to meet the growing capacity of its mills—now expanded to cut 90,000,000 feet and slightly later to cut 110,000,000 feet annually—was requiring from 15,000 to 25,000 acres of original growth a year.[38] Such a rate of cutting made it necessary to replenish constantly the supply of timber land even for a company like Knapp-Stout which had had the foresight to buy so far in advance of need. Some of the larger purchases of this firm between 1876 and 1882 are interesting as showing the persons from whom they were acquired and the prices paid (see Table 14, p. 232).

Among the Cornell lands was a block of pine land on the Red Cedar River in the vicinity of Rice Lake and Red Cedar Lake. Since Knapp-Stout owned all the mills and dams on the river and controlled the water flowage, in part, through the construction of flash dams, that company could reasonably expect speculators who owned land on

[37] *Barron County Chronotype,* March 22, 1877.
[38] *Chippewa Herald,* March 24, December 15, 1882.

TABLE 14

Sales of Land to Knapp, Stout & Co., 1876–1882 [39]

Seller	Acres	Price
George W. Riggs, Washington, D. C.	520	$ 2,600
William D. Washburn, Minneapolis	3,596	23,376
North Wisconsin Railroad Company	23,246	110,000
Chicago, St. Paul, Minneapolis & Omaha Railroad	21,358	136,475
John J. Haley, Newton, Mass. (mills at Cedar Falls and unstated area of land)		312,500

the Red Cedar to accept its terms for the purchase of their holdings.[40] Those who lacked the resources with which to carry their investments were forced to sell to the company at low prices, but Cornell University was in a different situation. Although pressed for funds, its officers preferred to wait until Knapp-Stout really needed timber before putting the block on the market.[41] In 1880 T. B. Wilson, a member of the firm, became so much concerned about the rapid depletion of its pine that he journeyed to Ithaca to consult with Henry W. Sage about the land on the Red Cedar. Thereafter Wilson, Douglass, and Tainter made frequent trips to Ithaca to bargain for the land, but the university was holding out for high prices which the firm refused to pay. Threats to sell the land to the Weyerhaeuser combination may have made the Knapp-Stout officials more ready to compromise.[42] At last, in September, 1880, Knapp-Stout agreed to purchase 28,279 acres of land, estimated to contain 216,476,000 feet of pine, for $16.31 an acre. In addition, 2720 acres of "farm land" were bought for $6 an acre. The total sum involved was $477,550.

Both sides gave way in the process of bargaining: Knapp-Stout raised the price that they were originally prepared to pay, and Cornell University agreed to accept the lowest figure it had received for pine for some time past, $2.13 a thousand board feet. That Cornell's concession was large is shown by the fact that the land thus sold was

---

[39] Compiled from Deed Records of Barron County.

[40] H. C. Putnam, Eau Claire, August 11, 1874, to Ezra Cornell.

[41] As early as 1867 Ezra Cornell reported that Knapp, Stout & Co. had applied for 20,000 acres on the Red Cedar River (E. Cornell, Nantucket, Massachusetts, July 22, 1867, to Andrew D. White).

[42] S. Robertson, Eau Claire, June 9, 30, 1880, July 29, August 1, 1881, to E. L. Williams, Ithaca; Williams, July 2, October 2, 1880, September 19, 20, 1881, to Robertson.

in a compact tract and bore one of the heaviest stands of pine that the university owned, averaging nearly 8000 feet of merchantable timber to the acre. The concession was probably unavoidable, for none but the Weyerhaeuser companies could dare intrude in the lumber barony of Knapp-Stout, and apparently they were not inclined to do so. In making this sale Sage and the other members of the land committee had driven the best bargain possible unless the university was prepared to withhold its land on the Red Cedar indefinitely. This would have been inadvisable. Taxes were high and difficulties frequently arose over paying them which created ill feeling between the residents of the locality on the one hand and the university and its agents on the other. The timber was ripe for cutting and should be logged with that on adjacent tracts, which were owned by Knapp-Stout. There seemed, therefore, no point in retaining the lands any longer.

News of the sale and of the average price—by acreage instead of estimated stumpage—was given widespread publicity and served to attract attention to the remaining land of the university.[43] It is interesting to note that the sale brought satisfaction to residents of Chippewa, Barron, and Burnett Counties, in which the lands were located, for they felt "that the taxes on the property will now be promptly paid, which has not hitherto been the case." [44]

Meantime negotiations were under way between Sage and Williams in Ithaca and Smith Robertson in Eau Claire, representing the university, and Frederick Weyerhaeuser for the purchase of a large block of land on the Chippewa and two of its principal tributaries, the Flambeau and the Thornapple. The Mississippi millmen had never invested in pine land on a large scale but had preferred to depend upon loggers operating upon the Chippewa for their annual needs. None of the firms which entered into the great Weyerhaeuser pool had bought Wisconsin land in any quantity from the government, and until the early eighties they had not needed to tie up large

[43] *Dunn County News* in *Phillips Times,* October 8, 1881; *Barron County Shield,* October 28, 1881; *Chippewa Herald,* November 4, 1881; *Bloomer Workman,* September 28, 1882; *Northwestern Lumberman,* November 12, 1881, p. 1.
[44] *Barron County Shield,* October 28, 1881.

sums of money in pine land.⁴⁵ Now, however, with Knapp-Stout, the Eau Claire Lumber Company, and other groups or companies being forced into the market for pine because of the exhaustion of their own stands,⁴⁶ the Weyerhaeuser pool, to protect itself, found it necessary to reverse its policy and to compete for the control of stumpage.

During the three years 1880–1882 the Mississippi River Logging Company, Weyerhaeuser & Denkmann, and other members of the pool bought 200,000 acres of the pine land, together with the great mill at Chippewa Falls, from Henry W. Sage, Francis Palms, and other owners of Chippewa pine land for nearly $2,000,000, and during the same period the Mississippi River Logging Company and the Chippewa Logging Company bought from Cornell University 6620 acres for the sum of $44,947. But this acreage was sufficient for the requirements of the pool for only a few seasons.

In 1882 Weyerhaeuser frequently discussed with Sage the purchase of all or a large part of the Cornell pine land on the Chippewa and also of a compact block of 24,900 acres of choice pine in the Penoke Range of northern Wisconsin. Weyerhaeuser is said to have offered $2,630,000 for the 197,522 acres of pine on the Chippewa and $269,000 for an option on the Penoke land.⁴⁷ By this time the university officials were finding that the earlier estimates of the quantity of pine on the Cornell lands were too low, and they were loath to make sales of land on which they had not as yet been able to secure new estimates. Consequently Weyerhaeuser's offer was not accepted. Continued bargaining finally brought Weyerhaeuser and Sage to the point where a sale to the Chippewa Logging Company was arranged,

⁴⁵ An exception to this statement is a sale of 50,000 acres by McGraw & Dwight to the Mississippi River millmen for $500,000 which was negotiated by Putnam in 1875.

⁴⁶ Following are some of the purchases of pine and land by Eau Claire and Chippewa Falls lumbermen in 1879–1882: Eau Claire Lumber Company, 3199 acres and stumpage, $34,755; McDonnell & Irvine, 3495 acres and stumpage, $25,000; Valley Lumber Company, 7069 acres and stumpage, $102,941. Smaller purchases were made by the Northwestern Lumber Company, Ingram, Kennedy & Co., the Daniel Shaw Lumber Company, the Badger State Lumber Company, and the Empire Lumber Company.

⁴⁷ Chippewa River Logging Company, April 12, 1882, to Sage and Boardman, *Transcript of Record, McGraw-Fiske Estate*, Supreme Court of the United States, 1889, p. 660; *Eau Claire Free Press* in *Chippewa Herald*, May 26, 1882; *Northwestern Lumberman*, June 17, 1882, p. 8; copy, F. Weyerhaeuser, Eau Claire, September 14, 1882, to H. W. Sage.

but it included neither all the land on the Chippewa nor the Penoke group. It provided for the purchase of 109,601 acres for the record price of $16.80 an acre. The estimated amount of pine on the land averaged well over 5000 board feet to the acre. A charge of $3 a thousand feet was made for the stumpage and 50 cents an acre for the land. The total price paid was $1,841,746.[48] This sale was the largest yet made by the university, not only in acreage but also in dollar value, and certainly the stumpage price was favorable. Needless to say much publicity was given to it in the local press and in the journals of the lumber trade.[49]

Although the sale to the Chippewa Logging Company caused the most rejoicing at Cornell University, there were other sales in 1882 which, though smaller in volume, brought a higher price by the acre and offered further proof that the Cornell lands contained some highly valuable stands of pine. The most profitable sale was made to the Valley Lumber Company of Eau Claire, a firm closely associated with the Weyerhaeuser companies, 1360 acres on the Big Elk River in Price County, bearing 6000 feet of pine to the acre, for $23.59 an acre. Another tract of 1906 acres in Chippewa County, having nearly 7000 feet to the acre, was sold to William Carson of Eau Claire for $21.85 an acre.

For the next few years Cornell did not press its lands on the market and sales were small (see Table 15).

TABLE 15

CORNELL UNIVERSITY'S SALES OF PINE LAND AND OF STUMPAGE, 1883–1886

Year	Pine Land	Stumpage
1883	3258 acres for $25,082	3640 acres for $35,507
1884	1360 " " 14,080	1012 " " 9,991
1885	4931 " " 46,773	320 " " 2,800
1886	5607 " " 82,851	No sale

[48] A "special" discount of $6847 was allowed on the contract, reducing the actual price from $1,848,593 to $1,841,746.

[49] *Chippewa Herald,* September 22, 1882; *Bloomer Workman,* September 28, October 19, 1882; *Phillips Times,* September 16, 1882; *Chippewa County Independent* in *Phillips Times,* October 14, 1882; *Northwestern Lumberman,* September 30, 1882, p. 9.

By the late eighties the swift strides of the lumbermen into the northern reaches of the Chippewa Valley had exhausted most of the tracts located on or in close proximity to the drivable streams. Those few tracts which were well located and remained uncut brought fancy prices. Furthermore, the high price of pine was making it possible to cut the smaller trees and was bringing into demand the Norway pine, previously not regarded as of much value. All this was upsetting the estimates of commercial timber on the Cornell land which had been made in the seventies, at the time of the purchase by Sage & McGraw. A decade later new and more favorable estimates had been prepared, but in a short time the Cornell officials came to realize that even these revised estimates were below those made by timber cruisers for prospective purchasers of Cornell lands. A blanket increase of estimates by 25 per cent was ordered, but even this soon appeared to be inadequate. Finally, in 1885, Sage and his associates were induced by the increasing pressure of lumbermen for pine to order new and most careful estimates to be made on the remaining lands. These new estimates were so much larger than any previously prepared that the land committee hastily ordered all offers cancelled. Special concern was felt for the Penoke land, on which an option had been given based on the old estimates.[50] When the option was permitted to lapse the officials breathed a sigh of relief, and for good reason, since the estimates on this tract soon showed that it had been greatly undervalued.

In the eighties Cornell kept a timber cruiser in the woods much of the time estimating stumpage, scrutinizing the cutting of stumpage buyers who were permitted to cut only in proportion to the payments they made, watching for timber stealing, and looking for windbreaks and fire damage. The reports of these cruisers enabled the members of the land committee to keep more closely in touch with the various tracts and to quote prices on them more intelligently than had been possible earlier.

The new estimates enabled the university to sell the choicer remaining tracts at prices even greater than Woodward and Putnam

[50] E. L. Williams, October 15, 1885, to Smith Robertson.

had once assured Ezra Cornell could be obtained. In 1886 a quarter section having 8500 feet of merchantable pine to the acre, which had been rejected by Sage & McGraw in 1872, sold for $39 an acre. The following year the pine on a compact group of 2000 acres in Chippewa County, estimated at nearly 9000 feet to the acre, sold for $45 an acre. At the same time the pine on a tract of 455 acres in Ashland County, estimated to average 14,000 feet, sold for $63 an acre.

In 1887 the last big sale of valuable stumpage was made. The Penoke tract which Weyerhaeuser had previously tried to buy was regarded by lumbermen as one of the most valuable blocks of pine remaining in the state. It was not only heavily timbered, but "it ran largely to uppers," and was close to the Wisconsin Central Railroad and the Bad River.[51] In 1879 a part of this tract had been offered for $5.50 an acre, but, on the insistence of Henry W. Sage, the price was raised to $6 an acre for the entire 24,900 acres.[52] Thereafter the price was increased so rapidly by the land committee that Wisconsin lumbermen must have felt that the university did not really intend to sell it. As each proposal for purchase came in, the price was raised. On September 27, 1880, $8 an acre was quoted; on February 8, 1881, $10 was named; then came the following quotations for the entire tract: March 7, 1882, $284,748; March 21, 1882, $325,748; September 18, 1882, $369,289; February 9, 1885, $390,000. By 1885 the excitement among Wisconsin lumbermen over the tract became so great that it was temporarily withdrawn from sale to permit a special investigation to determine its value. When the examination was completed it was found that the tract had some 50 per cent more white and Norway pine than earlier estimates had indicated. This called for a drastic revision of the price, which was now increased to $513,689. At this figure the pine only on the tract was sold to a group of New York capitalists consisting of Belden & McDowell of Syracuse and A. M. Dodge of North Tonawanda. Sage could well feel that his careful management was re-

[51] E. L. Williams, Ithaca, July 20, 1880, to Smith Robertson.
[52] E. L. Williams, Ithaca, October 10, 1879, July 20, 1880, to Smith Robertson; *id.*, October 11, 15, 1879, to G. S. Frost.

sponsible for the price of better than $20 an acre for a tract which just a few years earlier was going begging at $5.

Stumpage sales in 1887 totalled $746,561 for the pine on 35,809 acres, which made that year the second best in dollar value, being exceeded only by the record year 1882. During the next six years the volume of sales was smaller but the average of prices was high, since the very choicest tracts remaining in the university's hands were being sold. It may be interesting to record the most important of these sales (see Table 16).

TABLE 16
SOME CORNELL LAND SALES, 1887–1893

Year	Purchaser	Acres and Price	Board Feet By Acre	Board Feet Total	Amount Realized
1887	J. L. Gates, Milwaukee	152 @ $29	6 M	930 M	$ 4,436
1888	Early, Brown & Brewster, Chippewa Falls	160 @ 24	4 M	790 M	3,940
1888	John Paul, La Crosse	800 @ 40	7 M	6,242 M	32,740
1888	Gardiner, Batchelder & Wells, Lyons, Ohio	2,314 @ 20	3 M	8,194 M	47,760
1888	McDonald & Gilbert, Chippewa Falls	1,058 @ 26	5 M	5,615 M	27,845
1889	Goddard & Hemp	160 @ 56	9 M	1,550 M	9,082
1891	Mississippi River Logging Co.	3,200 @ 18	3 M	11,167 M	58,593
1891	Charles L. Colman, La Crosse	469 @ 50	8 M	4,185 M	23,784
1891	Joseph & George Herbert, Chippewa County	320 @ 37	7 M	2,260 M	12,120
1892	Daniel Shaw Lumber Co., Eau Claire	960 @ 26	4 M	4,536 M	25,523
1892	Empire Lumber Co., Eau Claire	320 @ 64	11 M	3,640 M	20,567
1892	Empire Lumber Co., Eau Claire	1,576 @ 32	6 M	9,337 M	51,107
1892	John Paul, La Crosse	720 @ 55	11 M	8,245 M	40,000
1893	E. Rutledge, Chippewa Falls	8,625 @ 17	3 M	27,649 M	150,000

Perhaps the richest piece of land the university had was a quarter section on a branch of the Eau Claire River in Chippewa County. The cruiser's estimate showed that this tract averaged 17,500 feet of pine to the acre. In 1891 it was sold to Charles Colman for the record price of $82 an acre. An annual summary of the stumpage sales for the years 1888 to 1893 shows the high prices being obtained for the university's choice timber during these years (see Table 17).

TABLE 17

CORNELL UNIVERSITY'S SALES OF PINE STUMPAGE, 1888–1893

Year	Acres	Value	Year	Acres	Value
1888	8,325	$159,912	1891	16,108	$203,731
1889	3,931	59,990	1892	7,224	179,799
1890	5,214	24,879	1893	11,857	175,042

All the most valuable timber on the Cornell University land was sold by 1893, but during the next eleven years a small business was done in the sale of second-growth pine and of spruce, white oak, pulpwood, ties, and poles. On 55,000 acres the stumpage of various descriptions was sold for $228,000. Not infrequently the pine would be sold to one buyer, oak to another, and spruce or pulpwood to still another. Such sales justified the policy that Cornell had always followed of keeping taxes paid on unsold land even though the valuable timber had been cut off or sold. Furthermore, the cut-over lands were not fully exploited as yet.

There was a surge of settlers into northern Wisconsin in the latter part of the nineteenth and the early part of the twentieth century. Thousands of homeseekers, deterred from going into the Great Plains by reports of drought, grasshoppers, and the approaching end of free land, were induced to try the cut-over lands of the northern Lake States. This movement was stimulated by state propaganda and the advertising of numerous settlement companies.

The Wisconsin State College of Agriculture, under the leadership of W. A. Henry, its dean, gave active support to the movement to settle the cut-over land in the north. The college published bulletins in which it decried the prevailing belief that northern Wisconsin was cold, its growing season short, its soil sandy and infertile, and the struggle for existence in that region harsh and unprofitable. In accordance with an act of the legislature of 1895, Dean Henry, with a corps of assistants, prepared an elaborate bulletin, *Northern Wis-*

consin: *A Hand-Book for the Homeseeker*. Its 192 pages, including numerous illustrations, picture northern Wisconsin as a most attractive region in which to start life anew.

Some of the old lumber companies turned into settlement and colonization companies. For example, the Weyerhaeuser property was conveyed in part to the American Immigration Company, the cut-over lands of Owen and Rust were conveyed to the Owen Lumber Company, and Henry W. Sage's land was sold in small lots to settlers by the Sage Land & Improvement Company. Other companies which sprang up to deal in and attract settlers to the cut-over lands were the Good Land Company, which owned 57,000 acres in Price County; the Chippewa Valley Colonization Company, whose interests were largely confined to Chippewa County; the Armstrong Land Company of Rochester, Minnesota, which claimed to own 2,000,000 acres of farming, hardwood, grazing, and mineral lands; and the Wisconsin River Land Company, with 200,000 acres of land in Price, Lincoln, and Ashland Counties for which it held tax titles. Other large dealers in tax titles who tried to attract settlers to northern Wisconsin were George B. Burrows and the Ramsay Land Company.[53]

Supplementing the work of these colonization companies were the land-grant railroads, the Wisconsin Central and the Chicago, St. Paul, Minneapolis & Omaha, both of which retained large areas in the Chippewa Valley long after 1900. Much earlier they had started a fairly systematic effort to bring in settlers by employing travelling emigration agents, distributing pamphlets describing their lands, and offering fare concessions to permanent settlers.

Aside from the land-grant railroads, the most active colonization work in northern Wisconsin was done by the J. L. Gates Lumber Company. Financed by the Pfister interests of Milwaukee, Gates bought cut-over land to the amount of 700,000 to 800,000 acres,

[53] B. M. King, agent for the sale of the Daniel Shaw Lumber Company's land, gives much detail about the sale of cut-over lands by these companies in his letters to Eugene Shaw and the Daniel Shaw Lumber Company (Daniel Shaw Lumber Company MSS, Eau Claire Public Library).

employed agents to work in populous cities where they could mingle with immigrants bound for the West, and attracted a steady stream of settlers to his lands.[54]

Cornell University did not fail to profit by the increasing interest being taken by immigrants in northern Wisconsin. In the eighties and nineties its agents sold many 80- and 160-acre tracts to settlers at an average of $10 an acre. Naturally those lands most suitable for farming were taken up first and the poorer lands remaining were slow to attract purchasers. To stimulate their sale the Cornell agent in Wisconsin got out special handbills in 1901 calling attention to the low price of the Cornell lands and what he chose to call their high quality.[55] Declining prices for the poorer lands and increasing taxes induced the university to sell about one-half of its remaining land to J. L. Gates, who was in a better position to retail it. He purchased 45,813 acres for $250,000. There was some timber on the land which the university had planned either to cut or to sell to others, but it was the demand for homes in northern Wisconsin which made it possible for Cornell to obtain this relatively high price for cut-over land.

It was in 1902 that the university finally abandoned Ezra Cornell's plan to establish a town and develop the water power at Brunet Falls. In 1866, when the business of founding towns was flourishing, William A. Woodward and Ezra Cornell had planned to lay out and develop a town at the Falls and had bought some 2000 acres for the townsite. The venture never got beyond the planning stage. After 1900, when the university was attempting to close out its interests in Wisconsin, its officials were glad to accept from the newly incorporated Cornell Land & Power Company $55,000 for the original tract at the Falls and an additional 2000 acres in the vicinity. At the suggestion of Charles McArthur, the Cornell land agent in Eau Claire, and L. V. Ripley, a timber cruiser long employed by Cornell, the

---

[54] In the Cornell MSS and the Daniel Shaw Lumber Company MSS are numerous documents dealing with the land business of J. L. Gates.

[55] E. L. Williams, Ithaca, October 30, 1901, to Charles McArthur; Charles McArthur, Eau Claire, August 13, 1900, October 23, 1901, to E. L. Williams.

new city established at the Falls was called Cornell as an act of courtesy to the institution which had previously controlled no small part of the Chippewa Valley.

Four other sizable sales of cut-over land to lumbering and colonization companies practically closed out the land business: 7655 acres were sold to the Northwestern Lumbering Company of Eau Claire for $50,000; 15,635 acres to the South Muscatine Lumber Company of Muscatine, Iowa, for $108,700; 5083 acres to Hugh D. Campbell of Washington County, Minnesota, for $27,500, and 26,393 acres to Charles M. Davidson and Edward H. Smith of Beaver Dam, Wisconsin, for $120,000. After 1906 there remained only a few scattered tracts to be marketed and the final deed was given in 1925.

From original entry to final deed the university had sold its 512,428 acres, including the small acreage in Minnesota and Kansas, for $4,542,563; in addition it had sold stumpage on some 190,000 acres for $2,211,617. Other income from damages paid by trespassers, the sale of hay, and the rent of land brought the gross proceeds to $6,779,677. A land business of this magnitude necessitated heavy expenses. Among the expense items the largest, amounting to $648,204, was for taxes. Then comes interest of $329,039, which was the result of two charges, namely, the interest paid to Ezra Cornell for all advances made in connection with the land business, and interest upon the capitalized value of the lands, which was used to meet current expenses of the university when it was waiting for proceeds of sales. The small income from the land business in its early days had induced the university's officials to use a part of the endowment for current expenses. The amount thus used was considered as interest upon the capitalized value of the land and was added to the interest account. Other important expenses were $160,831 paid Woodward for locating the land, $25,000 for the cost of the unnecessary Woodward suit, $146,219 for salaries, $43,577 for land examinations, and $22,513 for commissions. To these items should be added $309,200 which was paid into the Land Scrip Fund for the scrip at the rate of 60 cents an acre. After deducting the total expenses of $1,728,596 from the gross income there is left a net profit of five million dollars. To complete the picture of productive endowment funds derived from the Agricultural-College Act of 1862, it should be remembered that in addition to the five million dollars profit from the land business, paid into the Cornell Endowment Fund, there is also $603,002 in the Land Scrip Fund, part of which was obtained as explained above and the rest from the sale of the New York land scrip which Cornell did not use.

The Cornell land business was one of the outstandingly successful land speculations in American history, to be compared only with the landed operations of the western railroads which received imperial domains from the government. Its success was the result of the vision of Ezra Cornell, the keen judgment of H. C. Putnam, and the able management of Henry W. Sage.

Conclusion

WHEN the Agricultural-College Act was passed, its opponents predicted that it would not provide adequate endowments for the new colleges and that it would prove a harmful measure to the newly developing states and territories by making it easier and cheaper for speculators to acquire their land. For most of the states these predictions were to be amply fulfilled. The application of the Agricultural-College Act to the State of Wisconsin offers an excellent opportunity of testing the wisdom of its framers. This study is largely confined to the timbered section of northern Wisconsin, but, so far as the effect of speculation on the prosperity of new areas, on their local governments, on taxes, and on politics is concerned, there is much similarity between developments in the pineries of northern Wisconsin and in the prairies of Illinois or Iowa.

None of the states received through the Agricultural-College Act sufficient funds to place their agricultural colleges on a sound financial basis at the outset, and with the exception of New York no state east of the Mississippi River ever obtained from land or scrip what might be regarded as an adequate endowment. With two or three exceptions even the public-land states which had previous experience in administering Federal land grants were unable to profit much from their agricultural-college grants, so strong was western opposition to government speculation in lands. For example, the State of Wisconsin received 240,000 acres for its agricultural college which it speedily sold for $300,000. Since the interest on this sum would scarcely pay the salaries of more than six or seven professors, it was hardly sufficient to support a full college program. In consequence, the development of Wisconsin's agricultural college moved slowly in its early days.

CONCLUSION

If Wisconsin benefited only slightly from the government's bounty, New York State's land grant college, in contrast, obtained an endowment of $5,000,000 from the land it located in the pineries of the Badger State. Public opinion would never have permitted Wisconsin's officials to withhold its college land from sale for so long, but pressure could not be brought to bear on an absentee institution in the same way. Cornell University acquired an unfavorable reputation because it badgered the tax assessors, fought local levies, and opposed railroad subsidies and large expenditures for county buildings and roads, but discriminatory or confiscatory legislation directed at it was not adopted. Nevertheless residents of Wisconsin could well feel, as many did, that there was a great injustice in permitting Cornell to take such large profits out of the state to which it had contributed nothing.

Over 600,000 acres of land were entered in Wisconsin with agricultural-college scrip in addition to that acquired by Cornell. Much of this was secured by absentee owners like William S. Patrick, David Preston, and Francis Palms of Detroit; Sage, McGraw, and Dwight of Ithaca and Dryden, New York, and William A. Woodward of Vail's Gate, New York. Like Cornell University, these men were speculating in timber lands. They paid their taxes reluctantly, if at all, opposed local improvements as did Cornell, and harassed the county and town officials by frequent suits and threats of litigation. When the absentee-owned lands were sold to local residents the pinery counties breathed a sigh of relief.

Resentment engendered by absentee ownership of great blocks of pine land induced the residents of Wisconsin counties and towns in which such holdings were located to vote themselves extravagant and ill-conceived local improvements, the costs of which were levied chiefly on absentee owners by the expedient of assessing their land at disproportionately higher rates. Few early settlers in pinery counties owned much taxable property, and they had little incentive to minimize the costs of local government. This orgy of spending lasted only until homesteaders began to prove up on their claims or to

CONCLUSION

purchase land from settlement companies, but by that time large debts had been accumulated which made heavy taxes necessary for a long time to come.

As the tax burden on timber lands increased, absentee owners as well as many Wisconsin speculators were torn between their desire to withhold their land from sale until higher prices could be secured and the need to sell some of it to reduce the expense of carrying it. Only men and institutions with large capital resources were able to retain their land until the desired price level was reached. Many large owners were forced to sell; others who were interested in lumbering were induced by heavy taxes to cut their timber even though to do so at the time only contributed to an already overstocked market. In the seventies it was the lumbermen's constant lament that high taxes were forcing premature cutting of their timber and were thereby demoralizing the industry.

The rapidly rising tax burden had its share in encouraging abandonment of pine land once it was cut over. Since abandoned land paid no taxes, heavier burdens had to be levied on uncut lands to compensate for the loss of revenue. The vicious circle of increasing expenses, rising taxes, premature cutting, abandonment of land, and narrowing of the tax base continued to harass the holder of timber land in Wisconsin throughout the nineteenth century.

Reckless and prodigal cutting of timber was characteristic of lumbering operations in this period, but in Wisconsin the practice was to some extent made necessary by heavy taxation of timber land. Loggers gave little thought to the future, being concerned solely with immediate profits. The better grades of pine were ruthlessly logged, slash was left on the ground, and the inevitable fires destroyed the growing timber. A writer in the *Eau Claire Free Press* declared in 1880 that it seemed to be the order of the day "to send armies to the woods to slaughter pine by the hundred millions, to get them to market and to convert them to immediate dollars, without regard to any future use or benefit to the country. That's what's the trouble in Maine. They have stripped the state of its great pine forests in the north, and find now only a troublesome crop of grangers and greenbackers in their place." [1]

When the pine was gone many lumbermen abandoned Wisconsin to continue their destructive practices in the lush pineries of the South or the rich softwood regions of the Pacific Coast states. Isaac Stephenson, for example, transferred his interest to the South, Frederick Weyerhaeuser built giant mills in Minnesota and in Washington, and Henry C. Putnam roamed over Florida, California, and the Canadian provinces in his search for valuable lumber. Not all Wisconsin lumbermen followed their example. Others, like John S. Owen, William A. Rust, James L. Gates, and Henry W. Sage turned to the cutting of Norway pine, then hemlock, finally to the hardwoods and the small stuff used for pulpwood. Secondary industries sprang up to take the place of the great sawmills of the seventies and eighties, and the economy of the section was adjusted to the new conditions. These changes made possible the continued growth of such old mill towns as Eau Claire, Chippewa Falls, and Ashland. The second growth of pine and the inferior grades of trees lasted but a short time, however, and the lumbermen who had stayed to cut them were soon attracted to another field.

Around the turn of the century the lumber companies became settlement companies, their attention devoted to lavishing praise upon the north country to induce settlers to buy their cut-over lands. Northern Wisconsin never enjoyed the rush of settlers which made Oklahoma a boom territory in the nineties, but the immigration promotion work of the railroads, the numerous land and colonization companies, Cornell University, and the State Agricultural College directed a substantial stream of immigration into the cut-over counties. As the pine disappeared before the ruthless attack of the lumbermen it was replaced by the settler's tar-paper shack and his small piece of stump-free land cleared at the expense of the heaviest kind of toil.

In northern Wisconsin the struggle for existence was harsh and there were numerous failures. This could be said of the frontier process

[1] Quoted in *Northwestern Lumberman*, November 27, 1880, p. 1.

CONCLUSION 249

elsewhere, but the rate of failure among these new immigrants was high because much of the land on which they were induced to settle was unsuited for farming. Emigration promotion methods had been well tried out before northern Wisconsin was opened to settlement by the removal of the timber barrier. Experience had shown that immigrants could be directed to poor as well as to good land, and although the proportion of buyers who completed their payments on the former was low, efforts continued to be made to settle both classes of land. Settlers were located in remote and out-of-the-way places where roads and schools could be provided only at relatively high costs, and others were colonized on sandy and infertile soil unsuited to cultivation. The land companies and railroads were only interested in getting something out of their land and in "developing" the state by bringing in settlers. They gave little thought to the kind of land in which the newcomers were preparing to sink their little capital and years of toil.

A subsequent generation was to regret the destructive cutting practices of the lumbermen who destroyed irreplaceable resources in a generation, and it was to regret too the zealous work of the land companies which produced many submarginal farms and led to the settlement of areas which have since had to be abandoned. Cornell University had its share of responsibility for both misfortunes. Its insistence on a high price for its timber, together with the high interest charges on its land contracts, forced lumbermen-purchasers to cut the timber quickly and to wrest from the land the utmost profit at the least expense. This of course prevented careful cutting practices. The university, too, long engaged in efforts to settle its cut-over land as the best means of securing additional returns from it. It may be doubted, however, whether the investment of Cornell in Wisconsin was any more harmful to the state than it would have been had it been made by other absentee interests with the New York scrip.

While benefiting to the amount of $5,000,000 from its investment in Wisconsin pine lands, Cornell, like other lumbermen speculators, left the pinery counties nothing to compensate them for the wealth

CONCLUSION

which had been taken away. The project for the establishment of a town at Brunet Falls to be called Cornell was abandoned, although at a later time an ex-employe of the university was influential in having the community built around the new hydroelectric dam at that point named Cornell. Abstracts of titles to half a million acres of land on the Chippewa today all begin with the first transfer from the government to Ezra Cornell. A few local historians have recalled the visit of Ezra Cornell to the Wisconsin pinery; others have written with some bitterness of the part the university played in the pine-land business of northern Wisconsin. Otherwise, the Badger State has forgotten the connection it once had with the institution at Ithaca. Cornell alumni, students, and faculty, on the other hand, should cherish the memory of their founder's wisdom in undertaking the great land venture in Wisconsin; they should be familiar with the part Woodward and Putnam had in selecting the lands; they should never forget the superb management given to the lands by Henry W. Sage; nor should they be unaware of the cost of the investment to the State of Wisconsin.

Bibliography

THERE is little information in print on the pine-land business and the lumber industry in Wisconsin. Frederick Merk has two chapters in his *Economic History of Wisconsin during the Civil War Decade* which provide the best account of the Wisconsin lumber industry. Joseph Schafer delved deeply into land policy and land disposal in Wisconsin, but he barely touched upon the pine-land business. Local histories have been helpful, especially Thomas J. Randall's *History of the Chippewa Valley* and A. T. Andreas' *History of Northern Wisconsin*. Other books which are listed below have been of aid in providing the background for this study.

In the absence of scholarly and comprehensive treatments of the land and lumber business, main reliance had to be placed on manuscripts, local newspapers, trade journals, and government documents. Essential to any study of western land policy are the records of the General Land Office in the National Archives. Here is the Domesday Survey of America, prepared over a long period of years, complete in detail and easy to use, but requiring infinite patience to master. Complementary to the records of the General Land Office are the deed and mortgage records of the pinery counties, a study of which throws much light on the land business. Of equal importance for this study are the records of the Cornell land administration. Students of the economic and political history of Wisconsin cannot afford to neglect this significant collection. Other useful collections of manuscripts are listed below.

Two newspapers which are essential for the history of lumbering on the Chippewa are the *Eau Claire Free Press* and the *Chippewa Herald*. Official county newspapers like the *Lincoln County Advocate* and the *Phillips Times* contain the reports and proceedings of the boards of supervisors. All the pinery newspapers contain valuable information on floods, on the rafting of lumber through Beef Slough, on the promotion and construction of railroads, and on the wars of the railroads with the lumbermen and the land speculators. Wisconsin is fortunate in having extensive files of its local newspapers in the possession of the State Historical Society and in numerous local libraries and newspaper offices.

Among trade journals the *Northwestern Lumberman* was found to be most important. Its Wisconsin correspondents provided it with frequent news items concerning sales of timber tracts, the amount of pine cut annually on the various watersheds, the quantity of lumber sawn by the various mills, water flowage and flood conditions, river improvements, railroad construction, tax problems, and local government.

The *Congressional Globe,* the *Congressional Record,* the *Congressional Documents,* the *United States Statutes-at-Large,* and the statutes, journals, and documents of both houses of the legislatures of New York and Wisconsin have been used for the years covered in this study. The *Annual Reports* of the Board of Trustees of the Illinois Industrial University were of much value.

Unique published source material bearing on the lumber industry of Wisconsin as well as on the early history of Cornell University can be found in the records of two lawsuits. William A. Woodward, who helped locate the Cornell lands, brought suit against Ezra Cornell for additional compensation for his services, in the course of which much testimony was presented dealing with pine-land values and lumbering practices in Wisconsin. The testimony, letters, and other documents appear in *Woodward vs. Cornell,* record in the New York Supreme Court, Newburgh, 1872–1874, 2 volumes, 1388 pages. There is a copy in the library of the Cornell Law School annotated in the handwriting of Ezra Cornell. The five-volume *Return to the Court of Appeals in the Matter of the Estate of John McGraw, Deceased, and also in the Matter of the Estate of Jennie McGraw-Fiske, Deceased,* 1887, 2864 pages, contains a great quantity of information on the land and lumbering business of John McGraw and his associates, Henry W. Sage, W. J. Young & Co., Jeremiah W. Dwight, and others in New York, Michigan, Wisconsin, Iowa, and elsewhere. There is also material of a similar character in the transcript of record submitted in 1889 to the United States Supreme Court *In the Matter of the Estate of Jennie McGraw Fiske, Deceased, and also in the Matter of the Estate of John McGraw, Deceased. Cornell University, and Douglass Boardman, as Executor, etc., Plaintiffs in Error, vs. Willard Fiske and Others, Defendants in Error,* filed October, 1889, 838 pages.

MANUSCRIPTS

Cornell University Land Records.

In the Treasurer's Office, Morrill Hall, and in a vault in Prudence Risley Hall are kept the records of the land business of Cornell University. Sales books, account books, ledgers, plat books, tax receipts, and the correspondence carried on by Ezra Cornell, Henry C. Putnam, William A.

Woodward, and the officials of the university with lumbermen, agents, settlers and others in Wisconsin, Minnesota, Iowa, and Kansas are practically intact as they were when the land business was closed out.

Henry C. Putnam Papers, Boardman Hall, Cornell University.
Additional correspondence with Ezra Cornell, Jeremiah W. Dwight, Henry W. Sage, J. W. Williams, and William A. Woodward.

H. S. Allen Papers, Boardman Hall, Cornell University.
Concerning the lumbering and merchandising operations of H. S. Allen of Chippewa Falls, Wisconsin. Ledgers, daybooks, cashbooks, journals, delivery books, grain book, due bills, etc.

Andrew D. White Papers, Cornell University Library.
President White had little to do with the land business, which was left in the hands of a special committee of the board of trustees, the chief member of which was Henry W. Sage. These papers contain only a few allusions to land matters.

Ezra Cornell Papers, Cornell University Library.
Mostly concerned with the telegraph business.

Ezra Cornell Papers, De Witt Historical Society, Ithaca.
A few papers which were of some aid in tracing the beginning of the university.

Justin Smith Morrill Papers, Cornell University Library.
These papers relating to the Land Grant Act of 1862 are, for the most part, reminiscent in character. The Morrill Papers in the Library of Congress have been fully studied by Professor Earle D. Ross in *Democracy's College*.

Harrison Howard Papers, Cornell University Library.
Relate to the founding of People's College.

Catlin & Williamson Papers, Wisconsin Historical Society.
The firm of Catlin & Williamson represented prominent eastern land speculators. The collection is important for the light it throws on the business of lending to squatters.

Governors' Letters, Wisconsin Historical Society.

Ingram and Kennedy Papers, Wisconsin Historical Society.
Relate to the lumbering business.

Elisha Keyes Papers, Wisconsin Historical Society.
Important for the activities of the Republican boss of Wisconsin. The correspondence dealing with railroad matters is especially valuable.

Moses Strong Papers, Wisconsin Historical Society.
Of value for the story of speculation in wild lands and town lots in Wisconsin during the thirties, forties, and fifties. The contents are described by Frederick Merk in "Strong and Woodman Manuscripts in the Wiscon-

sin State Historical Library," Wisconsin Historical Society, *Bulletin of Information*, No. 78 (1915).

Cyrus Woodman Papers, Wisconsin Historical Society.

One of the most important collections of material dealing with land speculation in the nineteenth century. Described by Frederick Merk in *op. cit.*

Daniel Shaw Lumber Company Papers, Eau Claire Public Library.

Contain information on stumpage values and timber-land sales for the later years of the nineteenth century; also contain considerable correspondence dealing with the business of the J. L. Gates Lumber Company.

General Land Office Records, National Archives.

Abstracts of cash, warrant, and scrip entries for the Milwaukee, Mineral Point, Green Bay, La Crosse, Menasha, Eau Claire, Bayfield, Superior, St. Croix, and Hudson land offices. Also correspondence of the General Land Office.

Charles Mason Papers, Iowa State Department of History and Archives.

Mason was an influential speculator who dealt in Iowa and Wisconsin lands.

Francis Palms Papers, Burton Historical Collections, Detroit Public Library.

Palms was an influential lumberman of Michigan whose papers contain considerable information on the purchase and sale of agricultural-college scrip.

County Deed Records

of Ashland, Barron, Chippewa, Eau Claire, Lincoln, Marathon, Price, Rusk, and Taylor Counties.

NEWSPAPERS

Alma Express.

Ashland Press.

Barron County Chronotype (Rice Lake) and *Barron County Shield* (Barron).

Bayfield Press.

Buffalo County Journal (Alma).

Chippewa Herald, Chippewa Independent, and *Chippewa Union and Times* (Chippewa Falls).

Clark County Press and *Clark County Republican* (Neillsville).

Colby Phonograph.

Durand Times.

Eau Claire Argus and *Eau Claire Free Press.*

Hudson Star Observer and *Hudson Star and Times.*

La Crosse Democrat, La Crosse Leader, La Crosse Republican, and *La Crosse Tribune.*
Lincoln County Advocate (Jenny).
Madison Democrat.
North Wisconsin News (Hayward).
Phillips Times.
Polk County Press (St. Croix Falls).
Taylor County News (Medford).
Wisconsin River Pilot (Wausau).
Wisconsin State Journal (Madison).

PERIODICALS

Lumber Trade Journal (New Orleans), *Northwestern Lumberman* (Chicago), and *Wisconsin Lumberman* (Milwaukee).

BOOKS

Andreas, A. T., compiler, *History of Northern Wisconsin. Containing an Account of its Settlement, Growth, Development and Resources.* . . . Chicago, 1881.

Bronson, Walter C., *History of Brown University, 1764–1914.* Providence, 1914.

Cornell, Alonzo B., *Biography of Ezra Cornell, Founder of the Cornell University.* New York, 1884.

Gates, Paul Wallace, "Land Policy and Tenancy in the Prairie States," *Journal of Economic History,* i (May, 1941), 60–82.

——, "Southern Investments in Northern Lands Before the Civil War," *Journal of Southern History,* v (May, 1939), 155–185.

——, "The Homestead Law in an Incongruous Land System," *American Historical Review,* xli (July, 1936), 652–681.

——, *The Illinois Central Railroad and its Colonization Work.* Cambridge, 1934.

——, "The Role of the Land Speculator in Western Development," *Pennsylvania Magazine of History and Biography,* lxvi (July, 1942), 314–333.

Halliday, Samuel D., *History of the Agricultural College Land Grant Act of July 2, 1862. Devoted largely to the History of the "Land Scrip" which under that Grant was allotted to the State of New York and Afterwards given to Cornell University.* Ithaca, 1905.

Hewett, Waterman Thomas, *Cornell University. A History.* 4 vols. New York, 1905.

BIBLIOGRAPHY

Hibbard, Benjamin H., *History of the Public Land Policies.* New York, 1924.

Hotchkiss, George W., *History of the Lumber and Forest Industry of the Northwest.* Chicago, 1898.

Martin, Asa E., "Pennsylvania's Land Grant Under the Morrill Act of 1862," *Pennsylvania History,* ix (April, 1942), 85–117.

Martin, Roy L., *History of the Wisconsin Central* (The Railway and Locomotive Historical Society, *Bulletin* No. 54), Boston, 1941.

Mendenhall, Thomas C., editor, *History of Ohio State University.* 3 vols. Columbus, 1920.

Merk, Frederick, *Economic History of Wisconsin During the Civil War Decade* (State Historical Society of Wisconsin, *Publications, Studies,* I). Madison, 1916.

Powell, Burt E., *Semi-Centennial History of the University of Illinois.* Urbana, 1918.

Randall, Thomas E., *History of the Chippewa Valley.* Eau Claire, 1875.

Robbins, Roy M., *Our Landed Heritage. The Public Domain, 1776–1936.* Princeton, 1942.

Ross, Earle D., *Democracy's College. The Land-Grant Movement in the Formative Stage.* Ames, Iowa, 1942.

Roth, Filibert, *On the Forestry Conditions of Northern Wisconsin* (Wisconsin Geological and Natural History Survey, *Bulletin* I, *Economic Series*). Madison, 1898.

Schafer, Joseph, *History of Agriculture in Wisconsin* (State Historical Society of Wisconsin, *Wisconsin Domesday Book, General Studies,* i). Madison, 1922.

———, *Four Wisconsin Counties. Prairie and Forest (Wisconsin Domesday Book, General Studies,* ii). Madison, 1927.

———, *The Wisconsin Lead Region (Wisconsin Domesday Book, General Studies,* iii). Madison, 1932.

———, *The Winnebago-Horicon Basin. A Type Study in Western History (Wisconsin Domesday Book, General Studies,* iv). Madison, 1937.

———, *Wisconsin Domesday Book (Town Studies,* i). Madison, 1924.

Sheldon, Addison E., *Land Systems and Land Policies in Nebraska* (*Publications,* Nebraska State Historical Society, xxii). Lincoln, 1936.

Sherwood, Sidney, *The University of the State of New York: History of Higher Education in the State of New York* (United States Bureau of Education, Circular of Information, No. 3), 1900. Pages 318–425 contain a history of Cornell University by Ernest W. Huffcut.

Slater, C. P., "History of the Endowment Fund of the University of Illinois.

March 5, 1934." A manuscript in the president's office, University of Illinois.

Smith, Albert W., *Ezra Cornell*. Ithaca, 1934.

Stennett, W. H., *Yesterday and Today. A History of the Chicago and Northwestern Railway System*. Chicago, 1910.

Stephenson, Isaac, *Recollections of a Long Life, 1829–1915*. Chicago, 1915.

True, Alfred Charles, *History of Agricultural Education in the United States, 1785–1925* (United States Department of Agriculture, *Miscellaneous Publications*, No. 36). Washington, 1929.

White, Andrew Dickson, *Autobiography*. 2 vols. New York, 1905.

Index

Absentee land owners, areas blighted by, 23; frontier dislike of, 68; western efforts to penalize, 86-8, 246-7
Agrarianism in Wisconsin, 77-8
Agricultural-College act, movement for, 3 ff.; introduced in House of Representatives, 4; southern opposition to, 5; feared by the West as aid to speculators, 8-10; provides larger grants to eastern states, 10; supported by the East, 14; Greeley for, 15; combination for, 18; passes Congress, 19; sectional vote on, 19-20; Buchanan vetoes, 19; introduced again in 1862, 21; opposed by western representatives, 21-4; vote of 1862 on, 22; defeat for the West, 26; denounced in Wisconsin, 76-7; disappointment with results of, 34, 245
Agricultural-College scrip, disposal of, 27 ff.; low prices of, 28, 31, 57; rush to enter lands with, 30; market for, controlled by Lewis, 30; large tracts acquired with, 31-2; restrictions on use of, 32, 34-5; low income from sale of, 34 ff.; Rhode Island scrip, 36-41; Illinois scrip, 42-8; New York scrip, 56-8
Agriculture, schools of, 3
Allen, Hiram S., 124
American Immigration Company, 240
Anson, town of, 155, 160, 169, 187
Armstrong Land Company, 240
Ashland County, 151, 155, 164, 167, 169-70, 192
Ashland Press, 149, 161-2, 174, 198-9
Atchison, town of, 37-8
Atchison & Nebraska Railroad, 38
Atchison & Pikes Peak Railroad, opposes Brown University, 37 ff.; buys Kickapoo reserve, 38
Atchison, Topeka & Santa Fe Railroad, 38
Atwood Lumber Company, 133

Bailey, W. F., 149-50, 158, 162 ff., 167, 168-70, 171-2, 174, 175, 189, 198-9, 204, 207

Barron, H. D., 139
Barron County, 144, 156, 164, 165, 167
Barron County Shield, 141, 172
Bartlett, William P., 168
Bayless, V. W., 118
Becky, James, 103
Beebe, Thomas H., 67
Beef Slough, improvement of, 130-31
Beef Slough Booming Company, 131
Belden & McDowell, 237-8
Bell, John, 16
Bennett, Russell H., 71
Big Bend, 159, 160, 169
Black River, pineries of, 70
Black River Falls, 122
Bloomer Workman, 162
Bloomington Pantagraph, 6
Boardman, Douglass, 216
Boston & Western Land Company, 79
Bradley, Daniel W., 67
Brewer, A. P., 109
Bronson, Frederick, 66
Brown, John Carter, 36
Brown, Harry F., 70-2
Brown University, 36-41
Browning, O. H., 25
Brunet Falls, 209, 241
Buchanan, James, vetoes college bill, 20; vetoes homestead bill, 75
Buckingham, Alvah, 67
Buffalo County, 157
Burnham, George, 71, 112
Burrows, George B., 71, 165, 189, 204, 240

Cameron & Losey, 171
Carpetbaggers in pinery counties, 146-7
Carroll, Charles H., 66
Carson, William, 235
Carson & Rand, 104
Cedar Falls Manufacturing Company, 125
Chase, Elijah C., 62
Cheyney, Hazen, 67
Chicago, St. Paul, Minneapolis & Omaha Railroad, 156, 240

260 INDEX

Chippewa County, 101, 144, 146-8, 150-1, 153, 157-8, 167, 168-9, 204
Chippewa Current, 153-4
Chippewa Falls, 124, 131, 132, 187
Chippewa Falls & Western Railroad, 181
Chippewa Herald, 113, 117, 119, 134, 160, 165-7, 181, 187
Chippewa Independent, 162
Chippewa Logging Company, 119, 132, 235
Chippewa Lumber & Boom Company, 132, 133, 135, 136
Chippewa River, pineries of, 70, 128, 129, 131-2, 182-3
Chippewa River Improvement & Log Driving Company, 132
Chippewa Times, 175
Chippewa Valley, 77, 90, 182 ff.
Chippewa Valley & Lake Superior Railroad, 184
Chippewa Valley Colonization Company, 240
Chippewa Valley Bank, 118
Chippewa Valley Lumbermen's Exchange, 157, 170
Clark County, 148-50, 167, 169
Clark County Republican, 150
Clay, C. C., 5
Coburn, Abner, 85, 95
Colby, Charles, 191, 194, 195, 205
Colby, Gardiner, 191
Colby Phonograph, 149
Colfax, Schuyler, 25
Collamer, Jacob, 16
Colman, Charles L., 230, 238-9
Colonization companies, 240, 248
Columbia College, 49
Confiscation proceedings, see Easley & Willingham
Comstock Land Company, 165
Conkling, Roscoe, 32
Conservation, beginnings of movement for, 224 ff.
Cook, Charles, 51
Cooke, Jay, 32
Cornell, Alonzo, 184
Cornell, Ezra, favors amendment to liberalize use of scrip, 32-3; trustee of New York State College of Agriculture at Ovid, 50; sketch of, 53; sympathy for farmers and mechanics, 54; proposes to endow new university, 54-5; secures charter for Cornell University, 55-6; undertakes to enter western lands, 56 ff.; consults with Woodward, 59 ff.; with Elijah C. Chase, 62; enters land in Kansas and Minnesota, 62; consults with W. J. Cornell, 62-3; gets Woodward's proposal of monopoly of Chippewa pine lands, 97; employs Woodward to enter lands, 97; no financial agreement with Woodward, 99-100; unfamiliar with methods of controlling land entries at Eau Claire, 105; plans to enter 900,000 acres, 106; largest owner of pine land in Northwest, 106; breaks with Woodward, 114; urges tax exemption for university land, 138; unable to meet taxes, 142; responsibility for bungling of tax matters, 142; supports railroad to parallel Chippewa, 182-3; director, Chippewa Valley Railroad, 184; unable to meet costs of land business, 209; under financial strain, 218-19; results of his vision, 243
Cornell, W. J., 62-3, 103, 128
Cornell, city of, 209, 241, 242, 250
Cornell Endowment Fund, profits from land business, 243
Cornell Land & Power Company, 241
Cornell University, legislative manoeuvring for charter, 55-6; Ezra Cornell undertakes to enter lands for, 56 ff.; escapes notice in attack on pine-land ring, 116; future of, dependent on Wisconsin land venture, 137; tax burden of, 138; officials seek tax exemption for lands of, 139; attacks on, 141, 149-50, 174, 198-9; tax difficulties of, 141 ff.; opposes division of Chippewa County, 148; opposes division of Clark and Marathon Counties, 149; supports measure to reduce cost of tax lists, 154; critical of affairs of Luddington, 156; pays taxes slowly, 163; its policy respecting taxes, 167; fights assessments and expenditures of pinery counties, 167-70; presses for legislation to restrict county expenditures; 171 ff.; asks legislature for tax relief, 173; taxes not heavy, 175-6; its view of public aid to railroads, 182 ff.; opposes aid to railroads, 187; harmed by tax exemption of railroad lands, 195-6; its land title attacked, 200-2; argues with Wisconsin Central over right of way, 206; opposes Sawyer County aid to railroad, 207; takes over lands, 219

INDEX

Cornell University, land policy of, method of pricing, 219-21; abandons stumpage sales, 212; revives stumpage sales, 213; stumpage estimates required for sales, 220; prices increased, 236; estimates of pine, 236; dickering over Penoke tract, 237; hardwood and second-growth stumpage, 239; land policy and settlers, 241; success of land policy, 242-3

Cornell University, land sales of, retarded by panic of 1873, 208 ff.; sales to Sage, McGraw, and Dwight, 214-15; tables, 221-2, 231, 235, 238, 239; higher prices, 230, 237; sales to Knapp-Stout, 231-3; disposal of Penoke tract, 237-8; hardwood and second-growth stumpage, 239; sales to settlers, 241; summary of sales, 242

Corwith, Henry, 67, 71
Corwith, Nathan, 67
County orders, or tax anticipation warrants, 146, 159 ff.
County government, see Local government
County rings, 151 ff.
Crothers, John P., 31
Cushing, Caleb, 70, 82, 95
Cut-over lands, tax certificates on, 154-5; Cornell University's, 239 ff.; efforts to attract settlers to, 239-42

Davidson, Charles M., 242
Davis, Moses M., 131
Dells controversy, 185
Denniston, G. V., 66
Dix, Dorothea, 11-12, 17
Dix bill, 11-12
Dodge, A. M., 237
Dodge, William E., 71
Doolittle, James R., 25
Door County, 84
Dougherty, A. E., 95
Douglas, John H., 125
Douglas County, 192
Drummond, Willis, 115
Dunn County, 157
Dunn County News, 117
Dwight, Jeremiah W., 71, 108-9, 111, 116, 182-3, 184

Early, H. W., 111
Easley, James S., see Easley & Willingham
Easley & Willingham, 83-4
East, desires share of public lands, 11; favors Agricultural-College bill, 14; its vote on the bill, 20-22
Eastman, Ben C., 75
Empire Lumber Company, 238
Eau Claire, 127, 128 ff., 131
Eau Claire County, 101
Eau Claire Free Press, 74, 76-7, 91, 117, 141, 196, 247-8
Eau Claire Lumber Company, 71, 127, 133, 135, 136, 204
Eau Claire Telegraph, 69, 74
Edmunds, J. M., 38, 138
Ellsworth, Henry L., and Henry W., 23
Ellsworth, Pinckney W., 75-6
Elmira Female College, 51
Empire Lumber Company, 127

Fairchild, Lucius, 140
Farm mortgages, on western farms, 14; railroad farm mortgages, 78; see also Time entry business
Fernow, Bernhard E., 224
Field, George B., 67
Fifield, Sam, 174, 194-5, 198-9
Fiske, Jennie McGraw, 218
Fiske, Willard, 218
Fitzgerald, John, 67
Flambeau, town of, 157-8, 160, 168-9
Folwell, W. W., 34
Forestry, professional, 224
Funk, Isaac, and Jesse, 23

Gage County, Nebraska, 47, 48
Galena Gazette, 79
Gardiner, Freeland B., 67
Gates, John L., 165, 238, 241
Gates County, 151
General Land Office, 117
Genesee College, 52
Gilmore, George D., 71, 112
Goltra, Moore C., 43 ff.
Good Land Company, 240
Granger legislation, 177
Grant County Herald, 79-80
Great European American Emigration Land Company, 95
Greeley, Horace, 15, 18, 49-50, 69, 75
Green Bay & Lake Pepin Railroad, 188
Gregory, John M., 43 ff.
Griffin, William, 112
Guggenheim, Mark, 67
Gwin, William W., 9

Hale, Ebenezer, 66
Harlan, James F., 25
Hendricks, Thomas A., 32-3
Henry, W. A., 239-40
Hersey, Staples & Co., 163, 171
Hewitt, Henry, Jr., 71, 111, 163
Homestead Act, 1, 2, 4, 75, 76, 101-2
Holman, William S., 23-4
Homesteaders, 173
Hotchkiss, George W., 226
Hotchkiss, Giles W., 138
Hough, Franklin, 224
Howard, Harrison, 49
Howe, Timothy O., 10
Hubbard, Gurdon S., 66
Hubbard, Henry, 66, 85, 95

Illinois Central Railroad, 193
Illinois Industrial University, see Illinois, University of
Illinois, University of, 42-8
Irvine, Thomas, 134, 204
Irvine, William, 134
Ives, Robert H., 36

Jackson, M. E., and E. G., 71
Jenkins, James, 71
Jervis, William B., 67
Jewett, Samuel A., 67, 163
Jones, George W., 68-9
José, Malcom, 128
Joy, James F., 25
Julian, George W., 23-4

Keator, J. S., & Son, 230
Kercheval, Benjamin B., 66
Keys, Elisha, 177, 194, 197
Kickapoo Indian reservation, 38
Knapp, John H., 125, 139
Knapp, Stout & Co., 67, 71, 111-12, 123, 125-6, 133-4, 135, 136, 173, 204, 231-3
Knight, John H., 184

La Crosse Republican and Leader, 115-16
Lamb, C. J., & Co., 130, 135, 136
Land grants, given as subsidies, 1-2; proposed to subsidize care of insane, 11-12; proposed for Niagara Falls canal, 12; western opposition to, 13; to Atchison & Pikes Peak Railroad, 38; to Wisconsin railroads, 178 ff.; see also St. Croix land grant

Land, Log & Lumber Company, 155
Land policy, early, 1-2; land grants as subsidies, 2; clashes in, 2, 4 ff.; Agricultural College bill includes new principle, 10-11; proposal to subsidize care of insane by land grants, 11-12; West demands changes in, 14; permits large scale purchasing, 65 ff.; disposal of pine land unsatisfactorily handled, 70; opposition to land purchases of non-residents, 74; demand for end of large purchases, 74-5; attitude of speculators to Homestead Act, 75
Land sales, West asks for end of, 14; rush for, 103; excitement at Eau Claire sale of 1873, 112-13; by McGraw & Dwight, 217; by Sage & McGraw, 217-18; by Francis Palms, 229; see also Cornell University, Brown University, University of Illinois
Land scrip, see Agricultural-College scrip
Land scrip fund of Cornell University, 242-3
Land speculation, deplored by the West, 6; opposed by Iowa legislature, 7; retards settlement, 7; military bounty warrants contribute to, 8; revival of, 30-1; in Rock River area of Wisconsin, 6; in Wisconsin, 1834–1888, 65 ff.; pinery towns bitter against, 73-4; profits and losses from, 78 ff.; record of Boston & Western Land Company, 79; of Woodman, 80-2; of Mason, 81; of Pairo, 81-2; of White, 82-3; of Easley & Willingham, 83-4; hazards of, 86 ff.
Land speculators, 68, 196-8
Land warrants, 8, 29, 59, 90
Landlookers in pineries, 92, 102-3, 104
Landlord-tenant legislation in Indiana, 23
Lawrence, Amos A., 31
Lewis, Gleason F., 30, 31, 33, 42-3, 58
Lincoln, Abraham, signs college act, 21
Lincoln County, 147-8, 164-9, 189-90
Little, William, 225
Loan sharks, 59, 65-6, 68, 101-2
Local government in northern Wisconsin, abuses in, 144; salaries of county officers, 145; creation of new counties, 146; tax lists, 152-4; extravagance of, 155 ff.
Logging chance, 128
Long, Artemas, 204
Love, Horace, 37-41
Lovejoy, Owen, 25

INDEX

Luddington, misgovernment in, 156
Luddington, Stephenson & Co., 71
Lumber industry, development of, 122; capital requirements of, 122-3; need for expansion of, 135; in Wisconsin, 136; cutting practices of, 247 ff.
Lumberman's National Bank, 134
Lumbermen, characterization of, 121; opposed to pine-land purchases by speculators, 91; relations with local governments, 170; attitude to railroad subsidies, 181
Lyon, Lucius, 66

McArthur, Charles, 241
McCrea, Augustus, 67
McDonald & Gilbert, 238
McDonnell, A. B., 134
McGraw, John, 63-4, 71, 108-9, 116, 135, 182-3, 184, 214-19
McGraw, Thomas, 184
McGraw & Dwight lands, 215-17
Madison Democrat, 203
Mansfield, John W., 67
Marathon County, 148-50, 164, 188, 197
Marinette County, 173
Martin, Roy L., 206
Mason, Charles, 81
Mason, James M., 5
Menomonie, sawmill town, 122
Merrill, lumbering town, 122
Miller & Lux, 32
Milwaukee & St. Paul Railroad, 179, 183, 186
Milwaukee Sentinel, 194-5
Minneapolis Lumberman, 158
Minnesota, 43-8
Mississippi River Logging Company, organized by Weyerhaeuser, 119; account of, 130; operations, 132, 136, 217, 229, 230-4, 238
Mississippi River millmen, methods of, 128; combination of, 129
Mitchell, Charles J., 67
Montgomery, Alexander, 70
Morgan, Edwin D., 138
Morrill, Justin Smith, introduces bill, 4; speaks for bill, 15
Morrill act, see Agricultural-College act
Morrison, Dorilus, 67, 96
Mortgages, see Farm mortgages
Murphy & Gaynor, 230
Murray, Charles A., 66, 68-9; land business studied by Schafer, 85

Nelson, C. N., Lumber Company, 133
New York, State of, demands that original states share in public lands, 16; receives scrip, 49; struggle for control of fund, 51 ff.
New York Central Railroad lobby, 55
New York Lumber, Manufacturing & Improvement Company, 209
New York State College of Agriculture at Ovid, 49-51
New York Tribune, 18
Newberry, Walter L., 66
Newspapers profit by tax lists, 152-4
North Wisconsin Lumber Company, 133
North Wisconsin Railroad, 164-5, 186, 188, 202, 204
Northwestern Lumber Company, 127, 242
Northwestern Lumberman, cited, 135, 136, 227, 228

Ogden, William B., 67
Omaha Railroad, see Chicago, St. Paul, Minneapolis & Omaha
Oneida County, 155-6
Oshkosh, lumbering town, 122
Owen, John S., 119, 171, 200, 240

Pairo, Charles W., 67, 81-2
Palms, Francis, 32, 71, 104, 111, 128, 130-1, 229
Panic of 1857, 70
Panic of 1873, 70
Patrick, William S., 71
Paul, John, 238
Peck, D. M., 128, 133, 163
People's College, 51-2
Penoke lands, 234, 236, 237-8
Peoria Register, 79
Phillips & Colby Construction Company, 192, 197
Phillips Times, 147
Pierce, Franklin, vetoes Dix bill, 11-12
Pillsbury, Oliver P., 71
Pine, estimates of, 226 ff.; rising prices of, 230
Pine County, opposition to creation of, 146
Pine land, proposals for monopoly of, 95 ff., 97
Pine-land ring, 111-13, 117
Pomeroy, Samuel C., 9, 25, 37-8
Porter, Gilbert E., 91, 114-15
Porter, Moon & Co., 171
Pound, Thaddeus H., 124, 139, 185, 187

Pound, Halbert & Co., 71, 104
Powell, Burt, cited, 44
Prairie Du Chien Union, 117
Preston, David, 30, 71, 229
Price, William T., 177, 203, 204
Price County, 148, 164, 173
Pugh, George E., 9-10
Putnam, Henry C., land agent, 61, 63, 71; sketch of, 91-2; in control of Eau Claire land office, 91 ff.; plans monopoly, 95, 101, 107; engaged for Cornell entries, 100 ff.; deals with pine-land ring, 107 ff.; operations of, 109-19, 128, 139, 142, 149, 151, 162, 164, 182, 183-7, 192, 196-8, 216-17; as lobbyist, 185-6; conservationist, 224-5; his report for census, 225-9; sales by, 229; factor in Cornell's success, 243; wide interests, 248

Railroads in Wisconsin, 178-9, 181; see also individual railroads
Ramsay, Wayne, 165, 240
Randall, Thomas, 90-1, 125
Rantoul, Robert, 95
Receiver, importance of, 94
Red Cedar River, pineries of, 70; 125-6, 135
Red Cedar Improvement & Log Driving Company, 125
Register, importance of, 94
Rhode Island, land scrip, 36-41
Rice, Henry M., 9, 26, 36
Riggs, Elisha, 67
Ripley, L. V., 241
Robertson, Smith, 142, 170, 197-8
Rochester, University of, 52
Rusk, Jeremiah, 113
Rusk County, see Gates County
Russell, William S., 66
Rust, John F., 111
Rust, William A., 71, 111-12, 127, 200-1, 240
Rutledge, Edward, 103, 134, 238
Rutledge mill, 133

Sackett, Fred, 148
Sage, Dean, 184
Sage, Henry W., his large lumber interests, 63-4; partner of McGraw in Wisconsin investment, 71; alarms Woodward, 108; beneficiary of pine-land ring, 116; active in Wisconsin, 182, 183, 197-8, 204; argues for Cornell titles, 201; his large transaction in Cornell land, 214-17; put in charge of Cornell lands, 219-20; negotiates with Weyerhaeuser, 234; his wise management of Cornell lands, 243
Sage, William H., 184
Sage & McGraw, 171, 214 ff.
Sage Land & Improvement Company, 240
St. Croix & Lake Superior Railroad, 183
St. Croix land grant, 178, 183-6
Sargent, Charles S., 224, 225 ff., 228
Sawmills, on Mississippi and Chippewa Rivers, 118-19; of Union Lumber Company, 124; of Knapp, Stout & Co., 125-6; of Eau Claire Lumber Company, 127; of Eau Claire, 127; of Mississippi River towns, 127-8
Sawyer, Philetus, 71, 111-12, 117, 171, 177, 202
Sawyer County, 151, 160, 207
Schafer, Joseph, on profits from land speculation, 78, 85
Schulenberg, Frederick, 71
Schulenberg, Richard, 127
Schulenberg & Co., 163
Scott, Thomas B., 71
Scrip, see Agricultural-College scrip
Scully, William, 23, 47, 68
Sears, Barnas, 37, 39
Settlement companies, 240, 248
Settlers, 143-4, 180-1
Shaw, Daniel, Lumber Company, 171, 238
Shaw, Milton G., 229
Shawano Journal, 197
Shell Lake Lumber Company, 133
Sheboygan & Fond du Lac Railroad, 183
Sherry, Patton, 229
Shields, James T., 9
Simons, D. P., 160, 162
Slidell, John, 67
Smith, E. H., 242
Smith, George, 66
Smith, J. M., 149
Smith & Buffington, 71, 104
Smithson bequest, 3
South, opposed to government aid for colleges, 5; vote on college bill, 20-2
South Muscatine Lumber Company, 242
Spaulding, Jesse, 204
Spooner, John C., 177, 202
Staples, Isaac, 71
Starr, William, 71, 171
Stebbins & Porter, 41
Stephenson, Isaac, 71, 123, 124, 248
Stevens Point, 122

INDEX

Stout, Henry L., 125
Sylvester, Henry H., 95

Taintor, Andrew, 125
Taxes, 87-8, 138-44
Tax certificates, 164-5
Tax lists, 152-4
Tax titles, 83-4, 146, 165-7
Taylor County, 164, 167, 204
Tenancy, 24, 47
Thorp, Jim, 71, 111-12, 127, 139, 184, 185
Timber stealing, 70, 72, 73, 200, 211 ff.
Time entry business, 59-60, 92, 102
Turner, Frederick J., 78
Turner, Jonathan Baldwin, 17

Union Lumber Company, 123, 124

Valley Lumber Co., 171, 204, 235
Vandeveer, 23
Vermont, land scrip, 35
Vermont Agricultural Society, 17
Vocational education, movement for, 3

Wade, Benjamin F., 18
Wadsworth, Julius, 66
Walker, Thomas B., 117
Walker, Martin O., 66
Ward, David, 71
Washburn, Cadwallader, 66, 71, 96-7, 103, 117, 125
Washburn & Woodman, 67
Watson, James T., 66
Wausau, lumbering center, 122
Webster, Daniel, 95
West, opposes college land grants, 8 ff.; Dix bill would damage, 12; opposes cash sales of land, 14; vote on college bill, 20-2; tries to check speculation in land by non-residents, 74
Western Union Telegraph Company, 53
Weston, Samuel F., 67
West Wisconsin Railroad, 182, 183, 187, 188
Weyerhaeuser, Frederick, 119, 129-34, 204, 233-5, 248
Weyerhaeuser & Denkmann, 132, 137, 229
White, Albert S., 26
White, Andrew D., 52, 55, 105
White, Miles, 66, 82-3
Wilkinson, Morton S., 9

Williams, H. Clay, 91, 114-15
Williams, J. W., 196, 197, 220
Willingham, W. W., see Easley & Willingham
Wilson, Captain William, 118, 125, 139
Windstorms, damage by, 212
Wisconsin, favored college land grants, 17-18; land speculation in, 65 ff.; hazards of investments in, 78; growth of lumber industry in, 136; boss-ridden, 177; railroads in, 177 ff.; land grants to railroads in, 178-9
Wisconsin Central Railroad, sketch of, 190-1; in Chippewa County, 148; Clark and Marathon Counties, 148-9; ally of pine owners' lobby, 171; local subsidies, 179, 192; interest in St. Croix grant, 183; for new counties, 192-3; at odds with Cornell, 193 ff., 206; loses fight for longer exemption from taxes, 190-207; its colonization work, 240
Wisconsin River, pineries of, 70
Wisconsin River Land Company, 240
Wisconsin River Pilot, 150
Wisconsin State Register, 74
Wisconsin Valley Railroad, 149, 188, 189-90, 193, 204
Woodman, Cyrus, 28, 29, 66, 71, 79, 80-1, 96-7, 103-4, 110, 111, 117
Woodman, George, see Woodman, Cyrus
Woodward, William A., land broker, consulted by Cornell, 59 ff.; entries by, 67; loans to squatters, 66; profits of, 86; proposes monopoly, 97; put in charge of Cornell entries but without contract, 97-100; his methods, 98; his high charges, 100; depends on Putnam, 101; proposes usurious loans to settlers, 102; his bad advice to Cornell, 105-6; jealous of Sage and McGraw, 108, 214; works with McGraw & Dwight, 108-9; at Eau Claire sale, 111; breaks with Cornell, 114; in tax war, 138-9; failure of his plans, 142, 213; his agency costly for Cornell, 242
Woodward, Francis, 110, 114
Worcester, town of, 160
Wright, Joseph A., 24, 25

"Yale Crowd," 23
Young, W. J., & Co., 130, 135, 136, 171

www.ingramcontent.com/pod-product-compliance
Lightning Source LLC
Chambersburg PA
CBHW031346230426
43670CB00006B/451